SHALLOW GRAVES

For Susan, for your love and support.

Killers' Concealments

SHALLOW GRAVES

PAUL B KIDD

 LAKE PRESS

▲ LAKE PRESS

Lake Press Pty Ltd
5 Burwood Road
Hawthorn VIC 3122 Australia
www.lakepress.com.au

Some of these stories have been
previously published.
This edition first published 2020
Printed and bound in Australia at McPherson's
Printing Group, Maryborough, Victoria 5 4 3 2
LP21 101

A catalogue record for this
book is available from the
National Library of Australia

CONTENTS

FOREWORD

In a land of deserts, trees, deserted mines and tidal ocean sand hills, the term 'shallow grave' can invariably mean only one thing … that a body of some description is buried there. Besides an animal, the only other alternative is that the body is human. But in Australia's case, the term 'shallow grave' has many other connotations than its name implies.

A 'shallow grave' can, for instance, be a place where a body has been concealed by being covered with tree or bush branches or undergrowth, as were serial killer Ivan Milat's seven victims in New South Wales' Belanglo State Forest, not far south of Sydney.

Or perhaps it's where a body has been buried in tidal foreshore sandhills, to be unearthed years later by the constant lapping of the waves, as was Harvey Jones's skeleton twelve years after he was murdered and buried in the sandhills on the foreshore of Sydney's Botany Bay by gangster Neddy Smith.

Or how about any of the thousands of bottomless mines that dot the Australian landscape, left over from the mining days, which have become perfect burial sites for a murdered body? Bruce Burrell was suspected of concealing his victims Kerry Whelan and Dorothy Davis to become one of the very rare killers in Australian history to be convicted of double murder without the discovery of a body.

All of these are deemed to be shallow graves. You will find all of these stories in this book.

True, if Australia's bushland, forests, foreshores, sandhills or deserts could give up their secrets, there is little doubt that they would account for many of the people from all walks of Australian life who have mysteriously vanished without a trace over the years. Then there are the swamps, mineshafts, culverts and paddocks that may well be the last resting places of so many more.

When a murderer goes to extreme lengths to conceal a body, there is no mistaking that they don't intend the victim to ever be found … and most of them aren't. While it is a gross misconception that more murders occur in Australia than anywhere else, there is little doubt that concealing a body in Australia's vast wilderness, where chances are it will never be discovered, is easier to do than in most other places. Hide them as they may, however, there is no guarantee that the bodies will remain undiscovered.

On the other hand, there are those murderers who love nothing more than leaving their handiwork on display, with clues galore about the victim and murder site left for investigating police to find. They prefer to leave their victims in the public places where they killed them, on show, as if to taunt investigators in a horrific game of 'catch me if you can'. The Truro serial murders showed the reckless abandonment of the corpses of seven murdered young women in shallow graves after they were no longer of any use to their killers.

John Wayne Glover, aka the Granny Killer, bashed old women to death, then disarrayed their underwear to make it look as though he had sexually molested them on public streets in the Sydney harbourside suburb of Mosman, in broad daylight, leaving their bodies where he killed them, as if he were begging to be caught in the act or at least identified running away. He wasn't. You won't find his story in this book.

William 'the Mutilator' MacDonald stabbed his four male victims up to 60 times before slicing off their genitals and leaving their bodies on display, reclining on the toilet seat in a public lavatory in a busy city laneway, a public bathing area, in the foundations of a building he leased. When caught, MacDonald wondered what had taken police so long. He isn't in this book either.

Eric Edgar Cooke, the 'Night Caller' killer who shot, stabbed, strangled or ran over his seven victims in Perth in the early 1960s, made no attempt to conceal his crimes, and when apprehended he admitted he knew that it was only a matter of time before his flagrant attitude towards homicide would bring about his undoing. It did, and they hanged him. He's not in here either.

When caught, each of these serial killers admitted that he was glad it was over. But unlike these show ponies of Australian murder, others choose to hide their victims in the knowledge that, when a body can't be found, in most cases it is all but impossible to prove a case of murder against a suspect, no matter how strong the circumstantial evidence may be.

But it doesn't always work that way – as you will discover in some of the cases in this book. The best-laid plans of even the most devious killers go astray when their victims turn up unexpectedly ... usually many years later when they have been unearthed from their shallow grave, to forensically tell the tale of who killed them. Enjoy.

Paul B Kidd
September 2020

Chapter One

THE REID-LUCKMAN MURDER

On the night of 4 May 1982, 13-year-old Terry Ryan rushed into his family home in Marsden, a suburb of Brisbane, the capital of Queensland in north-eastern Australia, where he lived with his mother, father, older brother and younger sister, and told his mother Belita the most astonishing story. Terry said that he had been forced by two men to participate in the sexual assault and prolonged torture and murder of his best friend and that his friend's body had been buried in a shallow grave in scrubland about 60 kilometres south, over the New South Wales border, near the seaside hamlet of Kingscliff. Immediately, Belita Ryan rang police, and then accompanied her son to the nearby Beenleigh police station.

In the early hours of 5 May, Terry retold his story to Sergeant Wayne King and Detective Senior Constable Robert Guteridge of the Queensland Criminal Investigation Branch. At approximately 4.45 that morning, the detectives drove Terry and his mother over the border into New South Wales to Tweed Heads police station, where they were joined by Senior Constable Mark Ferguson, a local detective. On the boy's instructions, they first drove to and examined the contents of a garbage bin in nearby Faux Park. Then, they examined the sink, walls, urinal and cubicle of a local public toilet. From there, they proceeded south along the Coast Road to about three kilometres past Kingscliff until the boy told them to stop the car at a bush track leading in an easterly direction towards the ocean.

Terry led his mother and the detectives along the sandy track into the scrub, but the trail petered out to nothing. There was no bush grave as he had described. The detectives looked at each other. If this was a teenage prank, then it was quite an elaborate one. By the time they had explored another three bush trails with no result, the detectives' patience was wearing thin.

The fourth track they stopped at seemed to be more promising, with fresh tyre tracks on the sandy surface. Terry became excited and led the way, pointing enthusiastically at the tread marks. After about 200 metres, the track opened out onto a roughly cleared area and the tyre tracks disappeared into bushland on the other side of it. 'There ... in there,' Terry said as he pointed into the foliage. 'It's in there.'

The detectives led the way, and as they entered the track, they came across a grave-sized mound of earth off to the north-east. It was covered with small tree branches and twigs obviously broken from the nearby trees. Terry stepped back into his mother's arms and began to cry as the police officers approached the ominous mound and examined the freshly turned earth. In the dawn light, they saw spots of blood in the sand and a large, wet, blood-soaked section in the centre of the raised soil. Lying in the sand at the head of the bush grave was a dark sock and a knife in a sheaf. There were also numerous unstruck, chewed matchsticks lying about the gravesite.

What the police officers found beneath the mound almost defied their comprehension. It was as if there wasn't a part of 13-year-old Peter Aston's naked body that hadn't been defiled in one way or another. The fact that the boy was tall, more than six feet, made the discovery even more grotesque, as he had been bent to fit into the hastily dug hole that was not long enough for his gangly frame. A chewed, unstruck matchstick was caught in his pubic hair.

A post-mortem of Peter performed later that day by Dr John Follent at the Tweed Heads District Hospital revealed:

- multiple lacerations to the top of his head, as well as areas of the hair on his head that had been cut short, a deep cut to the back of his head and bruising to the left side of his head
- a depressed fracture of his skull with underlying brain damage
- leather punch marks and bruising on his left ear, plus lacerations to the front and back of the same ear
- bruising to his mouth, lips and chin
- lacerations to his right eye area and cheek
- a partial dislocation between his second and third cervical vertebrae, plus fractures of his vertebrae

- a large stab wound to the right side of his throat, and severing of the internal jugular vein and external arteries
- cigarette burns to his chest
- stab wounds to his left shoulder and severe bruises to his left wrist
- a stab wound to the left side of his abdomen
- shallow lacerations over his right loin and flank, plus bruising to his left buttock, scrotum and penis, and hair missing from his pubic area
- stab wounds to both legs below the knees and under the toes
- 15 more laceration wounds and 14 other types of abrasions, lacerations and bruises
- the presence of sand in his nose, mouth, trachea and bronchial tract, most likely caused by inhalation.

Dr Follent said that Peter could possibly have died from the skull fracture. However, due to the sand in his nose, mouth, trachea and bronchial tract, it was most likely that, after he had been bashed and tortured, he was buried alive and died of asphyxiation.

After he had recovered from the shock of revisiting the scene of the death of his best friend, Terry Ryan told the police every detail of what had happened the previous day.

🕆 🕆 🕆

Not long before Peter's death, he and Terry Ryan had become good friends. They met at Kingston State School and lived near each other in Marsden. Peter was a tall boy. He suffered from myopia and as a result had worn thick glasses since childhood. The combination of his thick glasses, lanky frame and recent arrival from Victoria made him the taunt of the school. As a result, Peter and Terry spent more time wagging school and shoplifting from department stores than they spent in class.

Terry told the detectives that he and Peter had wagged school on 4 May. That day, Peter intended to hitchhike to his hometown of Melbourne to join his elder brother, and Terry had agreed to keep him company as far as the Gold Coast, and then return home. He said:

> We met at a place called the Sands at about 8.30 that morning. It's a place in the bush and it's got sand and a little creek. From there we went to the nearby lake and played on the Tarzan swings.

*At about 10.30 am we went down to the Kingston railway station
and caught the train into Brisbane and got off at the Brunswick Street
Station. We went into Myers and got some shoes, jeans and a shirt
each. From there we caught the train to Woodridge and Peter went into
Kmart and got a carton of Winfield 25s – the red ones.*

*From there we caught a train down to Beenleigh and went into
Coles and bought a jacket each. By then it was early afternoon and we
walked down to the Gold Coast Highway and started hitchhiking while
we walked south. Not far down the highway we came across a yellow
4WD Daihatsu with the hood up and a bloke with his head under the
bonnet and another bloke sitting in the passenger seat.*

*We asked them if they would give us a lift down to the coast and the
bloke under the bonnet told us to hop in and that they were leaving now
as he had fixed what was wrong with the car.*

*They were both casually dressed in jeans and jumpers and told us
that their names were Bob and Paul. Paul was much younger than Bob
– who was driving – and Peter got in alongside him while I sat in the
back next to Paul. I told them our names were Peter and Terry and we
took off heading south.*

The boys had only been in the vehicle a short time when Paul produced a rifle from beneath a blanket on the floor and held it at Terry's head. The car pulled over to the side of the road, and Paul warned Peter that if he moved he would 'make a bullet in the head or the back'. With that, the men produced handcuffs from their pockets and at gunpoint secured both of the boys, then took off again down the highway. Terry told the detectives: 'They told us that they were police from Miami [a suburb south of Surfers Paradise] and we drove off again.' After a while, Peter told the men that his hands were getting tired, so Bob pulled up not far from Dreamworld (a theme park about 20 kilometres north of Surfers Paradise), undid his handcuffs, handcuffed him to the bar on the dashboard and took off again.

During the drive, the violence began to escalate. Bob hit Peter with his hand for no reason, and Paul jabbed him in the chin with the barrel of his rifle. Paul also hit Terry in the face with his hand. The vehicle then crossed the border into New South Wales, and when they reached Kingscliff, Bob drove onto a bush track and stopped. Paul got out, walked around to the other side of the vehicle and dragged Terry out. He made him spread his legs apart with his hands on the top of the vehicle, and after he had searched him, he fitted a pair of thumb cuffs (miniature handcuffs that fit around fingers instead of wrists) onto his hands. Bob un-cuffed Peter and dragged him from the car and threw him to the ground. Terry said:

Then they dragged both of us along the ground toward the beach. They were very rough with us and threw us around a lot. Then they made us lay on the ground with our legs apart and our arms out straight and took off all of Peter's clothes. He struggled against them but it was useless.

It was just going on dark but the moon was very full and I could see exactly what was going on. They made me lie on my stomach with my hands thumb-cuffed behind my back and watch while they really started knocking Peter about and kicking him. Then I heard something crack. It was the rifle butt. Paul told Peter to 'shut up' and then swung the rifle as hard as he could and hit him [Peter] in the jaw with it and then Peter fell to the ground. He hit him so hard that the rifle butt broke.

Then they let Peter rest for a bit and then they started stabbing him with knives they took from their pockets. They had about five knives in all. Peter tried to scream so they stuffed his ripped shirt in his mouth to keep him quiet. Then Bob came over to me and punched me in the face while I was on the ground and it made my nose bleed.

Bob produced a leather punch from his pocket and gave it to Paul who punched holes in both of Peter's ears with it. He put the pieces of skin he punched out of Peter's ears into a tablet bottle he had.

Then they made me suck Peter off. Bob made me lean over Peter and suck him off. Bob just said, 'Go on.' Then they made me eat his pubic hairs. The hairs from his privates. Bob cut some of the hairs off Peter's privates and stuffed them in my mouth and made me eat them. He said, 'Eat them.'

Although Peter had been repeatedly stabbed by both Bob and Paul he somehow managed to get up and he tried to run away with no clothes on. He was still handcuffed. Paul chased after him and brought him down while Bob had hold of me by the collar. Bob put the thumb cuffs on Peter's toes and said, 'Let's see if you can run away now.' Peter managed to get up again and started running off and Bob said, 'Shit, the little bastard got out of them,' and Paul took off after him and brought him back.

Then Bob took a shovel out of the back of the car and started hitting Peter over the head with it. The blows were very hard and he was hitting him with the sharp edge – the blade. Then one of them took the thumb cuffs off me – but left the normal handcuffs on – and Paul handed me the shovel and told me to hit Peter over the head with it, which I did, but as softly as I could. I can't remember how many times I hit him but they seemed to be satisfied.

That's when I asked them if I could join them so I could get out of it. I just said, 'Can I join you?' I'm not sure who said it then but he said, 'How can we trust you?' and I said, 'Well you seen me hit him on the head, didn't you?'

Peter was just laying there. His blood was everywhere. He was bleeding from the neck, back, front and the head. The blood was all over Bob and Paul. Then Bob put the thumb cuffs onto Peter's toes. Paul started waving the rifle around.

Then Bob shaved Peter's hair and cut his scalp. Paul was holding Peter's feet while Bob was shaving him. Then Bob stabbed Peter in the head. Paul was talking to Bob while he was stabbing Peter but I couldn't understand what he was saying.

Peter had just about had it when Bob took me to look for somewhere to dig a hole. Bob took my handcuffs off so that I could dig. The first place we tried had too many tree roots so we came back to where Peter was and started digging there.

When we got back Paul was standing over Peter doing up his fly. Peter was just laying on the ground, he had just about had it. Then they put him in the hole and covered it up with dirt and tree branches.

They got everything they had, put it in the car and drove off, and me too, and they drove me back home. While we were driving they told me that they were Satan worshippers and they had to do it [kill Peter Aston] for the sacrifice.

Along the way we stopped and put Peter's clothes into a bin and went into a toilet and cleaned ourselves. Bob threw Peter's hat off a bridge and Paul threw his [Peter's] glasses into a bin. They pulled up at a cafe and bought some food. I didn't eat any of it.

They wanted to know where I lived. Bob gave me a pocketknife. He gave it to me in case anyone tried to bash me or anything. When they dropped me off Bob got out, opened up the back and let me out. Bob shook my hand and made me promise I wouldn't dob. He said, 'If you dob the same thing will happen to you.'

I ran home. Along the way I went into the bush and took all the clothes off and I had my t-shirt and shorts on when I went home. I told my mother straight away what had happened and she called the police.

Although he was subjected to intensive questioning, there was a lot about the experience that Terry Ryan 'couldn't remember'. But detectives put this down to the fact that the boy was probably in shock and other events that had taken place would come back to him during later interviews.

Initially, the fact that the mysterious 'Paul' and 'Bob' dropped Terry at his home after murdering his friend in front of him had made the police suspicious. After all, it's not every day that police come across an eyewitness to a murder case, let alone one driven to his front door by the alleged perpetrators after the homicide has taken place. However, the discovery of Peter Aston's body in the bush grave removed all suspicion from Terry and told investigators that not only were they dealing with two murderers, but also, the killers were naively stupid. Police were confident of an early arrest.

⚰ ⚰ ⚰

In the early hours of 6 May, about 24 hours after Terry Ryan had taken police to the grave of his murdered friend, Private Robert Ponzetti was awakened by someone shaking his leg as he slept in his room at the Enoggera Army Camp on the outskirts of Brisbane.

It was 17-year-old Private Paul Luckman and 34-year-old Corporal Robin Reid. Ponzetti knew Reid well as he had shared a room with him for some time before they had a falling out. It was Reid's practice to share a room with each new army private when he came into the unit. About two weeks prior to that night, Luckman had come into the unit and been moved immediately into Reid's room. The pair had been inseparable ever since.

Reid and Luckman were both wearing jackets and jeans and Reid was clutching his stomach and appeared to be in pain. Luckman explained that he thought his friend had a severe case of food poisoning and asked Ponzetti if he could take them to the nearby hospital outside of the base. Ponzetti agreed. He dressed quickly, and the three men walked out of the barracks to Ponzetti's 1978 blue Holden Sunbird, which was parked in the car park opposite. He sat in the driver's seat and opened the front passenger door and the rear door for Reid and Luckman. Reid sat in the front and Luckman in the back.

As Ponzetti started his car, he felt the sharp blade of a knife across his throat. Luckman was holding the handle of the knife in his left hand and the end of the blade in his right.

'This is not a joke, Bob, just trust us,' Luckman said.

'What are you doing? You must be joking,' Ponzetti replied.

'No, it's not a joke, Bob. We need your car.'

By now, Reid had made a miraculous recovery from his chronic food poisoning. He produced a pair of handcuffs from his jacket pocket and cuffed Ponzetti's hands behind his back while Luckman held the knife to his throat.

'You don't need to do that,' Ponzetti said.

'It's for your own protection,' Reid replied as they bundled Ponzetti out of the car and into the back seat.

'No harm will come to you, I promise,' Luckman told the terrified Ponzetti.

With Ponzetti secured in the back of his car, Reid and Luckman walked over to a yellow 4WD Daihatsu that was parked about 10 metres away. They began to take gear from it and move it into the boot and back seat of Ponzetti's Sunbird. Their task complete, they then got back into the Sunbird and took off with Reid at the wheel. After about 15 minutes, Luckman turned to Ponzetti and said: 'That kid that was killed on the Gold Coast, that was us.' The discovery of Peter Aston's body had been in the news all the previous day.

'No, it wasn't,' Reid said.

'Don't lie, it was us. I am telling the truth,' Luckman replied.

'We just did it for kicks,' Reid conceded. 'It was a mistake. We just wanted to explore.'

'You've got to be joking,' Ponzetti exclaimed. 'I can't believe you did it.'

'Yes, it was a mistake we made,' Reid said. 'We don't want to do it again.'

When they stopped later at a petrol station for fuel, Luckman asked Ponzetti: 'Can I trust you if I take the handcuffs off?'

'Yes,' Ponzetti replied.

'Don't try anything,' Luckman said as he removed the handcuffs from Ponzetti. 'We have already made one mistake and we don't want to have to make another one. But we will if we have to.'

'Well, what are you going to do with my car?' Ponzetti asked.

'I promise you that the car won't be harmed,' Luckman replied. 'We are going to drive through Warwick and leave it about 200 kilometres past there.'

'We will park the car in a no-standing place so the police will find it,' Reid said. 'We are going to leave a note to notify your insurance company.'

When the group arrived at Warwick, Reid went into a newsagent and came out with two newspapers. There was a photograph of Peter Aston on the front page and a story about his murder. It prompted outrage from Luckman. He said: 'Most of this is a load of crap. The other 13-year-old kid, he helped. Where it says he was dumped on the road last. [That's] a load of crap too. We left him in front of his place. It wasn't 2.30 am. It was earlier than that when we got out of the car. He shook hands with us.'

As they approached Tenterfield, Luckman said to Ponzetti: 'We're getting close to dropping you off. Don't do what Terry did to us.'

'Who's Terry?' Ponzetti asked.

'The other 13-year-old creep that dobbed us in,' Reid said.

'No. I'm not going to dob you in,' Ponzetti replied.

'What are you going to tell the police?' Luckman asked.

'I'm going to tell them that the two blokes who stole my car are about 22 years old, one of them had blond hair and the other one had light brown hair,' Ponzetti told them. 'The one with the blond hair is wearing a blue T-shirt, black trousers and running shoes and the other bloke's wearing a white T-shirt, faded blue jeans and runners too.'

Apparently convinced, Luckman handed Ponzetti a dollar and some silver, a packet of cigarettes and a lighter, and told him to get out a few kilometres short of Tenterfield. Ponzetti had to wait only a short time for a lift into Tenterfield. When he arrived, he went immediately to a police station and told the police what had happened.

⚰ ⚰ ⚰

Around midday the same day, Constable Vincent Towns of the Tenterfield Highway Patrol was patrolling in a vehicle on the New England Highway. In response to a call on the police radio, he drove south at high speed. As he approached the Bolivia Post Office, he saw a blue Holden Sunbird travelling south at a speed of 60 to 80 kilometres per hour. Constable Towns followed the vehicle to a point 13 kilometres north of Deep Water to where it stopped in a truck parking area at the side of the road. The police vehicle stopped about 200 metres away from the Sunbird, and Towns observed a man get out of the car, walk around to the bonnet and open it. All the time the man was looking at Towns. After a couple of minutes, the man returned to the driver's seat of the Sunbird and drove off in a southerly direction. Constable Towns took off in pursuit at a safe distance. As they approached the outskirts of Deep Water, they ran into a police roadblock and had no alternative but to stop.

At 12.10 pm that day, Sergeant Jack Harvison at Glen Innes police station had received a radio message from Tenterfield Police. As a result, he and Senior Constable Goodall had rushed to a point on the New England Highway about half a kilometre north of the small town of Deep Water. There they had set up a roadblock with their police car and a large northbound truck on the western side of the highway.

Cautiously, Sergeant Harvison and Constable Towns approached the vehicle. They arrested Robin Reid and Paul Luckman without resistance. Reid came out with his hands in the air while Luckman was found cowering on the front seat.

⚰ ⚰ ⚰

After police had interviewed Terry Ryan during the day of 5 May, they issued a notice to be broadcast over the New South Wales Police Network for all officers to be on the lookout for a mustard-coloured Daihatsu 4WD. All local radio stations were given a description of the vehicle and of the occupants who answered to the names of Bob and Paul. Anyone seeing the vehicle was warned to stay away and to ring the police immediately as the occupants were armed and dangerous.

Acting on an anonymous telephone call in which police were informed that the vehicle might belong to two soldiers, 17-year-old Private Paul Luckman and 34-year-old Corporal Robin 'Bob' Reid, who answered the descriptions and were based at the Enoggera Army Camp on the outskirts of Brisbane, a squad of a combination of New South Wales and Queensland detectives descended upon room 29 of Barrack Block H9 to find the suspects gone. Detective Sergeant Bob Jackson and Detective Ian 'Spiro' Spiers from Murwillumbah Police, along with Detective Superintendent Mark Jackson of the Brisbane Homicide Squad and other Queensland detectives, were the first officers to arrive at the army camp. In the nearby car park, they found the Daihatsu 4WD that Terry Ryan had described. Looking inside the car, they saw that the interior and the car's contents matched the boy's description perfectly. From the vehicle detectives removed three knives and a baton. After examining the vehicle but before searching the suspects' room, Bob Jackson turned to Detective Spiers and said confidently: 'It looks like we've got the bastards, Spiro.'

By now aware that Reid and Luckman, who were on rostered army leave at the time of the murder, had left the camp (the commanding officer had had the whole area searched prior to the police arriving), the detectives set about searching the missing soldiers' room. Detective Sergeant Bob Jackson said:

> The room was untidy and divided into four sections with beds occupying the two front sections near the door. This area had two large wooden lockers which acted as a petition, leaving the back section as one large room. From papers found in this section it was apparent that it was the area occupied by Robin Reid.
>
> Inspector Jackson and I searched this section and took possession of 37 knives of different shapes and sizes which were on display in various parts of that room, as well as eight swords, one cutlass, one spear head and two scalpels which were on display on the walls and in the cupboard.
>
> We then conducted a search of the front area of the room and from the personal material found there it was obvious that this was the part occupied by Paul Luckman. We removed a pair of bone-coloured jeans and a red and white floral shirt of which both were bloodstained. I noticed a pair of steel crutches next to the bed.

Curious about the crutches, the detectives made inquiries at the army base hospital. It transpired that when Reid and Luckman had returned to the base after murdering Peter Aston, Luckman's foot was severely bruised and swollen from repeatedly kicking Peter. Luckman told the medic he saw that he had dropped a heavy suitcase on his foot, and after it was washed and bandaged, he was supplied with a pair of crutches.

A further search among the books in Reid and Luckman's room revealed a photograph album containing clusters of what appeared to be human hair cellotaped onto each page. Written on the page at the top of each sample was its identification, such as 'Bill W pubic', 'Bill W guts', 'Derek H ... under arms', and so on. In the same catalogue were pictures cut from magazines of naked and semi-naked youths either tied up or in bondage positions. Among the many books found was one in which the models had been cut out and pasted onto each other to create sexually suggestive positions. Bob Jackson continued:

> We had no idea what to expect when we went into that room but it didn't take long to realise that we had a couple of really strange bastards on our hands. On top of the arsenal of knives, the piles of [gay] books with the cutouts pasted on top of one another and the scrapbook with pubic hair samples, we also discovered dozens of books on Satanism. Some of the titles were The Devil's Prayer Book, Satan's Bible and The History of Witchcraft.
>
> In a notebook one of them had handwritten essays about leading a boy down a bush track at knifepoint and then holding him in a headlock with a knife at his throat while he undressed him. There wasn't much doubt that these blokes could help us with our investigations.

While Bob Jackson and the team of detectives were searching the room at the army base, news came through on the police radio that Reid and Luckman had been detained at Glen Innes police station.

⚰ ⚰ ⚰

Detective Sergeant Bob Jackson said later, 'Spiro [Detective Spiers] and I drove down to Glen Innes that night, taking with us the exhibits that we had taken from the suspects' room at Enoggera to use in the interviews if necessary. On arrival at Glen Innes both of the alleged offenders were being formally interviewed, Reid by Detective Sergeant Peter Dunston and Senior Constable Mark Ferguson, and Luckman by Detective Sergeant Eric Strong and Detective Eric Grimmond from Casino.' Each told conflicting stories, mainly blaming each other and Terry Ryan, the boy whom they had trusted but who had given them up to police instead. So preposterous were the allegations against Terry that the interrogating detectives could only conclude that Reid and Luckman had conspired to incriminate him as much as they could as a payback for 'dobbing' him in to police.

In his statement to police, Reid said:

> The boys told us that they'd stolen some cigarettes, I think 20 packets, and the clothes that they were wearing were stolen. We proceeded to get rid of him [Peter Aston]. I remembered that I had hit him, I don't

know how many times or how severe but I only used my hand. I am not normally a violent person. Nothing was said about the little one [Terry Ryan] but I think I hit him once.

The little one asked us if he could join us. We said, 'Yes'. The little one helped us. He burned the big one [Peter Aston] with a lighted cigarette. He put a hole in the big one's ear. He also kicked him. I can't remember a lot but I have a strong feeling that I stabbed the big one once because although they didn't like him, I didn't want to see him in agony.

Paul hit him with a shovel I think to quieten him and stabbed him. All three of us helped bury him because we were told to get rid of the body. That's as far as I can remember at this stage. Can I say at this stage that I deeply regret doing it. It's not something that I'm proud of and I am very sorry for my actions in this murder. It's murder, isn't it? I'll say murder.

In his statement, Luckman said that, after he and Reid had picked up the two boys, they had handcuffed and held them at knife- and gunpoint, and proceeded down a dirt track, parked and then walked them about 20 metres to a patch of sand and dirt. Here Bob (Reid) had ripped Peter's clothes off, grabbed his genitals and begun to crush them. He continued:

Peter went down then Bob shaved Peter around his genitals and told him [Terry Ryan] to go down and suck him off. While he was doing that Bob cut Peter's hair then he took Terry off and Terry turned around and said, 'Can I join in?' and Bob said, 'Yes'. And Bob and Terry walked about 20 metres inland with a shovel to go and dig a grave.

Whilst they were gone Peter said to me, 'What are you going to do with me?' I did not answer. Bob and Terry returned and Peter got up and ran inland. Terry and I ran after him to catch him. We caught him and took him back. Then Bob started crushing his genitals again then Terry grabbed a can of Aeroguard and matches and lit it towards Peter's hair on his head and to his genitals.

Then Bob put the thumb cuffs on Peter's big toes and told him not to run or he'd kill him. So Peter did and the thumb cuffs came undone. Terry and me ran after him and caught him and took him back. Then I said to Bob, 'It's time we left.' Then Bob said, 'You go first.' Then I cut his throat approximately four millimetres deep and stabbed him in the left or right shoulder. Then Bob stabbed him a few times, one in the back of the throat. Then Peter fell down on the ground and started spitting out

*blood and was dead I think. Then Bob dug a shallow hole and put Peter
in there and covered him up.*

Later that night, both men were formally charged with the murder of
Peter Aston. Reid was also charged with threatening to inflict bodily
harm on Terry Ryan.

The following morning, Reid and Luckman appeared before the Glen
Innes Court. Detective Sergeant Bob Jackson applied for them to be
'bail refused' and that they be remanded in his (Jackson's) custody to
be taken back to Tweed Heads. He said:

> *Spiro and I took Reid, and two detectives from the Sydney homicide
> squad who were working in the New England district on another
> murder case took Luckman. Reid was a tall, well-built man in jeans and
> a cowboy shirt and flat-heeled cowboy boots. Not a bad style of a bloke
> really. My first impression of him was that he was so conceited that he
> genuinely thought that he was completely in control of the situation,
> despite the circumstances.*
>
> *Along the way Reid asked me to stop and buy him a box of matches.
> The minute I gave them to him he put one in his mouth and chewed
> on it, like the cowboys do. That explained the matches found at the
> gravesite. Reid chewed them constantly. We figured that he thought it
> made him look tough.*
>
> *The following day Spiro and myself, along with a scientific
> investigator to take pictures, took Reid on a tour of the murder scene
> and he told us in intricate detail exactly what happened on the night of
> the murder. He was most obliging. He proudly told us about the whole
> night from start to finish including the actions of Paul Luckman and
> Terry Ryan. He pointed out where all of the weapons had been dumped
> and sure enough, when we went and looked, they were there.*
>
> *The sick bastard was enjoying his 15 minutes of fame. I kept telling
> him how clever he was to remember all those things and the more
> I pandered to his ego, the more he pumped himself up and strutted
> around re-enacting the murder, blow by blow, so to speak. He even sat
> on the sand around the grave and laughed. It was sickening.*

With Reid and Luckman safely behind bars, investigators began piecing
together the jigsaw in an effort to try to understand why the men had
committed such a heinous crime for seemingly no apparent reason.

⚰ ⚰ ⚰

Robin Reid was born in Hampshire, England, on 20 October 1948. He immigrated to Australia with his working-class family on 16 November 1961, and they settled in Queensland. He left school at 14 and worked as a labourer, spray-painter and salesman. Somewhere along the way – it isn't clear where – he developed a passion for bows and arrows and knives of all descriptions. Reid joined the army in 1972, and eventually wound up at Enoggera Army Camp. Here, he reached the rank of corporal and was put in charge of assignments for the privates. Because of his sexual preferences and willingness to participate at a moment's notice, he was known around the base as 'Head-job Bob'.

Paul Luckman was born in Melbourne on 1 November 1964, into a broken home where he had little or no relationship with his parents or step-parents. He didn't meet his real mother until he was 13, having been raised by his father and a stepmother. His mother lived with a violent alcoholic who bashed her constantly. In his early teens he was allegedly sexually assaulted by two men in their house over a five-day period. He left school at 16 and went on the dole but supported his meagre income by prostituting himself to men. In an attempt to get some guidance into his troubled life, he joined the army at 17. Within three months he was transferred from Melbourne to Enoggera Army Camp.

On his arrival at Enoggera, Luckman was sent to Corporal Robin Reid for allocation of accommodation. Immediately, Reid was entranced by the handsome young Luckman and arranged for the teenager to move in with him. The combination of Reid's passion for weapons, violence, sexual torture fantasies and Satanism and Luckman's willingness to be enticed into his dark world bonded the pair immediately, and from then on they were inseparable.

In hindsight, investigators realised that it was only a matter of time before the pair would attempt to make their fantasies a reality. After Reid and Luckman's capture, a young soldier, Peter Hoskins, came forward and told police of a conversation he had had with the pair on the night of 18 April, a fortnight before Peter Aston was murdered. Over a few beers the trio had chatted before going to a late-night movie. As always with Reid and Luckman, the conversation quickly got around to abduction and torture. Hoskins reported that Reid had said that he would like to kidnap a couple of 'coons' and torture and sacrifice them on a stone altar. He didn't want to kill them straightaway; instead, he wanted to inflict lots of pain before killing them. Then he wanted to bury their bodies in shallow bush graves where they wouldn't be discovered for up to 20 years. He had produced a medical book and pointed out how and where he would cut his victims, saying that he believed that cutting and burning them with cigarette butts would be the most effective method of torture without actually killing them. Producing two knives, Reid had held Luckman in a headlock and demonstrated his technique to the petrified Hoskins. The trio then went off to the movies.

It was also revealed that two days before they murdered Peter Aston, Reid and Luckman had picked up another young hitchhiker, John Bruce. They had blindfolded and handcuffed him at gunpoint and savagely beaten him before dropping him back at the spot where they had picked him up. Asked why they didn't kill John Bruce, Reid said:

> *I still had control of my reality and emotions in relation to John. We still had to abduct him and I thought we would terrorise him, okay, and we wouldn't take him to the police and my fantasies were being got at this stage.*
>
> *We set out to kill John Andrew Bruce but I couldn't and we let him go. But when we came to Peter [Peter Aston] it was getting stronger. Lack of sleep, other things, were building up within me. The fantasies had got to me at this stage but ... there was no feeling, there was no satisfaction or feeling in me when I set out to kill Peter.*

⚰ ⚰ ⚰

Reid and Luckman's committal hearing was held at Tweed Heads Court on 4 August 1982 before Magistrate Brian Hanrahan. From the outset the committal hearing was a debacle as media from all over Australia and an angry mob clambered over each other to get a look at the pair of monsters who had allegedly indulged in Satanism, torture and bizarre sexual rituals and butchered and murdered a boy. When Peter Aston's brother, Michael, went missing from his Melbourne home armed with a rifle after making threats to kill Reid and Luckman, the Tactical Response Group was called in to monitor everyone entering the courthouse. It was rumoured that the dead boy's mother had entered the courthouse armed with a knife, and although she sat within an arm's length of Reid during the proceedings, if she did have a knife, she refrained from using it. Satisfied that Reid and Luckman had a case to answer, Mr Hanrahan committed them for trial in the New South Wales Supreme Court in Grafton. But, given the gravity of the charges against the pair, the case was transferred to the Sydney Supreme Court to be heard in front of Mr Justice Adrian Roden and a jury of three women and nine men.

The trial began on 8 November 1982. Paul Luckman pleaded 'not guilty' and Robin Reid pleaded 'not guilty by reason of insanity'.

So appalling were the injuries to Peter Aston that the Crown Prosecutor, David Shillington QC, elected not to show photographs of the deceased to the jury. His reasoning for this decision was his belief that the photographs may psychologically block the jurors' minds and that they would then try to suppress the images and in turn fail to recall the brutality of the offence. Mr Justice Roden agreed with this strategy, and told the court that he believed it would be in everyone's best interests if the jury were spared the visual horror of what happened to Peter and instead heard it from the witnesses.

Given that there was no doubt Reid and Luckman had murdered Peter, the trial focused on which of the defendants played the major role in the atrocity. As the proceedings progressed, it was clear that Luckman intended to lay the blame squarely at Reid's feet. It was also clear that the pair's parting had been acrimonious. Among a multitude of allegations, Luckman claimed that he was forced to participate in the atrocities as a result of a direct threat on his life by Reid. He alleged that Reid had asked him to go on a drive to the Gold Coast, but when he was in the vehicle Reid pulled a knife, held it to his throat and said, 'We are going to kill someone tonight. If not, it will be you.' In contrast, Reid embarked on his defence of insanity by claiming that his bisexuality put him under much stress because, if his superiors found out, he would be discharged from the army. He also claimed that his job as a clerk in the Ordinance Corps put him under constant pressure and his obsession with the occult caused him to hear voices that, in turn, drove him to murder.

However, despite the pair's defence, Terry Ryan's evidence was damning and the jurors wasted no time in making up their minds. On 26 November 1982, the jury delivered a verdict of guilty for both accused. In sentencing Reid and Luckman to life imprisonment, Mr Justice Roden said that their crime was 'one of the most brutal and callous crimes ever to come before the courts in this state.' The prisoners were taken away to begin their sentences in separate jails.

⛫ ⛫ ⛫

In prison Robin Reid was kept in protective custody for his own safety. Mainstream prisoners didn't take kindly to men who sexually assault, torture and murder 13-year-old boys. Reid applied for a re-determination of his sentence on 26 November 1998, and was granted a maximum of life with a minimum term of 24 years. He was eligible for parole in 2006 but is still in jail and it seems likely he will be there until he dies.

Although deemed a child-killer, the feminine Luckman was treated with more respect behind bars than Reid. He survived in prison by selling his favours to inmates in exchange for money and other prison currency, such as cigarettes and drugs. As each year passed, he became more like a woman, and in 1989, he began hormone treatment after a visiting psychiatrist assessed that, in most respects, he was more of a woman than a man. In 1990 he had sex reassignment surgery in prison and changed his name by deed poll to Nicole Louise Pearce. On 20 October 1993, Nicole had her sentence redetermined to a maximum of 24 years and a minimum of 16 years. On 26 October 1999, she was released from the Kirkconnell Correctional Centre near Bathurst in New South Wales and moved into a house in Geelong, Victoria, amid vehement protests from the neighbours.

The years have not been kind to Terry Ryan, the innocent boy Reid and Luckman forced to perform a sexual act on his best friend before burying him alive. He became a pariah, the butt of jokes and taunts by his schoolmates and the community about his involvement in the crime, which was all laid bare during the trial. He was assaulted and spat upon. At the end of Reid and Luckman's trial, Terry attended the Wilson Youth Hospital for psychiatric assessment. He has been in and out of prison for a variety of offences, including assault and car theft. It was documented to the court in a pre-sentencing hearing that he showed anti-authoritarian behaviour and lack of anger management and suffered from alcohol and drug abuse. His mother says he still suffers from nightmares and flashbacks.

Commenting on Paul Luckman's release in 1999, criminologist and Dean of Bond University Professor Paul Wilson, who had researched and studied Luckman's case in 1984, said he believed that Luckman, now Nicole Pearce, should never have been released at any time. He continued: 'I had severe reservations about him then, being released this early. Although it has been many years since I have seen him, my view then was that it was very unlikely he would change. Not so much the pedophilic tendencies, more the psychopathic tendencies that worried me. He was someone that was easily manipulated and enjoyed violence.'

It is believed that Nicole Pearce has not offended since.

Chapter Two

THE MAD SCIENTIST

On Tuesday, 13 September 1983, a sewage treatment worker spotted the severed right middle finger of a woman's hand in effluent at Tasmania's Macquarie Point Sewage Treatment Plant.

At 9.45 am that day, Dr Rory Jack Thompson had reported that his estranged wife Maureen was missing from her home in West Hobart.

The Thompsons had moved to Australia from the United States in 1974. They lived in Perth and Sydney before settling in Hobart in January 1983. Maureen, 37, looked after their two children — three-year-old Rafi and seven-year-old Melody — while her 41-year-old husband, a specialist theoretical oceanographer, worked with the CSIRO.

Despite a happy start, the marriage soon deteriorated. Thompson beat his wife savagely in front of the children. In fear for her life, Maureen moved out of the family home a couple of months before Thompson reported her missing. With the assistance of state welfare agencies, she moved into a house in West Hobart to begin a new life.

As Maureen was broke with no access to her husband's income, she received a Supporting Parent's Benefit; she also took a part-time teaching job and left the children at a day-care centre. She took out a restraining order against her husband.

The situation mellowed and the couple began talking again. Maureen even allowed Thompson to take the children for one day and night per week. But the pain of losing his children slowly grew inside him.

After the severed finger was found, authorities visited Maureen's home the following day and found bloodstains on the hallway wall and pieces of human tissue in the bathroom. There was a large bloodstain by the bed. When told that his wife may have been murdered, and that the severed finger found in sewage could belong to her, Thompson appeared uninterested. He said that on the night police alleged Maureen had been killed, he had been in Kingston, and arrived home at about 9 pm. He put the children to bed and went to bed himself at about 10.15 pm, waking the next day around 7 am.

Three days later, Thompson went to the Criminal Investigation Branch (CIB) and asked for his car, which police had taken for testing. He said he wanted to take his children camping. Police told him they hadn't completed their tests and alerted detectives to Thompson's intentions. They had good reason to worry. The previous day Thompson had told Detective Inspector Ernest Roffe and Detective Sergeant Richard McCreadie that the 'good Rory' would not have killed his wife but the 'bad Rory' was still dominant. He also told investigators that he was concerned the 'bad Rory' could have been involved in his wife's death.

Rory Thompson was no stranger to dark and violent thoughts, referring to himself as 'Good Rory' and 'Bad Rory'. In his unpublished autobiography found by police, he admitted to having fantasised about murdering his first wife, and wrote of fantasies concerning Maureen's murder as well.

Roffe believed Thompson could be contemplating murdering his children and committing suicide. A close watch was kept on his home. The following night Rafi and Melody were taken away by uniformed police and placed in the care of the Social Welfare Department.

The next day, Thompson broke down and confessed to his wife's murder, claiming 'the bad Rory' had done it, and took police to her bush grave. The sewer pipes at the Hill Street house unearthed 83 pieces of her body. He had cut Maureen Thompson into pieces and flushed them down her toilet.

Thompson told police that at 10.30 pm on Saturday, 10 September 1983, he put on a long wig that covered his face, a scarf and mascara. He dressed in paint-splattered overalls covered by a thick wraparound skirt. In his carry bag he put the leg of a chair, rubber and cloth gardening gloves, a plumber's drain-clearing plunger, a meat cleaver, two knives, an oxyacetylene torch kit, two hacksaws with three spare blades and a garrotte made of orange rope. He then drove to his wife's house and waited in the garden until she went to bed.

Thompson said his initial plan was to garrotte his wife, but Maureen woke up after he pulled the quilt from her face. He struck her twice over the head with the chair leg, which he then dropped. Maureen picked it up and hit him over the head with it. She started to scream. Thompson then grabbed his wife by the throat and throttled her to death, saying, 'Maureen, I'm sorry it had to happen this way.'

Thompson dragged his wife's body to the bath and, using a meat cleaver and hacksaw, he cut her into small pieces and sat there for several hours flushing them down the toilet, until it became clogged. Finally, he burned what was left of her, bundled the charred remains in towels and put it all into a garbage bag. He then buried them and his bloodstained clothing in a hole he had dug at Lenah Valley earlier in the year, for the purpose of concealing any evidence of the murder.

At his trial on 23 February 1984, Thompson pleaded not guilty. He said he wanted to plead for mercy, and told the jury they had the power to acquit him. Thompson said he would never do anything 'like that again' and asked to be released so he could go back to his marine research where he could do more good for society than he could in jail.

He told the court that in the 12 months before the break-up he had planned to murder his wife. He had decided to bury her alive in the backyard. He even tried to dig a hole, but his small shovel was useless on the hard ground. Still, he carried a length of rope with him at all times, in case he got a chance to garrotte her. Thompson told the court that as he had been planning to dispose of his wife down the toilet, he had practised chopping up a side of lamb and some soup bones to see if they would flush.

Eventually Mr Justice Everett instructed that Thompson be dealt with as a mentally disordered person, and ordered him to be incarcerated in the hospital section of the overcrowded Risdon Prison until a decision was made on what to do with him. In June 1984, the Tasmanian Attorney-General declared that Thompson's period of detention at Risdon would be indefinite, and that he could only be released by the Governor when the Governor was satisfied, on advice, that detention was no longer required for the public's protection.

In 1990 the Mental Health Review Tribunal recommended that Thompson be released to an appropriate mental institution, but it was overruled. He stayed at Risdon. By this time Thompson had changed his name to Jack Newman by deed poll, and written a book titled *Mad Scientist*. He also kept in touch with the outside world and continued to conduct marine research.

Thompson published more than 50 scientific papers during his time at Risdon, and patents for a 3D television system and a solar oven were pending. But apart from his academic achievements in jail, Thompson found another love – gardening. The gardens became the pride of Risdon, and Thompson was encouraged to indulge his passion. Soon he was spending most of his time outdoors, alone in the fresh Tasmanian air with his beloved plants.

In July 1999 – with his freedom guaranteed in November that year – Thompson was working in the gardens outside Risdon Prison when he casually walked away, caught a bus into central Hobart, withdrew money from an ATM and flew to Melbourne, before he was arrested. Thompson wasn't given a sentence for the escape, but he was made to spend time in solitary confinement away from his beloved research books and garden. On 17 September 1999, he was found hanged by his shoelaces in his cell.

Chapter Three

PAUL CHARLES DENYER:
THE JOHN CANDY KILLER

In the midst of the Melbourne winter of 1993, the southern bayside suburb of Frankston was gripped by terror. A serial killer was on the loose. Women glanced behind them furtively and quickened their steps while walking home from railway stations and bus stops. Many locked themselves in at night. Real estate prices tumbled. The entire district was stricken with fear. The media fuelled the hysteria with regular reports as police set up a dragnet to find the killer.

The serial killer had already abducted and slain three young women. An 18-year-old student had been strangled and stabbed, her body discarded in a drain. A 22-year-old mother with a child less than a fortnight old had been brutally murdered and her body secreted in a bush grave. A 17-year-old secondary school student had been slain in the most macabre circumstances, her throat cut from ear to ear for no other reason than the gratification of her killer. And a 41-year-old woman had fallen into the killer's clutches but had managed to escape. When the serial killer was eventually apprehended, he told police that he believed he was destined to commit murder. He had waited all his young life to kill. He had selected his victims at random and for no other reason than that he wanted to kill. Chillingly, he told police: 'I've always wanted to kill, waiting for the right time. Waiting for that silent alarm to trigger me off.'

In a bizarre paradox, due to his 120-kilogram, 180-centimetre build, the killer was known as John Candy after the late funnyman who had made the world laugh. But, in fact, the 'Uncle Buck' look-a-like was a deranged psychopath named Paul Charles Denyer, who was just 21 years of age when he was arrested for multiple murder. And, in stark contradiction to his jovial nickname, Paul Denyer was a vicious sadist who took delight from the pain and suffering of others – especially women. The reason that the self-confessed misogynist ended the lives of 18-year-old Elizabeth Stevens, 22-year-old Deborah Fream and 17-year-old Natalie Russell was because he hated women. When the police asked him why all of his victims were women, Denyer replied: 'I just hate them.'

Denyer was a monster and it was a matter of time before he turned to murder. He was just ten years of age when he killed the family cat, slitting its throat with one of the knives he had in his burgeoning collection of home-made weapons. At 15 years of age he was charged with assault for forcing another boy to masturbate in front of a group of children. Obsessed with violence, Denyer used to watch movies such as *Friday the 13th* and *Halloween* again and again, his gaze fixed while the fake blood splattered across the screen. Yet celluloid violence would not ultimately satisfy Denyer. He needed the real thing. At his trial for triple murder, clinical psychologist Ian Joblin provided a detailed profile on Denyer. Joblin had spent long hours interviewing Denyer and reported that he showed no remorse whatever for his crimes. In fact, he recalled that Denyer seemed to get pleasure from recalling the pain he'd inflicted on his victims.

Denyer attempted to explain his actions to Joblin by saying that he was sexually molested as a young child. He made a number of accusations suggesting that his elder brother had interfered with him when he was an infant. He believed that this, combined with a tough upbringing at the hands of his father and long-term unemployment, had made him the wretched fiend he had become. As Joblin would tell the court, these were circumstances that many normal people endured in their lives, yet they did not resort to multiple murder. Joblin believed that Denyer possessed the most aberrant mind he had encountered. He told the court that the community should fear Denyer. He was a relentless sadist who derived pleasure from killing, and any satisfaction he derived from murder dissipated quickly, impelling him to kill again within increasingly shorter periods of time. He had displayed aggressive and cruel behavior since childhood. There was no effective psychological treatment for his personality; he had to be isolated from society, for society's sake.

On 20 December 1993, Mr Justice Frank Vincent sentenced Denyer to life imprisonment. There was no set non-parole period. Justice Vincent's sentence reflected the community's desire that Denyer should die in prison.

⚰ ⚰ ⚰

Paul Denyer was born on 14 April 1972 in Sydney. His parents, Anthony and Maureen Denyer, immigrated to Australia from northern England in 1965 and established themselves in Campbelltown, 50 kilometres south-west of Sydney. Paul was their third child. The Denyer household would ultimately comprise six children: five boys and a girl.

As an infant, Denyer had rolled off a table and sustained a minor head injury. Although he suffered no lasting injury from this incident, it became a running joke among the family. When he made an off-colour remark or behaved oddly, family members would look at one another and remark: 'That's because he fell on his head when he was a baby.' Nonetheless, Paul Denyer led a typical childhood. He experienced some difficulty in socialising with other children in his early years at primary school, but this awkwardness seemed to disappear as his education progressed.

At nine years of age, however, Paul's life was thrown into turmoil. His father had found employment as a restaurant manager in Melbourne and the family was forced to relocate. The Denyer family set up house in Mulgrave on the eastern fringes of Melbourne. All the children struggled in the new environment initially, but it was Paul who experienced the greatest difficulty in adjusting to the family's changed circumstances. He became withdrawn and isolated. At his new school, Northvale Primary School, he displayed learning difficulties and lacked the self-confidence to establish new friendships. He was changing physically too, growing taller and heavier by the day. He was bigger than most of his peers and his size became the subject of both derision and fear as the large youngster learnt how to use his size to intimidate others.

An unmotivated loner, Denyer drifted into a world of his own, a fantasy land in which he wielded knives and guns. He began to make and collect dangerous weapons. By the time of his tenth birthday, he owned a substantial assortment of home-made knives, shanghais and clubs. His sister often had to endure him decapitating her teddy bears and dolls with a knife. Many of her toys showed the bewildering signs of knife attacks. In 1982, Paul stabbed a kitten, killing the family pet and hanging it from a tree. Three years later, he was charged with car theft, but the matter was kept from the courts and police let the boy off with a caution. His luck ran out with the police shortly afterwards when he was charged with theft, wilful damage and making a false report to the Metropolitan Fire Brigade. This time he was charged. Denyer, not yet 14, made his first court appearance and was given a suspended sentence.

A student at Clayton Technical School, Denyer was bigger and heavier than most of his classmates. He became a bully, throwing his considerable weight around in the schoolyard. Most of his peers gave him a wide berth and with good reason. He left school at 15, shortly after his assault charge for forcing the boy to masturbate. He entered an adult world where his bullying would not be tolerated.

For a time Denyer worked at a suburban supermarket, stacking shelves and carting grocery stock around the store. At this time he met a woman called Sharon Johnston and fell in love with her. It was the only relationship Denyer ever had with a woman that could conceivably be described as positive. Johnston was unaware of his propensity for violence, and seemed to be attracted to the large young man. The pair became close, and when Denyer was 20 years old, they shared a flat in the Frankston district. Denyer's stay as an employee at the supermarket was, however, short-lived. He was dismissed after he knocked down a female customer and her child with a shopping trolley. He found other jobs but, due to laziness or incompetence, he either left them or was fired. His last paid job was at a marine workshop where he was dismissed after two goats were found slaughtered in a nearby paddock. Denyer, who spent most of his time making and using home-made knives instead of attending to his work, was the obvious culprit. His workmates found his violent obsessions disturbing and they were pleased to see him go.

Denyer then applied to join the Victoria Police Force but was rejected at an early stage due to his weight and low level of fitness. Thereafter, he joined the queues of the unemployed. He felt rejected by society, and this rejection clearly acted as a powerful trigger. He became isolated, spending much of his waking hours watching videos of horror movies and fashioning home-made knives. Meanwhile, Sharon worked two jobs, having found a part-time job as a telemarketer to add to her duties as a customer service assistant at the supermarket, to help pay the bills. With his board and keep subsidised by the labours of his girlfriend, Denyer made no serious attempt to find employment. Idle for much of the day, it was just a matter of time before he turned to crime.

⚰ ⚰ ⚰

Denyer and Sharon were living in a block of flats at 186 Frankston-Dandenong Road in Frankston. With plenty of time on his hands, he began to give his neighbours unwelcome attention. They did not suspect the stocky unemployed man of anything untoward. It was not until after Denyer was arrested for the murder of three young Frankston women that the truth was revealed.

One female resident returned home from work one evening to find that an intruder had broken into her flat. Nothing had been stolen but the place had been ransacked and her clothes ripped to shreds. Photographs of her had been slashed with a sharp knife. A number of residents became aware of a peeping Tom skulking about at night and peering in through their windows. One woman caught a glimpse of a large man looking at her through a window. She called the police, but as she was unable to provide a description of the man, an arrest could not be made.

To all outward appearances, Denyer was a caring and friendly fellow. When he was told about the peeping Tom, he told his neighbours that he would keep an eye out for the voyeur and give him a hiding if he caught him.

Both Denyer and Sharon had become friendly with a number of the other residents in the block, including a young woman named Tricia. Denyer used to chat idly with Tricia when he saw her or would give her a wave as they passed on the street. Tricia had a sister named Donna, and Donna and her fiancé, Les, and their newborn child lived in a block of flats nearby.

In February 1993, Donna and Les returned home late at night after Les had finished his part-time job as a pizza delivery man. They opened the front door of their home and, within seconds, sensed that something was wrong. Walking into the lounge room with their baby asleep in a bassinet, Donna and Les took in the scene with mouths agape. Their cat, Buffy, was lying in the middle of the floor, dead. The cat had been disembowelled and a picture of a semi-naked woman had been placed over its body. The words 'Dead Don' had been scrawled in blood on the television screen.

Incredulous, Donna and Les followed the blood trail throughout their home. The cat's intestines and organs had been strewn around the kitchen and smeared on the walls. On one of the kitchen walls, a cryptic message had been written in blood: 'Donna and Robyn – You're Dead'. Neither Donna nor Les knew anyone named Robyn. The laundry, too, was like a scene from a horror movie. Blood had been sprayed on the walls, ceiling and floor and all over a basket filled with soiled baby clothes. In the bathroom, the couple found two of Buffy's kittens lying in a pool of bloody water in the bath with their throats cut. There was more carnage in the bedroom. Cupboards and a chest of drawers had been smashed, and virtually every item of clothing that Donna owned had been slashed with a knife and left in tatters on the floor. The baby's clothing had also been cut to shreds, and a tattered photograph of a woman in a bikini had been placed in the cot where the baby slept. The intruder had written the names 'Donna and Robyn' in shaving cream on the dressing-table mirror.

Donna, Les and their tiny baby left the flat that night. They would never spend another night there. While they searched for alternative accommodation, they moved in with Donna's sister, Tricia. Tricia had a neighbour, a large man named Paul, who made all sorts of sympathetic noises when Donna told him her story. The big fellow had told Donna that he would take matters into his own hands if he came across the man who had wrecked their home and caused them such distress. However, the friendly next-door neighbour harboured a grim secret. It was he who had taken to trawling the streets with his home-made knives, peering in through windows, searching for a home where he could create mayhem. The psychopath was emerging, and it was just a matter of time before he spilt human blood.

⚰ ⚰ ⚰

An 18-year-old student, Elizabeth Stevens, became Denyer's first victim. On Saturday, 12 June 1993, Elizabeth's body was found in Lloyd Park on Cranbourne Road in Langwarrin. It looked like a frenzied attack. She had multiple stab wounds to her chest and a series of abrasions on her face and hands. Her nose had been broken, indicating that she had put up a mighty struggle before being overwhelmed by her assailant. The girl's clothing had been removed from her upper body. Her bra was pulled up around her neck. Along her chest and torso there was a series of four cuts running from her breastbone to her navel. Four more deep cuts had been made running across her chest in the other direction.

The young student had been a popular and friendly girl. She had died in a senseless attack, and initially police thought that Elizabeth had been the victim of a mugging but, for some reason, her attacker had lost control. She had been reported missing the previous evening by her uncle and aunt, with whom she had been staying. A bright girl, she was known to study in municipal libraries from time to time. Police investigated all possible leads, conducting house-to-house inquiries within the Frankston district. A roadblock was established near the bus stop where Elizabeth had last been seen alive. Police dressed a shop dummy in the same clothes she had been wearing the evening she disappeared in the hope that a motorist would recall seeing her and possibly identify anyone she was with. But there were no leads, and police were left mystified.

🏛 🏛 🏛

Less than month later, on Thursday 8 July 1993, a 41-year-old bank teller, Roszsa Toth, was attacked by a large man while she was returning to her Seaford home after work. Later, Toth told police that the man appeared to be carrying a gun in his jacket pocket and that he had held the gun to her head. Ordering her to comply or be shot, her attacker attempted to drag her off the footpath and into nearby parklands. She refused to comply and fought for her life. The man dragged her by her hair for a distance before she managed to bite his hand, removing herself from his clutches. She had bitten the man's fingers to the bone. He continued in his attempt to abduct her and pulled out clumps of her hair in desperation, but she maintained her strong resistance. Finally, she fought the man off, and with her clothing torn, she managed to get back to the road and flag down a passing car. She contacted police immediately, who attended the scene of her attempted abduction. However, Toth's attacker had fled. The extraordinary violence of the attack left her with the clear impression that she was lucky to escape with her life.

Later the same evening, police received more chilling news. Twenty-two-year-old Deborah Fream had gone missing while travelling to a shop near her home at Seaford to purchase milk and eggs. Debbie had given birth to a son, Jake, less than a fortnight earlier. Now, she had disappeared without a trace. The police believed that the murder of Elizabeth Stevens, the attempted abduction of Roszsa Toth and the disappearance of Debbie Fream were linked. Four days later, this belief was confirmed when the body of the young mother was found in a paddock in the nearby suburb of Carrum Downs. Debbie had been stabbed repeatedly about the neck, head, chest and arms. Her body bore witness to 24 separate knife wounds. She had been manually strangled. Although Debbie's jumper had been lifted up, there was no indication that she had been sexually assaulted.

The Frankston community now realised that a madman was on the loose. Instantly, the district was filled with fear. A serial killer who preyed on women was operating in this usually quiet area. Women locked themselves indoors at night, and the friendly, bustling suburban streets turned eerily quiet after dusk. Police established a support centre to provide women with assistance. The centre offered basic self-defence courses and instructed women on what to do in the event that they encountered the serial killer. They continued to pursue every lead and, with the local community in a vigilant mood, hoped that the psychopath might go to ground. At least then the killing might stop. But the target of the search had developed an appetite for murder. He would kill again. And soon.

⚰ ⚰ ⚰

On Friday 30 July, a 17-year-old Higher School Certificate student Natalie Russell went missing while riding her bicycle home from school. The young student from John Paul College in Frankston was reported missing by her parents. Eight hours later, Natalie's parents had their worst fears confirmed. Police had found her body in a park adjacent to the Peninsula Golf Club. She had been stabbed repeatedly in the face, neck and chest. Her throat had been cut. Forensic specialists quickly determined that the attack on Natalie had been extremely vicious, and more calculating and frenzied than those in the previous instances. The killer was escalating the violence. Again the post-mortem showed no evidence of sexual assault.

Forensic analysis proved to be crucial in the hunt for the killer. In the course of his maniacal attack on Debbie, the young mother, he had cut himself with his knife, leaving a large piece of his own flesh at the scene. Now, police had a vital piece of physical evidence.

Another lead was a car. A yellow Toyota Corona had been seen near the park around the time Natalie was murdered. A passing squad car had noticed the car and written down the registration number. A car fitting the description of the Corona had also been sighted around the scene of Elizabeth Stevens's murder. The car was registered to a Paul Charles Denyer.

🪦 🪦 🪦

Detectives Michael Hughes and Charles Bezzine paid a visit to Denyer's home, but Denyer was nowhere to be found. They left a card under the door, instructing Denyer to contact them urgently. His girlfriend, Sharon Johnston, was the first one home that day, and she saw the card and telephoned police to see what the problem was. She was told that it was a routine inquiry. The police asked her when her boyfriend would arrive home. She replied that Denyer was expected home at any time.

Police converged on the flat. A team of detectives knocked on the door, and Paul Denyer opened the door and let them in. They told the obese young man that his vehicle had been sighted near the scene of the recent murders in Frankston. Denyer told them that his car had broken down near the scene of Natalie's Russell's murder. On this occasion, he explained, he had driven to the railway station to pick up Sharon. The detectives noticed cuts all over his hands, including a large chunk of skin missing from his right hand. Asked what had happened to his hands, Denyer told the detectives that he got his hand caught in the fanbelt of his car while he was doing some mechanical work.

The detectives arrested Denyer on suspicion of murdering Natalie Russell and took him to Frankston police station for further questioning. Police interviewed him for several hours. He had no alibi for the times when the three young women had been murdered, but he continued to deny any knowledge of the murders. However, it was the piece of skin he had left at the scene of Natalie Russell's murder that sealed his fate. Police asked him for a blood sample and told him that they needed the sample to conduct a DNA analysis of the piece of skin found at the scene. They could prove it was his and Denyer knew it. He asked how long it would take for the results of DNA analysis to be confirmed and was told that it was a matter of a few days. He looked at Detective Darren O'Loughlin, weighing up his options. Suddenly, he told the detective: 'Okay, I killed all three of them.'

🔯 🔯 🔯

In painstaking detail, Denyer confessed to his crimes. What shocked police was his studied indifference to the suffering of his victims. He had killed the three young women callously, and now he coolly recalled the circumstances of their deaths in much the same manner as a person might describe a journey to a local shopping centre. What was clear to police, however, was that Denyer became excited and aroused when he told them *how* he had committed the murders.

Denyer confessed that, on 11 June 1993, he had waited behind a bush while the bus stopped and let out several passengers in Cranbourne Road, Langwarrin. It was a cold, rainy evening, and the passengers had scuttled from the bus quickly, eager to get home and out of the rain. Elizabeth Stevens had walked by Denyer, and he had known that he was going to kill her. He did not know the girl and had never met her before, but a silent alarm had gone off and the sadist was turning to murder for the first time. He had followed Elizabeth as she walked through the rain. He had then grabbed her from behind, telling her that he had a gun and if she screamed or attempted to escape he would shoot her. Denyer did not possess a gun but had joined a piece of metal pipe to a wooden handle. He had held the fake pistol in his jacket and led the young woman to nearby Lloyd Park.

In his statement to police, Denyer told how he committed his first murder:

> I started choking her with my hands and she passed out after a while.
> You know the oxygen got cut off to her head and she just stopped. And
> then I pulled out the knife and stabbed her many times in the throat, and
> she was still alive. And then she stood up and then we walked around

and all that, just walking a few steps and then I threw her on the ground and stuck my foot over her neck to finish her off.

Denyer demonstrated how he had pushed his thumb into Elizabeth's throat to strangle her, then he motioned wildly with his hands to show how he had stabbed the young woman. Later, he stood up and began shaking and jittering his entire body to show how Elizabeth had died. The murder was like theatre for Denyer; it seemed he thought he had the lead role in the drama. He continued to delight in his performance, without a moment of remorse for his victim or any apparent self-consciousness. He then told police how he had dragged Elizabeth's body to a drain where he had left it. His attack on the young woman had been so violent that the home-made weapon he had used had broken. He had disposed of the murder weapon on a roadside near where his victim lay.

Asked why he had killed the young woman, Denyer told police: 'Just wanted ... just wanted to kill. Just wanted to take a life because I thought my life had been taken many times.'

Denyer then recalled the events of 8 July 1993, the night he attempted to abduct Roszsa Toth, and how he had later murdered Debbie Fream. He told police he had been loitering around Seaford railway station when he saw a woman walk from the platform. He had gone up to her from behind and put his hand across her mouth. With his other hand he produced his fake gun and held it to the woman's head. Toth had struggled and bitten his hand while he attempted to muffle her cries for help. They wrestled on the ground before the woman broke free and ran onto the road to try to flag down a car passing by. None of the cars stopped, and Denyer told the woman to stop or he would shoot her. She seemed reconciled to her fate and stopped running. As he approached her again, she took off and made it back to the road where a car stopped to help her. Denyer ran from the scene, knowing that police would be there within minutes. When asked by police what he planned to do with the woman, he replied: 'I was just going to drag her in the park and kill her. That's all.'

Roszsa Toth's near miss left Denyer's urge to kill unsatisfied. He jumped onto the train at Seaford railway station and got off at Kananook, the next station on the Frankston line. He walked across the pedestrian bridge over the railway lines and spotted his next victim.

Debbie Fream had just got out of her car and walked into a milk bar to make her purchases. Denyer walked up to Debbie's Pulsar sedan and got into the back seat, waiting for her to return from the shop. He could hear her footsteps as she approached. She got into the car, placed a shopping bag on the passenger seat next to her, and then started the engine. Denyer told police:

> I waited for her to start up the car so no one would hear her scream. She put it into gear and she went to do a U-turn. I startled her just as she was doing that turn and she kept going into the wall of the milk bar, which caused a dent in the bonnet. I told her to, you know, shut up or I'd blow her head off and all that shit.

Denyer directed the young mother to the paddocks at Carrum Downs. He said: 'I told her when we got there that if she gave any signals to anyone, I'd blow her head off. I'd decorate the car with her brains.' Debbie was told to park her car near some trees. She was then ordered out of the car. Denyer came up behind her with a length of rope. He continued:

> I popped it over her eyes real quickly, so she didn't see it. I didn't want her to see the cord first. I lifted the cord up and said: 'Can you see this?' And she just put her hand up to grab it, to feel it and when she did that I just yanked on it real quickly around her neck. And then I was struggling with her for about five minutes.

Debbie lost consciousness and fell to the ground. Denyer pounced on her and drew his knife. He stabbed her repeatedly in the chest and neck. He continued to stab her in the neck, and then stabbed her once in the stomach. 'She started breathing out of her neck, just like Elizabeth Stevens,' Denyer stated. 'I could just hear bubbling noises.' He told the appalled detectives that he had lifted up Debbie's jumper to 'see how big her boobs were'. Once he caught sight of her naked flesh, he lashed out again with his knife, stabbing her in the chest. With his second victim lying dead before him, he felt nothing. He said: 'I felt the same way I did when I killed Elizabeth Stevens.' He could offer no reason for the murder: 'I just wanted to.'

Denyer then dragged Debbie's body to a row of trees and covered it with several branches. He took the murder weapon with him when he left the scene. He drove off in Debbie's car and parked it near his home. He must have noticed the child restraint in the back seat of the car. It is mandatory for children under the age of five to be belted in to an approved child restraint. Denyer would have realised that Debbie was a mother, but it made no difference to him. After Debbie's murder, he calmly drove his own car to the railway station to collect Sharon, his girlfriend. The next day, after Sharon had left for work, Denyer went back to Debbie's car and took out the shopping items and Debbie's purse. He tipped Debbie's milk and eggs down his kitchen sink, and disposed of the cartons by burning them at home. He buried the woman's purse at a nearby golf course.

Now more than six hours into his confession, Denyer turned his attention to the murder of Natalie Russell. While his victim was selected at random, it transpired that he had coldly calculated his next killing. He had chosen a bicycle track that runs the length of a municipal park. He decided to wait there, concealing himself behind trees. He had planned every moment of the abduction. Two days before he snatched Natalie and took her life, he had cut two holes through a metal fence with a pair of bolt cutters. Armed with a razor-sharp home-made knife with an aluminum blade and a leather strap to strangle his victim, Denyer planned to lie there in wait and grab the first young woman who walked past along the bicycle track.

At 2.30 pm on 30 July 1993, Denyer drove back to the park and took up his hiding place in the thicket behind the fence. The holes he had cut were big enough for him to drag his victim through and into the relative seclusion of the parklands. After a wait of about half an hour, he saw a young woman – Natalie Russell – entering the bicycle track. She was in school uniform. He followed her. As Natalie approached the second hole that Denyer had made in the fence, he struck, grabbing her from behind. He held the knife to her throat but managed to slash himself, slicing a big chunk from his right hand. He told her that if she moved or resisted in any way he would cut her throat. He dragged her through the hole in the cyclone fence and continued to hold her at knife point. Natalie may have realised she was face to face with the Frankston serial killer. She tried to negotiate her release, pleading to be spared.

'She said, "You can have all my money, have sex with me" and things,' Denyer told detectives. 'Just said disgusting things like that really.' Denyer was not tempted by sex. He wanted only to inflict pain and commit murder. He forced Natalie to kneel in front of him while he menaced her with the knife, easing it up to her eyeballs. He then slashed her face. Trying to escape, Natalie struggled to her feet and screamed for help. He told the detectives: 'And I just said, "Shut up. Shut up. Shut up. Shut up." And, "If you don't shut up, I'll kill you."'

Denyer forced Natalie back to the ground in a kneeling position. The young woman was sobbing and terrified. He then tried to strangle her. He said:

> I put the strap around her neck to strangle her and it broke in half. And then she started violently struggling for about a minute until I pushed – got her on her back again – and pushed her head back like this and cut her throat.
>
> I cut a small cut at first and then she was bleeding. And then I stuck my fingers into her throat ... and grabbed her chords and I twisted them.

Denyer told the horrified detectives that he had plunged his hand into the young woman's throat in an attempt to kill her. 'My whole fingers – like, that much of my hand inside her throat,' Denyer told them, indicating a line up to his knuckles. He continued: 'She sort of started to faint and then when she was weak, a bit weaker, I grabbed the opportunity of throwing her head back and one big, large cut which sort of cut almost her whole head off. And then she slowly died.'

The detectives asked again what motive Denyer had for killing the young woman. He said: 'Just the same reason as before, just everything came back through my mind again. I kicked her before I left.' Denyer also told the detectives that he had slashed the young woman's face one more time. He then walked back along the bike path with his blood-soaked hands thrust deeply into his pockets. As he got back to his car, he saw two uniformed policemen looking closely at his vehicle, jotting down the registration details. He turned around and walked home the other way.

When he got home, Denyer showered, washing the blood from his hands. He concealed the knife he used to kill Natalie Russell at the back of his flat. Later, he collected Sharon from the railway station and spent the night dining with Sharon at her mother's home.

Denyer's stunning confessions had taken more than six hours. Denyer revelled in telling police every sordid, despicable detail. The only time he showed any emotional response to the crimes was when he expressed contempt for Natalie Russell for offering him sex in a desperate attempt to avoid death. But he hadn't finished. Later that day, he told police that he was responsible for breaking into Les and Donna's home and torturing and killing their three cats, smearing blood on the walls and threatening to kill Donna. He revealed that he had gone to the flat for the sole purpose of killing the young mother. When he arrived there to find no-one home, he broke in regardless and vented his psychopathic fury on the hapless felines.

Later, Denyer explained to detectives why all of his victims were young women: he detested women. He told Detective Darren O'Loughlin: 'I just hate them.'

'I beg your pardon,' replied O'Loughlin.

'I just hate them,' Denyer repeated.

'Those particular girls,' O'Loughlin asked. 'Or women in general?'

'General.'

Denyer's girlfriend, Sharon Johnston, had no idea of the type of man she was living with. She was stunned and shocked when police informed her that Denyer had confessed to the murders. She simply had not seen that side of him. Denyer had treated her well. Clearly, he did not see his girlfriend as an enemy. He told the detectives: 'Sharon's not like anyone else I know. I'd never hurt her. She's a kindred spirit.' It was the only positive remark he made throughout the course of his confession.

⚰ ⚰ ⚰

Paul Denyer was charged with the murders of Elizabeth Stevens, Deborah Fream and Natalie Russell. He was also charged with the attempted murder of Roszsa Toth. Later this charge was reduced to abduction.

At his trial on 15 December 1993 in the Victorian Supreme Court, Denyer pleaded guilty to all charges. Five days later, Mr Justice Vincent delivered the sentence: Denyer was to serve three terms of life imprisonment with no fixed non-parole period. He received a further eight years for the abduction of Roszsa Toth. One of the most experienced judges of the Victorian Supreme Court, Mr Justice Vincent could not conceal his revulsion for Denyer's crimes. He told the convicted murderer:

The apprehension you have caused to thousands of women in the community will be felt for a long time. For many, you are the fear that quickens their step as they walk home, or causes a parent to look anxiously at the clock when a child is late.

Denyer appealed his sentence to the Victorian Supreme Court. On 29 July 1994, the Full Bench of the Supreme Court determined that Denyer might one day be released. He was granted a 30-year non-parole period. Theoretically, he may walk free from jail in 2023. When the sentence was announced, the families of his victims and victim support groups were outraged. There had been no mercy granted to Denyer's victims. It did not seem right that leniency be ascribed to Paul Charles Denyer. His psychological profile concluded that he was, and remains, a threat to society. While he continues to be deemed a risk, he will remain behind bars.

Paul Charles Denyer will be 51 when he becomes eligible for parole. By then, chances are that the comic name John Candy will be long forgotten. Hopefully, the crimes of the 'John Candy Killer' will not be, and the families and loved ones of the young women he callously murdered will petition the authorities to see that he never breathes the air outside prison walls as long as he lives.

Chapter Four

THE SNOWTOWN SERIAL MURDERS

Never before in the annals of mass murder has there been a gang of serial killers. Couples, yes. But never a gang of four torturing and killing in harmony. Never, that is, until a series of depraved events that became known simply as Snowtown.

Before Thursday 20 May 1999, Snowtown, about 150 kilometres north of the South Australian capital, Adelaide, was best known as a sleepy rural hamlet with a nostalgic feel to its quaint streets and ideal conditions for sheep grazing and wheat growing. But that all changed for the population of around 550 when, in the closing stages of a year-long missing persons investigation, authorities found various remains of eight different victims decomposing in hydrochloric acid in six black 44-gallon plastic barrels in the vault of a disused branch of the State Bank of South Australia. The death toll connected to the 'bodies in the barrels' case would eventually rise to 12, shocking the nation and making it by far the most prolific body count in Australia's sordid history of serial murder.

Knives sat on top of some of the barrels. A variac machine used to give electric shocks was also found in the red-brick building on the small town's main street. Police wearing breathing apparatus located clothing and random body parts inside the barrels, including severed hands and 15 human feet. Detective Steve McCoy, one of the officers on hand that day and the first to find the barrels, later recalled the shocking scene. 'The stench was unbearable,' he remembered four years after the gruesome discovery. 'It was the stench of what I would say was rotting flesh, rotting bodies, human bodies. It was putrid. It permeated your hair, your clothing; everything you had on, the stench got into. It was horrific.'

Speaking for the prosecution in the eventual court case, Wendy Abraham QC described how rubber gloves, handcuffs, rope and tape used in the torture killings were found strewn throughout the bank. She said, 'A number of [victims] had been dismembered, with legs and feet removed from their bodies, or they had been cut. One had his hands handcuffed behind his back and his legs tied together. More than one of the bodies had marks consistent with burn marks.'

There were ropes around necks, and heads with gags still stuffed in their mouths. 'It was a scene from the worst nightmare you've ever had,' said another police officer who attended the scene. 'I don't think any of us was prepared for what we saw.'

An examination by a leading pathologist would later conclude that prolonged torture had taken place using common everyday tools such as pliers, pincers and clamps, examples of which were found in the disused bank. After the victims were tortured, they were strangled or asphyxiated.

One of the victims was placed in a bath after being viciously attacked with clubs. The murderers then beat him repeatedly about the genitals and crushed a toe with a pair of pliers before garroting the man with a piece of rope and a tyre lever. Another victim received electric shocks to his testicles and penis. After his toe was crushed and his ears and nose burnt with lit cigarettes, he choked to death on his mouth gag.

Information received by the authorities suggested the remains had been in storage behind the vault's 10-centimetre-thick metal door for up to three months, but the roots of the 'bodies in the barrel' case went back much further.

The man believed to be the first victim, Clinton Douglas Trezise, was just 22 when he was killed and buried in a shallow grave at Lower Light, 50 kilometres north of Adelaide, in August 1992. Trezise's skeletal remains weren't uncovered until 16 August 1994. When the discovery of the body was reported on the *Australia's Most Wanted* television program, John Justin Bunting is alleged to have told James Spyridon Vlassakis, an accomplice in later murders, 'That's my handiwork.'

Bunting was 32 years old at the time police found the bodies in the barrels. He met his main accomplice in the horrifying string of murders, Robert Joe Wagner, in 1991 when he moved into Wagner's house in Waterloo Corner Road – the address where authorities would later find the remains of two bodies. Described by neighbours as 'brooding' and 'illiterate', Wagner was 27 when the bodies were found. For the most part, Wagner and Bunting remained reclusive strangers in the small community. As a result, the people of Snowtown tended to leave them to themselves.

Though not a lot has come to light about Bunting's past, it is believed he was the victim of sexual abuse, and he harboured a strong and deep resentment for those he believed to be gay or a paedophile – people he would allegedly describe as 'dirty'. Indeed, observers of the Snowtown trial soon came to believe that the heart of the case seemed to rest within Bunting's seething hatred; it seemed he had made it his life's work to seek revenge upon and punish people he suspected to be gay or a paedophile.

His friend Wagner was said to be a white supremacist who is alleged to have been a member of the National Action group. He told neighbours that he 'and his friends' hated gay people and Asians. Wagner had been taken away from his family and reportedly forced into a gay relationship at the age of 14 by convicted paedophile Barry Lane, who liked to go by the name Vanessa. Lane would later become a victim in the bizarre murder spree.

Those responsible for the killings – Bunting, Wagner, Vlassakis and another alleged accomplice, Mark Ray Haydon – would come to be described by authorities as 'a group that preyed on itself'. The men also seemed to live in their own world, a world where the shocking was commonplace and vulnerable people were routinely singled out for a brutal slaying. Even after their victims were tortured to the brink of death and then murdered, the men would continue to raid their bank accounts, stealing near $100,000 in social security benefits over time.

Thanks to information already gathered in the missing persons case relating to Clinton Trezise, police swooped the day after the bodies were discovered in the acid-filled barrels. Bunting, Wagner and Haydon were arrested and charged with one count of murder 'of a person unknown between August 1, 1993 and May 20th, 1999'. Authorities expected to lay further charges in the future. All men were remanded in custody while police made a grim search for more bodies.

Still, police wouldn't know the full extent of what had happened to the Snowtown victims until the arrest of Vlassakis, then 19, on 2 June 1999.

Vlassakis would go on to plead guilty in 2001 to four killings and he turned star witness for the Crown, an action that saw his eventual sentence reduced and brought to light some of the most shocking tales of torture to be heard in Australian courts. The young man spilled information on everything from the stench of death in the barrels to the sound of the victims' screams. He also told of toes being crushed by pliers, decapitated heads being held up and offered for kisses, and sparklers being inserted into the penis of one victim.

Like Wagner and Bunting, Vlassakis had been sexually abused as a teenager. When he was at his lowest, filled with self-loathing and being molested by his half-brother Troy Youde, he met Bunting through his own vulnerable mother, Elizabeth Harvey. Vlassakis was tormented by his hate, thanks also to what he felt was an inability to save himself and his siblings from the unwanted attentions of family friend and paedophile Jeffrey Payne. Bunting set about drawing the distressed teenager out of his shell. The older man took the youth riding on his motorcycle and soon became something of a father figure to him.

Before long, Bunting became the first person Vlassakis trusted enough to tell the tale of his abuse. Feeling guilty, Vlassakis moved away from the family home and went to live with Bunting, who set about grooming the youngster for violence by using the same hatred that burned inside him.

Bunting became so obsessed by what could be perceived as his mission against those he saw as 'dirty' that he created what came to be known as 'the Spider Wall', referring to the colloquial term for paedophiles, 'rock spiders'. Pinned to the wall in a small bedroom in the Waterloo Corner Road house, the Spider Wall was a detailed diagram that had names and contact details for people he believed were paedophiles or gay. The diagram was covered in post-it notes and cross-referenced by links of coloured wool. According to one witness who had visited the house, 'On a few occasions the Friday night thing was to go into the room ... [Bunting would] close his eyes and walk up to the wall and whichever card he'd touch he would take down and ring the person and abuse them over the phone.'

Also stuck on the wall was a chart that had been written on the back of an anti-paedophile leaflet. In the centre of the chart was a single name, 'Barry' – Barry Lane, the paedophile who had forced the teenage Wagner into a gay relationship. From Lane's name spread a twisting maze of lines connecting him to dozens of other people Bunting considered to be paedophiles, many of whom they'd learnt about from Lane.

It was only Bunting's friendship with Wagner that loosened Lane's psychological grip on him. In Bunting's eyes, Lane was a pivotal figure in his self-proposed mission because of the abuse he had rendered on Wagner.

Lane and Wagner had lived together in Salisbury North, a block away from the Waterloo Corner Road house, for eight years. Lane was known for his flamboyant dress sense – he often wore bright pink hotpants and had dyed his hair blond before renaming himself Vanessa. Neighbours described him as 'outgoing', but he was sometimes persecuted by the local community because of his paedophilia convictions. The abuse was mainly verbal, though there were times when Lane and Wagner's house was pelted with eggs. The pair – both of whom received disability benefits – would eventually build a two-metre-high fence around their home. They also kept four Doberman dogs on the property.

Lane was closely linked to the assumed first victim in the Snowtown murders, Clinton Trezise. The young man from Adelaide's northern suburbs was a lover of Lane's, and Wagner and Bunting had met Trezise though Lane. Neither came to be formally charged with his murder.

The next victim, Ray Davies, was also a friend of Lane's. Davies lived in a caravan at the back of Suzanne Allen's house, near Bunting and Wagner's Waterloo Corner Road residence. Allen is believed to have had a crush on Bunting. Bunting, meanwhile, was convinced Davies was a paedophile. On 26 December 1995, Allen's daughter found out Davies had allegedly abused her children. After the news got out, Davies was stabbed and later strangled to death by Wagner. His body was buried in the backyard at 203 Waterloo Corner Road.

It wasn't until late 1996 that the next killing took place. Suzanne Allen's remains were found stuffed in 11 separate garbage bags and buried in the same backyard as Davies, but Bunting maintains that she was already dead from natural causes when he and Wagner found her. Like eight of the victims, Allen's social security benefits were accessed after her death.

Bunting referred to their next victim, Michael Gardiner, as 'the biggest homo'. An obvious enemy for Bunting because he was gay, Gardiner disappeared in September 1997. Bunting and Wagner took him to Bunting's home at the time in Murray Bridge, 80 kilometres north of

Adelaide, and strangled him in the shed. Gardiner has the unfortunate distinction of being the first victim whose body ended up in a barrel.

Considering the seething hatred inside Wagner and Bunting, it's little surprise that Barry Lane himself was their next victim. Lane was in a relationship with a Thomas Trevilyan when he disappeared in October 1997, and it is alleged that Trevilyan played a part in the torture and murder of his lover.

Lane was beaten and tortured before he died. His toes were squeezed between pliers, among other indignities, but according to Vlassakis, talking about Lane's murder had little effect on Bunting or Wagner. 'It's like, you know, when you go to a shop with a young kid and you buy them a toy and the kid gets really excited ... [Their reaction] was like that,' Vlassakis later explained. 'When they squeezed the toenail, Barry screamed more, which obviously hurt more.'

After a while, Wagner finally strangled Lane, putting him out of his misery. In Wagner's own words, according to Vlassakis, the cross-dresser had been 'made good'. His body was then put in a barrel and later taken to the bank vault.

Whether or not Trevilyan did indeed have anything to do with Lane's murder will never be known for sure, because he was the next victim in a seemingly endless trail of terror.

After Lane's death, Trevilyan moved in with Wagner and a woman he was having a relationship with named Vicki Mills, in a house in Elizabeth Grove in Adelaide's north. But on Melbourne Cup Day in November 1997, Mills told Wagner and Bunting she wanted the man out of the house. Trevilyan's body was eventually found hanging from a tree in Kersbrook.

The next victim was Gavin Porter, a drug-addicted drifter. Porter was Vlassakis's best friend – the pair had even received treatment together on the same methadone program. Porter now lived with Vlassakis's mother, Elizabeth Harvey, as well as Bunting and others. Bunting and Wagner tried to strangle the young man in April 1998. After a failed attempt in which the rope got caught around the helpless victim's nose, the men eventually succeeded. They then stashed the body in the Murray Bridge shed before it was transported to the bank vault.

It was in this shed, confronted by the bodies of Lane and Gardiner in barrels, with Gavin Porter dead on the floor, that Vlassakis realised the shocking stories of murder the others had told him were true.

Vlassakis's half-brother Troy Youde was the next to meet a gruesome death – his was also the first murder in which Vlassakis played an active part. Youde was the one who had sexually abused Vlassakis on a number of occasions when Vlassakis was 13. In 1998 Youde was living with Vlassakis, their mother, Elizabeth Harvey, and Bunting. One night in August that year, he was woken by Vlassakis, Bunting and Wagner. Mark Ray Haydon was allegedly also in the murder party. The men then attacked and handcuffed Youde before taking him to the bathroom, where Bunting and Wagner tortured him. As Vlassakis later recalled in his testimony, 'John [Bunting] said, "We'd better make sure Troy's dead." So Robert stood on Troy's chest and the air from Troy's lungs came out of his nose and it made a grunting noise. John and Robert laughed and Robert kept pushing on Troy's chest.'

Vlassakis delivered the final act by strangling his older tormentor. Youde's body was another that eventually showed up in a barrel in the bank vault.

Even with so many dead, the grim toll continued to rise at an alarmingly regular rate. Fred Brooks – nephew of another later victim, Elizabeth Haydon – disappeared in September 1998. Hated by Bunting, he was tortured horrendously over an extended period before finally being killed and moved to the Snowtown bank vault. With Vlassakis again taking part, Brooks was handcuffed and thumbcuffed. He had a 'smiley' face burnt into his forehead with a lit cigarette, and he received electric shocks via the variac machine. Water was injected into his testicles with a syringe, and sparklers were inserted into the eye of his penis and left to burn down.

The next man to die, Gary O'Dwyer, lived near Bunting in Murray Bridge. He had drinks with Wagner, Bunting and Vlassakis on the night he was murdered. While the men were sitting around, Wagner grabbed him. O'Dwyer was then beaten by all three men before Wagner and Bunting tortured and killed him. His body, like so many others, was moved to the bank vault. The group also accessed his bank account.

Another thing O'Dwyer shared with several other victims was the voice recording of his so-called confessions before he died. Some of these were even later played down phone lines to the deceased's family and friends to convince them the victims were still alive.

The 'voices from the dead' were also played in court during the eventual trial. It is obvious O'Dwyer is in pain when he is made to say,

'I'm Gary O'Dwyer, I'm a paedophile. Now I'm really happy I've had treatment.' A voice identified as Bunting's then asks, 'Did you like the treatment you got?' to which O'Dwyer replies, 'No.' After admitting the treatment 'hurt', O'Dwyer is asked, 'Are you ever going to fuck another little girl or boy?' He answers, 'No I'm not ... I know I will get hurt if I hurt someone else.'

The next victim was Elizabeth Haydon, the wife of Bunting's best friend Mark Haydon, a woman Bunting is alleged to have referred to as 'scabs 'n pus'. In November 1998, Bunting told Vlassakis that he and Wagner had strangled her to death in a bathtub before moving her body to the Snowtown bank vault.

The final victim was Vlassakis's 21-year-old stepbrother David Johnson, killed on 9 May 1999. Bunting told Vlassakis to tell Johnson about a cheap computer for sale in Snowtown, and when Johnson arrived at the disused bank with Vlassakis, Wagner grabbed him from behind and Bunting handcuffed him. Johnson was later beaten and tortured, and another 'voices from the dead' tape was made. His ATM card and PIN were then stolen. Bunting sent Wagner and Vlassakis to access the account at a highway roadhouse, but they were unsuccessful. When they returned, Johnson lay dead on the floor. Bunting said the man had grabbed a knife and fought for his life until Bunting strangled him. The men then cut up Johnson's body to fit it into a barrel.

⚰ ⚰ ⚰

The authorities got their first real break in the missing persons case regarding Barry Lane when they checked Lane's bank account and found that it had been accessed from a service station in the north of Adelaide. After checking surveillance tapes, they identified Wagner. Bunting's name came up as an associate.

The information gathered from investigations into this missing persons case led to the discovery of other victims, and on 3 July 1999, Wagner, Bunting and Haydon were jointly charged with 10 counts of murder. Vlassakis was charged with murdering a then-unnamed person, later discovered to be Barry Lane. No charges were laid in relation to the death of Clinton Trezise. The investigation into his murder continues.

After pleading guilty to four murders, Vlassakis was given a life sentence with a non-parole period of 26 years. The judge said that if he hadn't given evidence against his accomplices, the non-parole period would have been 42 years.

Bunting was later found guilty of 11 murders, Wagner of seven. They each received automatic life sentences – mandatory under South Australian law. Neither Bunting nor Wagner showed any emotion as the judge handed down the court's finding. Marcus Johnson, the father of David Johnson and stepfather of Troy Youde, told a reporter, 'I feel there's no remorse there, none at all.'

At his trial, which concluded in December 2004, the jury of six men and six women unanimously convicted Mark Haydon on five separate counts of assisting John Bunting, Robert Wagner and James Vlassakis in five of the murders. He was eventually sentenced to 25 years in jail with a non-parole period of 18 years. The jury failed to reach a verdict on a sixth charge of assisting the killers in another murder.

After a further deliberation of almost 37 hours over five days, the jury could not arrive at a decision on the two murder charges Haydon had faced relating to the death of his wife Elizabeth and Troy Youde in 1998.

South Australian Supreme Court judge John Sulan bound Haydon over until a date to be set in 2005, when he would determine a sentence on the guilty verdicts and decide whether or not Haydon would face a retrial on the two murder charges and the sixth charge of assisting in murder. All of the charges were eventually dropped on appeal.

With its 12 victims and four perpetrators, to this day Snowtown remains the most prolific case of serial murder in Australia's history, committed by the only gang of serial killers in the world.

Chapter Five

THE TRURO SERIAL MURDERS

On Saturday, 17 February 1977, Christopher Worrell, James Miller and Deborah Skuse were driving back to Adelaide after spending a night at the South Australian border town of Mount Gambier. Worrell was at the wheel. He had been drinking heavily all day and was driving erratically and at dangerous speeds. Skuse had fallen in with Worrell and Miller after they had appeared unexpectedly at her home looking for her ex-boyfriend – a former prison friend of theirs. She was getting nervous and begged Worrell to slow down. Worrell ignored her.

Driving along the Princes Highway north of Millicent, Worrell lost control of the car, a 1969 blue and white Valiant, swerving to miss an oncoming vehicle. The car left the road and rolled four times, throwing out all three occupants. Christopher Worrell and Deborah Skuse died instantly, while Miller escaped with a fractured collarbone, cuts and abrasions.

The fatal accident added to South Australia's burgeoning road toll. But the death of Worrell had more significance. With Worrell, a 23-year-old convicted rapist, dead, the streets of Adelaide had become a much safer place.

At Worrell's funeral, James Miller confided to Worrell's girlfriend, Amelia, that he and Worrell, who had been constant companions, had a dark secret. Miller told Amelia that Worrell had been murdering young girls. At first, Amelia, who would later come forward and help police solve the murders, did not take Miller seriously. But when bodies started turning up near Truro, she realised the ghastly significance of what Miller had told her.

On 25 April 1978, just over a year after the car accident in which Worrell and Deborah Skuse died, William Thomas was looking for mushrooms in a flat paddock next to Swamp Road in a remote and uninhabited area outside Truro, a tiny country town 80 kilometres north-east of Adelaide, when he came across a bone protruding from the soil. Initially, Thomas thought that the bone belonged to a cow, and was the remains of an unfortunate creature that had strayed from the herd and got caught in the marshy, flood-prone soil. But something about the scene unsettled him, and five days later he returned with his wife. This time, Thomas examined the bone closely and knew instinctively that the remains were human. He also saw that the skin was in good condition. On closer scrutiny, he observed that a shoe remained on the foot that was visible and that the toes of the foot were painted with nail polish. Then Thomas discovered a skull and some other bones in the immediate area, and he contacted the police.

The police conducted a thorough search of the area and found some personal effects that identified the victim as 18-year-old Veronica Knight, who had last been seen shopping in Adelaide's City Cross Arcade on 23 December 1976.

This grisly find would eventually lead to the discovery of the bodies of six other young women. The seven bush graves, five of which were located around the small country town of Truro, became the subject of one of the most notorious crimes in Australian criminal history. But South Australian police, called to the scene after William Thomas and his wife had stumbled across the remains of the young woman, had no reason to suspect that the marshlands contained more bodies. It was not until a year later, on 15 April 1979, when four bushwalkers discovered a skeleton in a swampy paddock almost a kilometre from where the body of Veronica Knight was found, that police began to realise they may have a serial killer on their hands. From clothing and jewellery found at the scene, police were able to identify the remains as that of 16-year-old Sylvia Pittman, who had disappeared from outside Adelaide railway station on 6 February 1976.

Missing persons files showed that five other young women had disappeared from the Adelaide city district between December 1976 and February 1977. Police had considered that the disappearances were highly suspicious and were part of ongoing investigations. The officer who headed the Truro investigation, Detective Superintendent

K Harvey, said that several thousand people were reported missing in South Australia every year. Generally, all but a few were eventually located. When the seven young women had disappeared in the 1976–1977 period without a trace, Harvey knew it was more than a coincidence. Harvey ordered a search party to scour in and around the area where the bodies of Veronica Knight and Sylvia Pittman had been found. He believed the search may lead to the discovery of more bodies. He said:

> We don't know what we will find. We will be looking for any clues to the killing of the two girls we have found but we can't overlook the fact that we may find the bodies of some of the other missing girls.

Sadly, Harvey's hunch would be proven correct.

A large search party of uniformed police officers, homicide squad detectives and forensic investigators conducted an exhaustive search in the area for 11 days before coming across the skeletal remains of 16-year-old Connie Iordanides and 26-year-old Vicki Howell, two of the missing girls. Both bodies had decomposed, and evidence at the scene of discovery left police with little to go on. Investigations of serial murder can be fraught with difficulty. Faced with appalling crimes, homicide detectives are invariably frustrated by an apparent lack of motive and the seemingly anonymous nature of the perpetrators. Superintendent Harvey appealed to the public for help to solve the Truro murders. His appeals were fruitful. Some weeks after the search at Truro had concluded, police got a call from a woman named 'Angela' advising them that she may be able to assist them with their inquiries.

Angela reported a conversation she had had with a man she knew as James Miller at a funeral she had attended in February 1977. She had gone to pay her last respects to a friend who had died in a car accident. The friend was Christopher Robin Worrell. Angela told police that an inconsolable Miller had approached her and told her about girls being 'done in'. Miller told her that he and Worrell had 'done something terrible'. Miller had told her, 'I did the driving and went along to make sure that nothing went wrong. They had to be done in so they would not point the finger at us.' He went on to say that the girls were 'just rags', indicating that he considered their lives were worthless. He said that one of the victims had enjoyed it. 'But it was getting worse,' Miller continued. 'It was happening more often. It was perhaps a good thing that Chris had died. If you don't believe me, I will take you to where they are.' Miller then told her that Worrell had said he had 'done away with two in WA'.

🪦 🪦 🪦

Born into a family of six children on 2 February 1940 in the West End, the then poorest part of Adelaide, James William Miller was well known to police. At age 11 he had been committed to the local Magill Reformatory, at 15 he was in Long Bay Jail in New South Wales, at 16 he was back in Magill, and he spent his 17th birthday in Adelaide's Yatala Jail. A habitual criminal with 30 convictions for car theft, larceny and breaking, entering and stealing, Miller would, upon release from prison, return to a life of crime and end up before the courts and straight back in jail. It was not surprising, then, that he had spent most of his adult life behind bars. But while Miller was a multiple felon, he had no prior convictions for violent crime.

It was not hard to locate Miller. Penniless and living on the streets, he would be found in only a few places in Adelaide. Officers of the Major Crime Squad observed Miller as he went about his business, running odd jobs for the Adelaide City Mission in return for a bed at night. For days, eight detectives monitored his every movement. Miller attempted to flee when he became aware that police were following him. He was arrested on 23 May 1979.

With Miller in custody at Angas Street Police Headquarters, the officers of the Major Crime Squad knew they were in a bind. As the uncorroborated statement from 'Angela' was the only link between Miller and the Truro murders, they knew that he could easily evade their questions and stonewall the investigation. After all, he had plenty of experience in being interrogated by police. The officers who conducted the interview with Miller, Detective Sergeant Glen Lawrie and Detective Peter Foster, knew that, in the absence of hard evidence, they needed a confession. Without it they knew that Miller would go free.

Initially, Miller denied any knowledge of the killings and disputed having a conversation with 'Angela' at the funeral of Christopher Worrell. Advised by the detectives that 'Angela' was in fact Worrell's girlfriend, Amelia, Miller became evasive but continued to refuse to acknowledge that he knew her at all. He was shown photographs of Worrell and Amelia together, and then he quickly changed his tune. He told the detectives that he knew both Amelia and Worrell but continued to deny that he had had any conversation with Amelia at Worrell's funeral. Asked why Amelia would say such things, Miller replied, 'Maybe she's short of money.' This was an obvious reference to the $30,000 reward the South Australian Government had offered to any person who could provide information that might lead to a conviction in the Truro murders.

With the interview in progress for six hours, Miller's defences began to falter. According to the record of interview, Detective Lawrie continued to present Amelia's statement that indicated Miller's direct involvement in the murders. Finally, Miller said, 'On second thoughts, maybe she's done what I should do. Can I have a few minutes to think about it?' Detectives Lawrie and Foster left him in the interview room to consider his next move. They returned shortly afterwards and noticed that Miller looked resigned to his fate. Miller stated:

> If I can clear this up, will everyone else be left out? I suppose I've got nothing else to look forward to whatever way it goes. I guess I'm the one who got mixed up in all of this. Where do you want me to start?

Miller then provided a detailed statement describing his involvement in the Truro murders.

> I drove around with Chris and we picked up girls around the city. Chris would talk to the girls and get them into the car, and we would take them for a drive and take them to Truro and Chris would rape them and kill them. But you've got to believe that I had nothing to do with the actual killings of the girls.

Detectives Lawrie and Foster gently persuaded Miller to tell the whole, terrible story. Perhaps relieved that the dreadful secret he had carried for more than two years was out, Miller told the two detectives, 'All right then, there's three more. I'll show you.' Detective Sergeant Lawrie hastily organised a police escort for Miller, who then directed them to two separate graves: one near Port Gawler, where they found the body of Deborah Lamb, 20, and the other at the rear of the Dean Rifle Range at nearby Wingfield, where the body of Tania Kenny, 15, was found. Later that night, police travelled with Miller to Truro where he showed police where he and Worrell had concealed the body of 16-year-old Juliet Mykyta.

⚰ ⚰ ⚰

Miller, who was gay, admitted during the police interviews that he had become obsessed with Christopher Worrell when they had first met in prison. Miller was doing a three-month sentence for breaking into an Adelaide gun shop. Worrell had been convicted of a particularly vicious rape and sentenced to six years' imprisonment. When sentencing Worrell for the crime, the judge described the then 20-year-old Worrell as a 'disgusting and depraved human being'. Miller and Worrell had shared a cell while on remand, and after they were convicted for their crimes, both were transferred to South Australia's Yatala Jail. Miller doted on the handsome young Worrell, and the two became inseparable. While in prison Worrell accepted sexual favours from his submissive and obsessed new friend.

Miller was released after serving his three-month sentence, but, as on so many occasions in the past, he returned to his life of crime. He was convicted of stealing 4000 pairs of sunglasses after being caught hawking the stolen goods around Adelaide's bars and hotels. On this occasion he was sentenced to 18 months' imprisonment and returned to Yatala Jail to continue the sexual tryst with his slim, dark-haired lover.

After serving his sentence, Miller was released, and less than a year later, Worrell walked from Yatala Jail on parole. The duo continued their relationship beyond prison walls. Miller had taken up residence with his sister and her two daughters in an Adelaide suburb. Worrell became a regular visitor, and shortly afterwards the pair began sharing a flat at Ovingham in Adelaide's inner northern suburbs. It became apparent to Miller that, while Worrell had enjoyed their sexual encounters in prison, Worrell preferred women. Miller often performed fellatio on Worrell while the younger man read pornographic magazines portraying acts of bondage and cruelty towards women. Eventually, these episodes ceased altogether, and Miller's infatuation with Worrell manifested itself in his unquestioning loyalty and devotion to his young friend.

Often Miller was troubled to find that Worrell would fly into fits of inexplicable and uncontrollable rage. Sometimes, Miller would quieten him down, but generally he cowered away and waited for the storm to pass. Regardless of Worrell's behavior, Miller always returned. His infatuation with the younger man would soon lead him to act as a willing accomplice in the commission of multiple murder.

The pair found employment working for Unley Council as labourers on the roads in Adelaide's inner suburbs. With both men in gainful employment and living under the same roof, Miller described this period as the happiest of his life. But all that began to change when the fury welling up inside Worrell took them onto the streets of Adelaide to satisfy his lust for rape and violence.

Worrell possessed a gift for the gab that young women often found irresistible. Now 23 and with shining, shoulder-length dark hair, he was very aware that women found him attractive. With Miller driving Worrell around in a 1969 blue Valiant, the two would cruise the city in search of young women who were out on their own, isolated and vulnerable to Worrell's slick patter. Girls at bus stops, railway stations and hotels were often targets, and Worrell would implore them to get into the car to go for a ride. Miller would then drive to remote spots on the outskirts of Adelaide. He would park the car and go for a walk, leaving Worrell to his own devices. Worrell would rape the girls in the back of the car. Often, he would tie them up, rendering them helpless to his advances. With Worrell's urges sated, Miller would return from his stroll and drive them back to town. This pattern continued for some months, and according to Miller, there was nothing to suggest that Worrell would progress to murder.

Miller's unsigned statement indicated that he and Worrell would travel through the streets of Adelaide on an almost nightly basis in search of new prey. Miller never challenged his friend and dutifully drove the old Valiant while Worrell maintained a lookout for young women to accost.

† † †

On Thursday, 23 December 1976, the streets of Adelaide were filled with shoppers looking to purchase last-minute gifts before Christmas. Worrell and Miller were cruising around the city shopping centres and Worrell's attention was sparked by the number of young women out shopping. He told Miller to stop the car. He got out and walked into the shopping centre, instructing Miller to drive around the block while he was inside. Miller did as he was told and returned in the car a short time afterwards. But he could not see Worrell outside the shopping centre and was forced to drive around the block a couple of times. Finally, he saw Worrell at the front of the Majestic Hotel and noticed that he was accompanied by a young woman. She was 18-year-old Veronica Knight.

Veronica had been shopping with a friend but, with the City Cross Arcade packed with shoppers, they had become separated. Veronica was walking around looking for her friend when Worrell approached her. She lived nearby in the Salvation Army Hostel in Angas Street, and was persuaded by Worrell to join him. He told her that he could give her a lift home. Veronica and Worrell got into the car, and Miller drove off. Not long into the voyage, Worrell used all his powers of persuasion to entice the young woman to go for a drive in the Adelaide foothills.

Out of the crowded city, Miller pulled the car onto the side of a quiet road. Continuing with their routine, Miller got out of the car and went for a walk in the nearby bushland. He returned about 30 minutes later to find Worrell now sitting in the front seat. Veronica was nowhere to be seen. As he got closer to the vehicle, he saw Veronica lying motionless on the floor in the back of the car. Worrell casually told Miller that he had just raped and murdered the girl. Incredulous, Miller noticed that the girl was still clothed but that her hands had been tied. The bruising on her neck told him that she had been strangled.

Now it was Miller's turn to fly into a rage. 'You fool, you fucking fool,' he screamed at Worrell. 'Do you want to ruin everything?' Usually submissive, Miller then grabbed Worrell by the scruff of his neck and roughly pulled him towards him. According to Miller's statement, Worrell produced a long-handled knife and held it to Miller's throat. He threatened to kill Miller if he refused to cooperate. Worrell ordered him back in the car and to drive it towards Gawler. So Miller drove the car along the Sturt Highway to Gawler, and was then told by Worrell to drive on towards Truro. He turned into Swamp Road and stopped the car next to a clump of eucalyptus trees. He told Worrell that he wanted nothing to do with the body, but the younger man brandished the knife so he then helped Worrell remove Veronica's body from the car. They both carried the body to the wooded area. 'He asked me to give him a hand to carry her into the bushes,' Miller said. 'We got through the fence and dragged her under.' The pair lay Veronica's body on the ground, covered her with branches and leaves, and then returned to the car and drove back to Adelaide.

Miller recalled that neither he nor Worrell ever discussed the murder afterwards. Instead they attended work at Unley Council the following day as scheduled as if the gruesome murder of Veronica Knight had never happened. Miller stated that he could not go to police as he feared Worrell and believed that he might kill him if he reported the murder. Miller's fear and fixation with Worrell would lead to the murders of six other young women.

🪦 🪦 🪦

Fifteen-year-old Tania Kenny became the next victim. Early on the morning of 2 January 1977, Miller and Worrell were out driving around Adelaide. As it was a public holiday, the shopping centres in and around Rundle Mall were packed with shoppers. It did not take long for Worrell's keen eye to spot another victim. He told Miller to pull the car over, and he got out and began walking towards Rundle Mall. He told Miller to meet him around the other side of the mall. When Miller arrived there in the blue Valiant, Worrell was waiting for him accompanied by Tania Kenny.

Tania had been hitchhiking earlier that day and had travelled to Adelaide from Victor Harbour, a seaside town 70 kilometres south of Adelaide. Apparently Tania had no reason not to trust the two men and sat in the front seat between them. Miller drove Tania and Worrell to his sister's home. He determined that his sister was not at home and then Worrell and Tania got out of the car and went inside. Miller waited in the car for them.

About a half an hour later, Worrell returned to the car and immediately Miller knew that Tania was dead. He went inside and into the playroom and saw Tania's body bound tightly with rope. She had adhesive tape across her mouth. Like Veronica Knight, she was fully clothed, but Miller saw the telltale signs on her neck and knew that Worrell had strangled her. According to Miller, another argument ensued between him and Worrell. Again, Worrell threatened to kill him if he did not help hide the body. So they concealed Tania's body in a cupboard and left the house, returning later that evening when the cover of night offered them the best protection against would-be witnesses who might see them transporting the body to Miller's car.

During the day Miller and Worrell had dug a shallow grave at the back of the Dean Rifle Range at Wingfield in Adelaide's west. Miller helped Worrell lift the body into the car and assisted in transporting the body to the grave. Miller told police later that he had only done this because he did not want his sister to be involved in the murder. Once again the opportunity for Miller to tell police and stop the killing presented itself. Yet he was besotted with his violent friend, and chose to go along meekly with Worrell's murderous spree. He decided to continue his role as chauffeur while Worrell trawled the streets of Adelaide for his next victim.

☦ ☦ ☦

At 9.00 pm on 21 January 1977, Worrell met 16-year-old Juliet Mykyta on the steps of Adelaide's Ambassador Hotel in King William Street. Juliet was a student at Marsden High School, and had taken a summer job selling jewellery from a stall in Rundle Mall. Earlier that evening, Juliet had telephoned her parents to tell them that she had been asked to work back and would be home late. When approached by Worrell, Juliet was sitting on the steps of the hotel's entrance, waiting for a bus to take her home.

The offer of a lift home must have been too hard for young Juliet to resist, and she happily got into the car with Miller in the driver's seat. Worrell got into the car and on the other side of her. Miller then drove to a secluded place off Port Wakefield Road. Just moments after Miller parked the car, Worrell forced the young girl into the back seat. Miller remained in the car and saw Worrell tie Juliet's hands together with a length of rope. She tried to fight Worrell off, but he was too strong and bound her limbs tightly. Miller left the car, walked a short distance away and waited for Worrell to perform his perverted acts. He heard Worrell and Juliet shouting, and then saw Juliet struggle out of the car before falling to the ground. Worrell kicked her and forced her onto her back. With Juliet subdued, he placed both his knees on her chest and proceeded to strangle her with rope.

Miller later told the police that he had sought to intervene to prevent Worrell from murdering the young girl. He had grabbed at Worrell's arm, but Worrell had pushed him away and threatened to kill him if he intervened again. Miller tamely walked away. Miller claimed that when he returned, Juliet's body was already in the back of the car. Worrell was in a dark and violent mood, and when he ordered Miller to drive the car to Truro, Miller did as he was told. He drove the hour's journey to the tiny country town and headed towards Swamp Road as before. However, acting on Worrell's instructions, he drove past where they had placed the body of Veronica Knight. On this occasion Worrell selected a site near an abandoned farmhouse as the place for disposing of Juliet Mykyta's body. Both men carried the fully clothed body into thick trees and covered it with branches and leaves. Miller then drove Worrell back to Adelaide.

⚰ ⚰ ⚰

On 6 February 1977, Worrell commenced a killing spree that led to the murders of a further four young women in just six days. Clearly his appetite for murder had increased. James Miller acted as his accomplice throughout the rampage.

Sixteen-year-old Sylvia Pittman was accosted by Worrell while waiting for a train at Adelaide Station. Sylvia got into the car with Worrell, and Miller drove to the Windang area. As soon as Miller had parked the car, Worrell told him to get out and go for a walk. Miller claimed that he returned about 20 minutes later to find Sylvia's body already in the back seat of the car, partially covered by a rug. He noticed that a pair of pantyhose had been used to strangle her. Worrell bluntly ordered Miller to drive the car to Truro. He now knew that Worrell became sullen and uncommunicative after committing a murder, and underneath the cold, morose silence Miller believed the threat of violence was never far away. The two made the grim drive to Truro again. Sylvia's fully clothed body was taken to a fresh site next to Swamp Road and left there under a scattering of leaves and branches. For some reason Worrell had not, on this occasion, felt the need to tie or gag his victim.

Less than 24 hours later, Miller received a telephone call from Worrell, who told him to meet him outside the Adelaide GPO at 7.00 pm that evening. When Miller arrived at the designated spot in his car, he saw that Worrell was with a young woman. She was 26-year-old Vicki Howell. Vicki and Miller struck up a conversation, and Miller took an immediate liking to the friendly and outgoing young woman.

Miller drove the car along the Barossa Valley Highway past Gawler again, but this time, he claimed, he had few concerns about the safety of his passenger. Worrell appeared to be in good spirits, and when they passed Nuriootpa, Vicki asked Miller to stop the car so she could use a toilet at a service station. Worrell allowed Vicki to leave the car and Miller believed this was a sign that Worrell would do her no harm. Afterwards, as they drove on, Miller had to stop the car so he could relieve himself. He left the couple chatting amiably in the car. He returned a few minutes later and found the two continuing the conversation. He went off into the bush again, feeling confident that Worrell would not hurt his new friend.

Shortly afterwards, Miller returned to the car and was shocked to find Worrell leaning over the front seat, gingerly placing a blanket over the body of Vicki Howell. She had been strangled. Miller berated Worrell. He could not understand why the likeable woman had to die. But, by then, the black cloud had descended over Worrell, and when Miller's anger subsided, he began to fear for his own life. Worrell and Miller drove to Truro in silence with Vicki Howell's body on the floor in the back of the car. Miller later recalled that he was terrified of Worrell when he (Worrell) was in this kind of mood. He believed he was obliged to do Worrell's bidding, no matter how ghastly it was. Worrell instructed Miller to drive to Truro, where they hid the body under foliage, then drove back to Adelaide.

⚰ ⚰ ⚰

On 9 February 1977, Miller and Worrell were again driving through the streets of Adelaide. Worrell had noticed a girl — 16-year-old Connie Iordanides — standing on the roadside. An effervescent teenager, Connie was full of life and like many young people was not prone to distrust strangers. Miller turned the vehicle and pulled up alongside the teenager. Connie, naïve and easygoing, accepted the offer of a lift and climbed into the front seat next to Worrell. The car sped off, and moments later, the young girl suspected something was terribly wrong. Screaming and fighting with Worrell, she was forced into the back seat. Miller drove a further 20 kilometres to a quiet spot near Wingfield and left the car, fully knowing what horrors awaited Connie. He went for a walk, and when he returned, Connie Iordanides' lifeless body lay in the back seat. Worrell had raped her, then strangled her.

Miller drove the car along the well-beaten trail to Truro and again helped Worrell to dispose of the body along Swamp Road. Driving home to Adelaide, the rigours of murder weighing heavily on their bodies and minds, Miller and Worrell parked the car at a racetrack and slept there for the night.

On 12 February 1977, seven days before his own death, Worrell committed his last murder. This time his victim was 20-year-old Deborah Lamb. Driving around one of their popular haunts near the City Bowl, Worrell saw Deborah hitchhiking. Miller was told to pull the car to the kerb and Deborah was offered a lift. Worrell told her that he could take Deborah as far as Port Gawler, the location of one of his previous murders. Eager to be on her way, Deborah accepted the lift and jumped into the car. When the trio arrived at the beach at Port Gawler, Miller claimed he left Deborah and Worrell alone and took off for a walk along the sand dunes. When he returned, Worrell was outside the car, busying himself by kicking sand into a hole with his foot. Miller claimed he could not see the girl anywhere. Two years later, however, he was able to lead police directly to Deborah Lamb's grave.

According to forensic evidence obtained after the discovery of Deborah Lamb's body, she may have been buried alive. At Miller's trial, the Director of Forensic Pathology at the Institute of Medical and Veterinary Science, Dr CH Manock, told the court that it was possible that Deborah had been alive when Worrell had placed her in the makeshift grave. Dr Manock stated that, despite the advanced state of decomposition of the body when it was finally found on 23 May 1979, '[t]he sand and shell grit would have formed an obstruction to the airway and prevented air from entering the air passages'. When Dr Manock examined Deborah's body, he noticed a pair of pantyhose wrapped seven times around her mouth and jaw. She would have invariably asphyxiated in any case, but Dr Manock's evidence led the court to believe in the distinct possibility that Deborah may have died the most terrifying of deaths.

⚰ ⚰ ⚰

As the victims' bodies remained undiscovered, it took the death of Worrell for the killing finally to cease. On 19 February 1977, just one week after the murder of Deborah Lamb, Worrell was killed in a motor vehicle accident while driving home from Mount Gambier. Miller, the sole survivor of the murderous duo, was charged with seven counts of murder. His trial began in February 1980 in South Australia's Supreme Court. Miller pleaded not guilty to all seven charges.

Miller's defence was that he had not participated in the murders and that his love for Worrell, according to Counsel for Defence, KP Duggan QC, had led him to be 'trapped in a web of circumstance'. His defence was predicated on the argument that he was the scapegoat for the murders. With Worrell dead, the defence asserted, the police had pursued Miller as if he was the sole perpetrator of the unspeakable crimes. According to Mr Duggan, 'He was just waiting for Worrell and there was no joint enterprise as far as he was concerned. Although Miller admits that he handled the situation incorrectly, he maintains that he is not a murderer.'

The prosecution took the view that Miller's actions made him as guilty of the murders as Worrell. The Crown Prosecutor, BJ Jennings SC, argued that Miller and Worrell had collaborated to pick the girls up and that Miller was well aware of the fate that awaited the seven girls each time he pulled his car to the kerb to allow Worrell to entice them in the vehicle. In his summing up to the jury, Mr Jennings ripped the defence to shreds:

> Mr Miller referred to the girls as 'rags'. That was the attitude that led him to throw in his lot with Worrell. No rapist and murderer could have had a more faithful or obliging ally. You will never know the truth. But have no doubt that it is a horrible truth that these young women were murdered because they were going to point the finger at the young man who tied them up and sexually abused them. They could also point the finger at the older man who ignored their plight and their terror. If a man assists another by driving him to a place where a girl is going to be raped and killed, then he is guilty of murder.

On 12 March 1980, the jury returned with a verdict. Miller was found guilty of six counts of murder and not guilty of the murder of the first victim, Veronica Knight. The jury believed that Miller had not known that Worrell intending killing Veronica on the night of 23 December 1976. As Miller stood passively in the dock, Mr Justice Matheson sentenced him to six life sentences. As he was taken from the court, Miller glared at

Detective Sergeant Lawrie and screamed: 'You filthy liar, Lawrie – you mongrel.'

🪦 🪦 🪦

Over the years Miller continued to protest his innocence. Back at his old home in Yatala Jail in its notorious maximum-security wing, he went on hunger strikes and on one occasion drew attention to his case by staging a 43-day 'strike' from the rooftop of the jail. Interviewed after he was talked down from the prison roof, Miller stated:

> *Nobody turns into a cold-blooded murderer overnight or helps commit murder. I'm just an ordinary thief, no killer. I have never been a violent man. I was there at the time and for that I am guilty of an unforgivable felony. I fully deserve the life sentences I am currently serving. I am serving out a life sentence for Chris. But I never killed any of those girls. That's the truth.*

Later, in an interview, Miller said: 'They can give me life for knowing about the murders and not reporting them. But they charged me with murder as a payback for not informing on Worrell. It's a load of bullshit.' In the same interview Miller showed his true colours when he said: 'Chris Worrell was my best friend in the world. If he had lived maybe 70 would have been killed. And I wouldn't have dobbed him in.'

In 1999, 19 years after being sentenced to life in prison, Miller applied to the South Australian Supreme Court to have a non-parole period attached to his sentence. South Australia's Chief Justice, John Doyle, granted Miller's application and fixed a 35-year non-parole period on Miller's original sentence. James William Miller, fixated and obsessed with Christopher Worrell, became an accomplice and collaborator to the evil that became known as the Truro Murders.

On 22 October 2008, James William Miller died of cancer in Yatala Jail, aged 67.

Chapter Six

THE BABY FARMERS

As it would be for many years to come, times were tough for single mothers around the turn of the 19th century; society looked down on any woman who had a baby out of wedlock. To make matters worse, contraception was far less reliable, and abortions were difficult to obtain and highly dangerous.

As a result, with few mothers wanting to adopt their children out, 'baby minding' became big business. This practice saw the infant child placed in the care of a minder for a weekly fee. The baby would generally be cared for by staff in the nursery of a large house, with the parent or parents being able to visit regularly. Once the child had grown to school age, he or she would be returned to the parent and (usually) introduced as the niece or nephew of a dead relative. This way, both the child and the parent avoided the stigma society would place on them.

But while most baby-minding centres were honest and provided reliable care and attention for the children placed in their charge, there were inevitably cases of unscrupulous people cashing in on the misfortune of others. Some centres sold babies to desperate childless couples, others took the mothers' money – handed over in good faith – in the belief that it was going towards food, care and medical bills, and then let the infants live in squalid conditions. More often than not, these children would die from starvation or disease. The heartless murderers of these tiny innocents became known as 'baby farmers'.

In 1893, there were more than 60 official inquests for babies who had either been found dead and abandoned or died through neglect. More than 20 of those cases were treated as murders, but those responsible had usually moved on, leaving no trace. Many more infants had gone missing, presumed sold.

One of Australia's most shocking baby farmer cases came to light on 11 October 1892, when a local drainer, James Hanoney, was digging in the soft dirt of a backyard in the Sydney suburb of Macdonaldtown, not far from the CBD.

About 2 metres down, he found the cause of the blocked drain he had been called to see to – two bundles of foul-smelling baby clothing. James removed the material and was horrified to find the decomposing remains of two babies. He called authorities immediately, and they uncovered the remains of five other infants in the yard.

Detectives used tenancy records to find another dwelling of the cottage's previous tenants, 50-year-old John Makin and his 47-year-old wife Sarah, in nearby Redfern. The remains of more babies were found there.

Police tracked the Makins to their latest home, in Chippendale, and found more infant corpses buried in their yard. This brought their tally to 12. The entire family – John, Sarah and their four daughters, Florence, 17, Clarice, 16, Blanche, 14, and Daisy, 11 – were arrested. John and Sarah Makin were charged with murder. The nation was, understandably, appalled.

At the Makins' trial, the Sydney Supreme Court heard that the family were professional child minders who cared for children for a weekly fee until the mothers were in a position to reclaim their offspring, or suitable parents were found to adopt the children. It was also said that in some cases, the Makins made it possible for the mother to continue visiting her child after it was placed with new parents.

The prosecution said that these claims, while fine in theory, were incorrect. The Makins, they said, used deception to stop the mothers seeing their children, all the while collecting money from them every week.

The first witness called was Amber Murray. In March 1892, Amber, 18 years old at the time, gave birth to a son she named Horace. Unmarried and finding herself in no position to care for the infant, she placed an ad in the *Sydney Morning Herald* seeking a loving mother to adopt her baby. She added that she was willing to pay a weekly fee for the child's support.

It wasn't long before she received a reply from the Makins, at that time living in Redfern, saying they'd care for Horace for 10 shillings a week. Amber called on the family the next day. She met John and Sarah and two of their daughters. The four Makins all claimed to fall in love with Horace instantly.

They said they couldn't wait to have little Horace live with them, and intended to give him much love and support. They also told Amber that they had lost a young son of their own. The Makins explained away the five or six other babies in the house at the time by saying they were looking after them for friends.

After agreeing to the fee, Amber left, with the Makins' agreement that she could visit Horace. That was the last time she ever saw her child alive. John Makin made sure he called upon Amber each week to collect the 10 shillings, but every time she asked to see her son, she was given another excuse.

John Makin eventually told Amber his family was moving from Redfern to the south-western suburb of Hurstville. He said he would forward her their new address in around six weeks. Meanwhile, he continued to call and collect his weekly fee.

Instead of Hurstville, however, the Makins relocated to nearby Macdonaldtown, where they moved in under the cover of night. Their daughter Clarice would later tell the court that there was no sign of young Horace during the move. The child had already been murdered, but John still collected the weekly 10 shillings. Before long they moved again, this time to the house in Chippendale.

At the trial, Amber Murray and three other mothers identified clothing that Sarah Makin had pawned as belonging to their babies. Yet another couple claimed they had given the Makins a substantial up-front payment and agreed on the 10 shillings weekly fee for caring for their child until they could sort their affairs out. But within days they were told their baby had died. They then handed the Makins £2 to go towards a funeral.

When questioned, Sarah and John Makin were no match for the prosecution. Despite constantly denying that they'd murdered the 12 babies, their own children eventually turned against them. Clarice Makin identified clothing found on one of the dead infants as something that she had seen in her mother's possession. Daisy Makin testified that only two baby girls were with the family for the move from Redfern to Macdonaldtown.

There was little doubt in the court. Mr Justice Stephen sentenced John and Sarah Makin to death by hanging. John Makin held his wife as she collapsed. None of the Makin children had a conviction recorded against them. After two appeals, John Makin was hanged in Darlinghurst Prison. Sarah Makin won a reprieve and was sentenced to life in prison with hard labour. She was released in 1911 after serving 19 years and was never heard of again.

Chapter Seven

HUSBAND, FATHER, PREACHER, CHILD KILLER

On a cold winter's day on 29 June 1991, six-year-old Sheree Beasley disappeared while riding her bicycle at the Victorian seaside tourist town of Rosebud. In the early afternoon, Sheree had gone around to the shops on her treasured pink bicycle to pick up some grocery items for her mother. She pedalled back home with a shopping bag slung over her shoulder containing some of the things her mother had asked her to buy. At home her mother discovered that Sheree had forgotten a few of the items on the list, so Sheree headed out again on her bicycle, with her pink helmet strapped firmly on top of her head. It was just after two o'clock, and Sheree's mother, Kerri Greenhill, watched as the little girl headed back to the shops. It was the last time she would see her little girl alive.

In September 1991, Sheree's body was found in a bush grave in an advanced state of decomposition. Her tiny six-year-old body had been forced into a stormwater drain, 15 kilometres from where she had been abducted.

A seemingly respectable 56-year-old man was charged with Sheree's abduction, sexual assault, murder and concealment of her body. Robert Arthur Selby Lowe was a husband, father and church elder who lived in the heart of Melbourne's eastern suburbs at Glen Waverley. But in fact, Lowe, a travelling salesman, lived a double life. Unbeknown to his wife and children, he preyed on young children and teenagers and had a long list of convictions for public exposure and indecency. At Lowe's trial in October 1994, in the Victorian Supreme Court, Justice Phillip Cummins wept openly as he heard evidence that alleged that Lowe had abducted

Sheree Beasley and murdered her. 'Take me home to Mummy. I want my mummy,' Sheree reportedly screamed, begging for release from the monster. Lowe ignored Sheree's pleas as she choked to death while he forced her to perform oral sex on him.

⚱ ⚱ ⚱

A number of witnesses had seen the little girl riding her bicycle on that afternoon. A small boy, the same age as Sheree, had seen a man pick up Sheree and place her in the passenger's seat of a small blue car before he drove away. One woman saw Sheree on her bicycle near the shopping centre. She remembered that she saw the little girl crying as she sat in a small blue car. The witness did not get a good look at the driver of the car. She could not even say if the driver was male or female. In her statement to police, she said, 'I know there were only two people in the car, being the young girl and the mature-aged person. I don't know whether they were male or female, but they didn't have a beard or moustache. I know the car was very small and I recall it being a hatchback.'

It was clear to police that Sheree had been abducted. While Kerri Greenhill waited anxiously for news of her daughter, police turned to the witnesses. A statewide manhunt began to find Kerri's little girl. The witness who had seen Sheree bundled into the car was, with the assistance of officers of the Victoria Police, able to successfully identify the vehicle as a late-model Toyota Corolla hatchback. Police trawled through registration records and came up with a long list of people who owned the particular make and model of vehicle the witness had identified. There were hundreds of people who owned blue Toyota Corolla hatchbacks, and police were required to contact each one to determine if they had been in the Rosebud area at the time Sheree had gone missing.

As part of this routine and exhausting exercise, police contacted Robert Arthur Selby Lowe, a sales representative whose company provided him with a blue Toyota Corolla hatchback. While out on the road for work, Lowe received a call from police. Clearly, he was in no hurry to assist them as it took him over a week to return their calls. He curtly told police that he was nowhere near the Rosebud area at the time Sheree Beasley had been abducted. He had been home that day with his wife and two teenaged boys. Police grew suspicious of Lowe when he refused to give them his home telephone number in order to check his alibi. They checked the 54-year-old man's criminal record, and immediately alarm bells rang.

In 1984, Lowe had been placed on a 12-month good behaviour bond when he was found guilty on a charge of obscene exposure. He had been arrested after he was found exposing himself and making sexually suggestive remarks to a group of schoolgirls at a suburban shopping centre. Four years later, he was arrested in Traralgon in Gippsland, 150 kilometres east of Melbourne, and questioned by local police. A number of teenage boys and girls had reported a middle-aged man accosting them, exposing his penis and masturbating in front of them. Police determined that Lowe was a person of interest in relation to these crimes, but had been unable to prove that he was the flasher in question. He was subsequently released without charge.

In 1990, Lowe was arrested and charged with obscene behaviour after he approached a number of schoolgirls at busy Flinders Street railway station. The girls had been carrying balloons, and Lowe told them the balloons they carried looked like 'big dicks'. Exposing himself to the girls, Lowe had propositioned them, asking them to go with him to have sex. Horrified, the girls fled, running out of the railway station to a waiting police officer who listened to their story before he took off after Lowe. Lowe was discreetly making his way from one of the railway platforms when he was arrested. He was ultimately convicted and fined $700.

Since his 1984 conviction for obscene behaviour, Lowe had been seeing a psychotherapist, Margaret Hobbs. Hobbs had prepared a pre-sentence report for the defence in relation to Lowe's attitude to his crimes. In the report she stated that she felt it was clear that Lowe considered his activities to be inoffensive. She implied that Lowe should be imprisoned in order to stress the community's outrage at his crimes. She wrote:

> I am of the opinion that he [Lowe] truly believes that he is indulging in harmless behaviour ... It does unfortunately need the intervention of the courts to instill in him the illegality of his actions. The censure of the courts at this time will assist with any ongoing therapy once it has been clearly demonstrated ... his behaviour is unacceptable to the general community.

Lowe's defence counsel did not release the report at his trial in 1990. It is likely that such a damning finding would have led to a period of imprisonment if presented to a magistrate prior to sentencing. The psychotherapist believed that Lowe was a risk to the community and that the slap-on-the-wrist sentences from the courts to date had spurred him on to more perverse crimes, in the belief that he was beyond the reach of the law. One can merely speculate whether Sheree Beasley would still be alive today had Lowe been imprisoned in 1990. Instead, he was convicted and received only a fine.

⚰ ⚰ ⚰

Robert Arthur Selby Lowe appeared to be a solid member of society. His wife, Lorraine, was a deeply religious woman, and her husband seemed to share in her devotion to her church, her faith and her God. They had married in 1972 and had two sons who attended private schools. The Lowe family was a model of middle-class morality. Living in Glen Waverley, they were friendly, although circumspect, with their neighbours. Every Sunday morning, they would attend the local Baptist church, where Robert and Lorraine were held in high esteem as elders of the congregation. Lowe was a Sunday school teacher, with a group of children in his care each Sunday morning. During holidays, the Lowe family headed off to their flat at the seaside town of Rosebud on Port Phillip Bay.

Under the cover of respectability, Lowe lived a double life. Once the bourgeois veneer was stripped away, it was apparent that he lived in the shadows. He had felony convictions in three countries, and had been sent to prison on two previous occasions for sex offences. He had immigrated to Australia from New Zealand, where he had developed a reputation as a recidivist criminal, his police file heavy with convictions for indecent assaults on young men and women. Residing in Australia, he routinely and regularly exposed himself to young boys and girls, often masturbating in front of them and making lewd sexual advances.

Lowe was born in 1937 in northern England. He was the second of three children, all boys. In 1956, he had been convicted of stealing a car and of injuring a police officer while attempting to avoid capture. The 19-year-old youth was spared a prison sentence on this occasion. Three years later, he and his family emigrated from England to New

Zealand and settled in the nation's capital, Wellington. Shortly after his arrival, he was charged with an indecent assault on a young male. In 1961, he moved to Auckland, and shortly afterwards, he received his first custodial sentence for sex offences. He returned to Wellington and the family home after his first experience of prison. It did little to rehabilitate Lowe as he was convicted of wilful and obscene exposure in 1964 and sent back to prison. Shortly after his release, Lowe was convicted for theft.

Lowe had become a profound source of embarrassment and shame to his family, who were prominent in the business community in New Zealand. They encouraged him to travel to Australia to take up residency there. With a burgeoning criminal record in New Zealand, he took up the offer of starting afresh. He started a new life in Melbourne. His family was relieved to hear that he intended to wed and that he had settled in to his new home well. He turned to religion and appeared to become a devout and earnest adherent of the Christian faith.

But Lowe lusted after his life in the shadows and began exposing himself to young boys and girls on an almost daily basis. He appeared to show no fear of apprehension for his crimes, and while police had taken him into custody on numerous occasions, the mild-mannered Lowe was often able to convince police he was harmless and had caused no great hardship to his victims.

🚪 🚪 🚪

The investigation into Sheree Beasley's disappearance continued apace. Knowing that the sex criminal Lowe drove a car similar or identical to the one observed by witnesses in the abduction of the six-year-old girl, police stepped up their inquiries of the tall, gaunt figure. It transpired that there was an ongoing investigation of a man who had exposed himself to young boys in March 1991 at a suburban swimming pool. The man had fled the swimming pool when approached by several adults. The adults had seen the man get into a blue Toyota Corolla hatchback and had noted the registration number of the car. It was the car driven by Robert Lowe.

Lowe became a prime suspect in Sheree's abduction when police received an anonymous tip from a woman who claimed that she knew a man who had a long history of sex offences and exposing himself to children. The man had a holiday flat in Rosebud and drove a blue Toyota Corolla hatchback. His name was Robert Arthur Selby Lowe. The anonymous caller also told police that Lowe was undergoing psychotherapy for his behaviour. Police would later identify the caller as Dr Margaret Hobbs, who had been treating Lowe since 1984. Dr Hobbs feared that Lowe's crimes would escalate and believed it was possible that he would harm one of his victims at some point.

Police decided to put Lowe under surveillance. Specialised surveillance officers, referred to in police vernacular as the 'Dog Squad' because their primary activity is to follow suspects in much the same way as a canine follows its master, maintained a constant vigil outside Lowe's home. The Dog Squad followed him to his workplace and his every movement elsewhere. They observed Lowe loitering around public places such as swimming pools and municipal parks. They saw him approach prostitutes on the streets. They witnessed him masturbating in public toilets. Clearly, the church elder was leading a double life.

It was now time for the police to move in, and they obtained a warrant to search Lowe's home. In August 1991, a team of detectives and uniformed police knocked on the door of the Lowes' Glen Waverley home. They searched the house high and low, but any hopes they'd harboured of finding incriminating evidence were dashed. Police could find nothing in the house to link Lowe with the abduction of Sheree Beasley, and Lowe himself steadfastly denied any involvement in the crime.

Finally, he was taken into custody and questioned at length about his movements on 29 June 1991, the day Sheree Beasley disappeared. Lowe stuck to his alibi, that he had been at his Glen Waverley home with his wife and children. Without any physical evidence linking him to the scene and with his alibi intact, at this point, police were obliged to release their prime suspect. But the heat was on. The surveillance continued in the hope that Lowe would make a critical slip or, in their wildest dreams, even lead police to Sheree Beasley's body.

Meanwhile, all was not well in the Lowe household. Lowe's wife was in a state of shock. For the first time, she was becoming aware of the awful truth: her husband of 19 years was a convicted criminal, with a long record for sex offences. Now, he was under investigation for the abduction and possible murder of a little girl. Shock gave way to anger, and the pious Lorraine Lowe ordered her husband from the family home. And Lowe's denials were falling apart. His wife now recalled where he had been on 29 June 1991: he had been on his own at the Rosebud flat. She was certainly not going to provide him with an alibi. She told police that she could not recall seeing her husband that day. Her two sons also gave statements to police, saying they had not seen their father until about 5.00 pm on the day in question. Further, news of Lowe's convictions for sex offences and his alleged involvement in the disappearance of Sheree Beasley had reached his employer. Lowe found himself homeless and out of a job.

Then, on 24 September 1991, almost three months after she had disappeared, the body of Sheree Beasley was found. Two teenagers riding horses around the paddocks of Red Hill, a town on the Mornington Peninsula, came across the tiny body. Sheree had been forced into a stormwater drain, some 15 kilometres from where she had been abducted. Police converged on the location to begin the grim task of examining the scene for the presence of physical evidence. They hoped to find evidence that would incriminate Lowe. An autopsy later revealed that Sheree had died of asphyxiation.

Around this time, Lowe returned to psychotherapist Margaret Hobbs for further treatment for his behaviour. It appears that he trusted Hobbs, and under the pretext of his ongoing therapy, she tried to persuade him to tell her about his involvement in the crime. He was unaware of Dr Hobbs's decision to assist police with their investigation. Every time she met Lowe, Hobbs recorded the conversations. It was a painstaking process, taking many months. Slowly but surely, Hobbs managed to connive various admissions from Lowe. Initially, he gave her scant details, but later as his trust in her grew, he drove her to the scene of the abduction, and then on to the stormwater drain to show the horrified woman how he had concealed the body. With each admission made, detectives would be sitting nearby, listening to every word.

Twenty-one months after the abduction of Sheree Beasley, detectives finally arrested Robert Arthur Selby Lowe and charged him with her murder. Lowe was remanded in custody at Pentridge Jail's K Division, and spent much of his time locked away with other violent offenders.

⚰ ⚰ ⚰

At last, the police believed they had a strong case against Lowe. But the evidence obtained by Margaret Hobbs could prove to be inadmissible in court. Police wanted his conviction assured. The opportunity to seal Lowe's fate for the murder of Sheree Beasley presented itself when Peter Allan Reid, an inmate at K Division who was serving a life sentence for the murder of a police officer, came forward. Reid told police that Lowe had approached him and told him about the abduction and murder of Sheree Beasley. Reid was a violent offender but he felt revulsion at the thought of the sexual assault and killing of a young child. For once in his life, the convicted murderer decided to assist police.

Apparently, Lowe felt at ease with Reid. Presumably, he believed the convicted cop killer would be an ally and unlikely to divulge the substance of any of their discreet conversations. But the criminal code of silence did not extend to child murderers. Reid provided a detailed statement to police that helped convict Lowe. He stated that Lowe had approached him not long after arriving in K Division: 'On the 6th of April, 1993, another inmate of the prison, Robert Lowe, was transferred to my unit. I became reasonably friendly with Lowe; he seemed to want to talk about why he was there. He told me he was a married man with two children. I knew he had been charged with the murder of Sheree Beasley.'

Lowe told Reid how he had abducted and killed Sheree Beasley on 29 June 1991. He had told his wife and children that he was going to the Rosebud flat to fix some tiles. The repair job was merely a pretext; he had no intention of doing any do-it-yourself work at the flat. He had intended to abduct Sheree Beasley that day. Reid stated:

> Lowe stated he did not go down to Rosebud on the day of Sheree's abduction purely to fix the tiles in his flat. He said he just used the tile-fixing story as an excuse to justify being away from his wife. Lowe had made a comment that he had been watching the little girl for some time and that she had been at the shops before.

According to Reid's statement, Lowe had seen Sheree on previous occasions. Reid's allegations led police to the chilling conclusion that Lowe had intended to abduct and sexually assault Sheree and had been planning to do so for some time. He continued: 'I asked him how many times he had seen her in the past and he said numerous times.' Reid alleged that Lowe provided details on how he had abducted Sheree. He said:

> He left his place about 2 pm. He drove up to an area about seven kilometres away where he saw a little girl riding a pushbike 'all over the place'. He said he pulled over up the way a bit at a T-intersection or X intersection. He said he got out of his car and waved to the little girl to pull over. He said that she had a blue and pink tracksuit on with a pink and blue helmet.

Sheree did not want to get into the car, so Lowe physically threw her into the front seat of his car. 'He said that he told the little girl that her mummy had said for him to take her home as her mummy was ill,' Reid recalled. 'He said the little girl became suspicious of him and added that he opened the car door and forced her into the front of his car.' Allegedly, Lowe then told Reid how the little girl had died. Reid said:

> He said he then put a seat belt around her and drove about fifteen kilometres to an inland country area and forced her to do the 'dirty acts'. He said that from terrifying fear and the act she was forced to do, she choked to death. Lowe would not comment much on the actual 'act'. I don't know why he wouldn't.

According to Reid, Lowe felt no remorse for his crimes. In fact, he seemed to delight in recalling them. 'Lowe told me he decided to take the girl's helmet off when she was choking,' Reid stated. 'He also made a couple of comments that sickened me. He stated, "They say the little girl would have been submissive as her mother was a prostitute."' He added that Lowe also 'told me that before the little girl choked, she screamed, "Take me home to Mummy. I want my mummy"'.

Lowe needed to dispose of the body and all the evidence linking him to Sheree's murder. According to his conversations with Reid, he did so painstakingly and with every intention of avoiding suspicion. He burnt his semen-stained clothing and disposed of Sheree's clothing in a dumpster in Blackburn, a short drive from his Glen Waverley home. He had left her bike on the roadside where he had abducted her, but Sheree was still wearing the bicycle helmet, which concerned Lowe as he thought that it may have his fingerprints on it. Reid stated:

> Lowe and I discussed the possibility of Sheree Beasley's missing helmet being found and what it would mean to Lowe. Lowe wrote me out a

*short letter about how his fingerprints may have come to be on the bike
helmet. He said he had been warned by police in Rosebud not to ride his
bicycle without a helmet, so he went to Kmart and picked up a number
of helmets to see if he could buy one. He said that if a helmet turned up
later with his prints on it, then he could fall back on this excuse as to
why they were there.*

Lowe provided Reid with a map, showing where he had buried Sheree's
helmet. Reid stated: 'Lowe marked a map with a circle and a cross.
These marks show where he reckons he buried Sheree Beasley's
helmet.' The helmet was never found.

There were bloodstains on Lowe's car seats, and he told Reid how he
had scrubbed and cleaned away any sign that Sheree had ever been in
his car. Reid said:

*He told me he had first vacuumed the car on Sunday, 30 June, the day
after the abduction. He said he did his wife's car at the same time. He
said he used a chamois to clean blood off the edge of the front seat and
he also used a detergent to clean it. I asked him where the blood came
from and he said, 'The little girl vomited it up when she was choking.'*

*He also said he had taken his own clothes off when he got home
later that afternoon. He said he washed his clothes the same day as
they had dirt all over them and there were other stains on them.*

*He told me he removed mats from the front of the car and scrubbed
them. He also told me he took some blood-stained paper out of the car,
but couldn't tell me anything about it, or whose blood it was. He told me
he cleaned all of the inside of the car with detergent.*

*He then told me he hosed the outside of the car down, cleaning
everything, including the wheels and the underside. After that he said
he drove the car off the driveway and hosed down the driveway as well.
He added that he paid special attention to the seats in his car.*

Lowe had meticulously set about throwing the police off his trail. And
when his wife would not support his alibi, he set about creating a new
one. He told Reid that he would concoct a story that he was fixing a
fence on the day of Sheree's abduction and murder. It was intended to
establish reasonable doubt in the minds of the jury. Lowe was trying to
evade the justice he deserved. Reid recalled:

*He told me he'd say a Chinese fellow helped him to build a fence on 29
June 1991. He also told me he dug a hole and planted an apple tree. He*

said his son came in via a back gate after 5 pm. He said the reason his son never saw him was because he'd concealed himself behind the tool shed while he was working.

Lowe told me that if the neighbours said he wasn't at home on the day, he would say he went up to McEwans to get some nails so he could help the Chinese fellow fix or build his fence.

Lowe wanted all of the incriminating evidence out of the way. At the request of Margaret Hobbs, he had typed out a confession. He knew that police could obtain the confession by analysing the typewriter ribbon. Allegedly, he asked Reid if he knew of a way to dispose of the typewriter. Reid said:

He said the written confession he made was half-typed and half-written because it took him about a month to type it out and at the same time he was writing it at home and at Margaret's [Hobbs] place as she was, in his words, 'advising' him. Lowe asked if I knew anyone who could destroy a typewriter for him as the police would need this typewriter as evidence against him, and that it would be damaging to him if it was found.

Lowe wanted to tie up all loose ends. Now that his wife was assisting police, he allegedly told Reid, he wanted to kill again, this time to avoid conviction. He also discussed organising the murder of Kerri Greenhill, Sheree's mother. Reid stated:

Lowe stated that his wife had divorced him and that she had taken out a restraining order against him. He told me he wanted her dead, as she was working for the police. He stated she was very sick and he wished she would die. He said that Sheree's mother was in Queensland and that he wanted to get her too. By 'get' her, I believe he meant to kill her. Lowe told me he had $2000 in a bank account and that the bank book or cheque book was being held by his legal advisers. He said he would use this money to have his wife fixed.

The calculating child killer would stop at nothing to avoid conviction. There were other items of evidence that Lowe wanted destroyed. He told Reid about them all. He provided maps and sketches of the scene of the abduction and where he had travelled to the paddock in Red Hill to dispose of Sheree's body. In some cases, he actually signed the maps before handing them over to Reid for safekeeping.

Reid was appalled by the murder of six-year-old Sheree and disgusted by Lowe's vivid recollections of the awful crime, so he turned everything over to the police. His detailed statement to police shortly afterwards described his almost daily conversations with Lowe between 6 April and 16 June 1993 in relation to Sheree's murder. This was all police needed to ensure a conviction.

⚰ ⚰ ⚰

At his trial on 27 October 1994, held in the austere surroundings of the Supreme Court of Victoria, Lowe must have known he was sunk when Reid's evidence was produced. The Crown also showed the evidence provided by Margaret Hobbs, the psychotherapist whom Lowe had trusted, which provided a limited confession of his involvement in Sheree's murder. Lowe's defence relied on his assertion that he was not at the scene of Sheree's abduction and that the Crown case was a simple instance of mistaken identity.

The jury pondered its verdict for five hours before returning to the courtroom. Lowe was found guilty on all counts. Mr Justice Philip Cummins ordered him to be led away while he considered an appropriate sentence.

Two days later, Lowe was brought before the judge for sentencing. Mr Justice Cummins told Lowe that he accepted Peter Reid's evidence that Sheree Beasley had died by choking while being forced to perform oral sex on Lowe. Cummins noted that Lowe had shown no remorse for his crimes. Recalling Reid's evidence, the judge said that, if anything, Lowe appeared to revel in his notoriety as a child killer. Cunningly trying to avoid prosecution for months, Lowe was described by Mr Justice Cummins as 'very intelligent, very articulate and very manipulative in your dealings with the police'. The judge told the prisoner: 'What you did was every child's fear and every parent's nightmare.' He then sentenced the 57-year-old Lowe to life imprisonment without the possibility of parole. The judge added that, in this instance, 'Life means life'. Lowe will never be released from jail.

In prison, Robert Arthur Selby Lowe is now an old man. Prison life has aged him further, beyond his years. As he stares at the patchy sunlight as it shines through the bars in his cell, one wonders if the devout Christian has ever really accepted responsibility for the murder of helpless little Sheree Beasley. He may have sought solace in religion. He may even have asked God for mercy. Here, on earth, he will remain unforgiven.

Chapter Eight

THE MYSTERIOUS DEATH OF SAMANTHA KNIGHT

It was one of Australia's most enduring mysteries that saw the face of Samantha Knight become deep-etched in the memories of Sydneysiders who lived through that terrible time.

And then, as is so often the case when children come to harm, Samantha's killer was there all the time, just a heartbeat away, a trusted friend of the family.

But it took many years to catch the beast and during that time he assaulted countless other children on his way to his cell in protective custody, away from the other prisoners who would gladly tear him to shreds if they could get their hands on him.

At 4.30 on the afternoon of Tuesday, 19 August 1986, nine-year-old Samantha Knight left her Bondi flat, where she lived with her mother Tess and their black cat Midnight, to go to the shops in nearby Bondi Road to buy some lollies and a pencil.

Samantha made her purchases and soon after was positively seen by a neighbour walking alone along Bondi Road. Three other witnesses said that they *may* have seen Samantha walking – perhaps hand in hand, but not for certain – with a man that afternoon, but it couldn't be confirmed. Besides that, the little girl in the urchin's cap simply vanished.

Samantha's disappearance triggered one of the biggest investigations in Sydney's history, which saw her face on posters put up everywhere throughout Sydney and its suburbs and as far away as Newcastle. They asked the question, 'Have you seen this girl?' But no-one had. There were countless alleged sightings, the majority from well-meaning citizens and the rest from cruel hoaxers, but none offered the slightest positive clue as to what may have become of Samantha Knight.

Despite relentless campaigning by Samantha's family to keep the case in the public's awareness, a $50,000 reward offered by the New South Wales Government for any information, and the press running stories at the slightest opportunity to keep the case alive, it wasn't until 14 years later that relentless investigators revealed that at last they had a definite suspect.

On 11 February 2000, convicted Sydney paedophile Michael Anthony Guider, 49, was convicted of sex offences against two five-year-olds between 1982 and 1985. He was already four years through a 10-year sentence for 60 counts of drugging and molesting 11 children aged two to 16, and possessing thousands of pornographic pictures of children that he had taken.

Although found guilty, Guider wasn't given any additional jail time on top of his existing sentence. 'There is little point in my imposing an additional term – he's already looking at six more years, which in my opinion is long enough to deal with any problems that he has,' Judge O'Reilly told the court.

Apparently, back in 1996, shortly after Michael Guider was initially sent to Lithgow Jail for 10 years, detectives questioned him about the disappearance of Samantha Knight. He was questioned about the matter again in 1999, and again before, and after, his 2000 conviction. It seemed that Michael Guider had once been a family friend who had acted as babysitter on several occasions to Samantha Knight and some of her friends.

On 21 February 2001, a year after his 2000 conviction, Guider stood before the court at his committal hearing charged with the murder of Samantha Knight, more than 14 years earlier. Those who had known him gasped as he was brought into the court.

Dressed in prison greens, his bespectacled face was almost completely covered in a prison-grown bushy grey beard and long unkempt hair hung down over his face and shoulders. Guider was unrecognisable. He had grown the ultimate disguise.

Documents presented to the court stated that Guider, a former North Shore landscaper and gardener, had admitted to witnesses that he had drugged Samantha to take naked pictures of her, but he gave her too many sleeping pills and she accidentally died. Documents also said that Guider had admitted to molesting and taking pornographic pictures of many children over the previous 20 years. Two of the victims were Samantha's friends.

The documents said that Guider was a friend of their family. He had initially endeared himself to Samantha when she was five and living at Manly. Samantha had two friends of similar age, and when she moved to Bondi at the age of seven, she stayed friends with the girls; she would regularly visit their homes, including for sleepovers. During the following years Guider occasionally babysat for Samantha and her two friends, drugging them with sleeping pills in soft drink and taking obscene pictures of them while they slept.

Medical records verified that Guider regularly bought the prescription drug Normison, a sleeping pill that could undoubtedly cause toxic overdose, especially in a nine-year-old child, if too many were taken. Guider had purchased Normison in the month leading up to Samantha's disappearance.

Samantha's mother Tess and father Peter O'Meagher, who separated before their daughter went missing, sat intently through the proceedings. They listened as, one by one, three prisoners who had been in jail with Guider told of his confessions to them.

One told the court that Guider had told him he had given Samantha too much Normison and that if police had looked under bushes in nearby Cooper Park, they would have found her.

Another said that Guider had told him he was the man the three witnesses thought they saw Samantha with, and that he had taken her to a cave in North Sydney. There, he drugged her and photographed her, then went home. When he came back some time later, she was dead. He buried her in a park, then dug her body up later and put it in the garbage. It was then taken away, never to be found.

Michael Guider was committed for trial, where he pleaded guilty to the manslaughter, not the murder, of Samantha Knight after arriving at a deal with the Crown, with the approval of Samantha's family. It carried a maximum of 25 years in jail. Guider received 17 years with a minimum of 12, to be served concurrently with the term he was already serving. This means that potentially, all he may have got for killing Samantha Knight was eight years. That's if he behaved himself.

It turned out that one of the three prisoners who gave evidence against Guider was his own brother Tim, who was serving a 10-year sentence for matters relating to an armed robbery. Given that it was alleged that it was Tim's information against his brother that brought about the conviction, Tim was given a pardon and released from jail.

Michael Guider was released from prison on 5 September 2019, at age 68, under strict conditions and an extended supervision order. No-one has any idea what he looks like these days. Keep your children close.

Chapter Nine

THE BIRNIE MURDERS

In general, serial killers operate in the shadows. Solitary figures, they practise their evil secretively. Their victims are interred in shallow graves or dismembered and disposed of in the quiet of night. Robert K Ressler, a former FBI profiler and Director of Forensic Behavioral Science at the Bureau's headquarters in Quantico, studied many serial killers. This, in his opinion, is the profile of a serial killer: the killer is male, white and generally of below average intelligence. There are a few examples of women serial killers, but it is unusual.

Husband and wife serial killers are even rarer, but there have been some chilling examples. England's Fred and Rosemary West tortured, raped and murdered 12 victims over a 20-year period, including two of Fred's young daughters. They buried their victims in the cold ground at 25 Cromwell Street, Gloucester – a place the media dubbed the 'House of Horrors'. In 1965 Ian Brady and his live-in lover Myra Hindley were convicted of the murders of five children, whose bodies they buried on the Saddleworth Moors in northern England.

In Australia there are fewer instances of this bizarre confluence of sadism, sexual perversion and blood lust. But a series of murders that few will forget appeared on the outskirts of Perth, Western Australia in 1985. In a plain two-bedroom bungalow, Catherine and David Birnie, a common-law husband and wife, tortured and murdered four young women before Western Australian police halted their spree. A 16-year-old girl abducted by the Birnies on 9 November 1985 managed to escape from them and alert police, who were already investigating the disappearance of four Perth women in the belief that a serial killer was operating in Perth. When the teenager came forward after her hellish experience, the suspicions of police were confirmed. Heavily armed officers swooped on the Birnie household and arrested Catherine Birnie. Her husband was arrested at work later that same day.

Catherine and David Birnie abducted their victims and drove them to their modest home at 3 Moorhouse Street, near the Fremantle docklands, where they then carried out their perverse sexual fantasies. When the couple had had their fill of their victims, they murdered them. Sometimes, they drugged their victims before strangling them. At other times, the pair bludgeoned them with an axe or stabbed them in frenzied attacks. David Birnie had an extraordinary sexual appetite, which included a taste for bondage and sodomy. With Catherine as a willing partner, his perversions led them to prey on young women who were forced to endure acts of sexual depravity.

In the spring of 1986, over a 27-day period, four women disappeared from Perth. Their bodies were later found in shallow graves when police caught up with the Birnies. Twenty-year-old Mary Frances Neilson, 15-year-old Susannah Candy, 31-year-old Noelene Patterson and 21-year old Karen Denise Brown lost their lives at the hands of the couple. Their final hours were spent in terror as the sadist David Birnie repeatedly raped them, his partner at his side urging him on. When the pair showed police the graves, David remarked, 'What a pointless loss of young life.'

⚰ ⚰ ⚰

David John Birnie was born in 1950 in the inner-city Perth suburb of Subiaco. He was the eldest of six children. His family was impoverished, and what little money was available was usually spent on his parents' desire for alcohol. As a result, from time to time, Birnie and his brothers and sisters were placed in foster homes or in government institutions when authorities considered that their parents could not care for them properly.

Not long after Birnie's 12th birthday, he was separated from his siblings and placed in a foster home. By this time he had already come to the attention of police and the courts for petty crime, mainly stealing offences. The die was cast for Birnie at this early age. He was on the way to becoming a recidivist criminal, periodically moving from court to prison, and back into the community. Then he would commit further crimes, and the cycle would begin again. But no-one suspected that the sickly, pale and frail youth would graduate to murder.

Catherine Birnie was born on 31 May 1951. Before she reached her first birthday her mother died, and so Catherine spent her formative years travelling between the home of her father, who took up residence in South Africa, and the home of her grandparents, who lived in Perth. Her grandparents were impossibly strict and would not permit Catherine to play with other children. She was a lonely little girl, without a mother's love and desperate for affection.

In 1964 a callow youth moved in next door to her grandparents' home. Catherine immediately took a liking to him. The slim young man was working as an apprentice jockey, and he offered Catherine the hope of some love in her life. He introduced himself as David Birnie. The two became lovers when Catherine was just 14 years old. Thus began Catherine's obsessive dependency on David Birnie. But Birnie moved away from the doting Catherine to continue training to become a jockey under the tutelage of trainer Eric Parnham. According to Parnham, Birnie showed plenty of promise as a jockey and could have become a good one if he had stuck at it. But Birnie was incapable of applying himself to anything else but crime. Parnham was forced to sack his young apprentice when he discovered that Birnie had bashed and robbed an elderly man who owned a boarding house where Birnie had stayed.

Now, without prospects for gainful employment, Birnie turned to a life of crime. He had found an ally in Catherine and took the young woman with him. Catherine was a willing accomplice in his crimes. She loved Birnie and knew there was nothing she would not do for him. She proved this repeatedly, perpetrating crimes with her lover. Such was her obsession with Birnie that she would, one day, willingly commit murder at his urging.

On 11 July 1969, David and Catherine pleaded guilty in a Perth Magistrates Court to 11 charges of breaking, entering and stealing. Court records show that the pair had stolen blowtorches and other oxyacetylene equipment and used them in a futile effort to open a safe at a suburban drive-in movie theatre. With his already prodigious criminal record, David Birnie was sent to prison for nine months. Catherine, who was pregnant, escaped a custodial sentence and was placed on probation. Less than a month later David and Catherine were ordered to stand trial in the Supreme Court on eight further charges of breaking, entering and stealing. The judge handed down a three-year sentence to David and Catherine had her probation period extended by four years.

On 21 June 1970, David Birnie escaped from prison. On the run, his first port of call was Catherine and she did not need to be invited to join him. She was excited at the prospect of joining her lover; it was an adventure in her otherwise miserable existence. Happy at David's side, she ignored the consequences and the likelihood that she would go to jail if caught. Police caught up with the pair three weeks later and charged them with 53 counts of stealing, breaking and entering, receiving, unlawfully driving motor vehicles and being unlawfully on premises. David was also charged with escaping from custody. Frighteningly, a police search of their vehicle showed that the pair was driving around with 100 sticks of gelignite, fuses and detonators. Birnie was sentenced to serve a further 30 months in prison. Catherine, who had been testing the courts' patience for some time, was given her first custodial sentence. Her child, less than three months old, was taken from her and placed in care while she served six months.

When she had served her sentence, Catherine left prison and started to rebuild her broken life. She took her child and went to work as a maid for a family in Fremantle. The son of the family for whom she worked, Donald McLaughlan, fell in love with her, and they married on Catherine's 21st birthday. With David Birnie still in prison, his influence over her dissipated and she began to live what appeared to be a normal life. She had six children with Donald. Their first child, a boy named Donald Junior, was killed in a car accident when he was just seven months old. Catherine seemed to take this tragedy in her stride, but as time passed it became apparent that she longed to be with David Birnie. Nevertheless, she remained with McLaughlan for the next 12 years, but their marriage was doomed. Catherine could not cope with the demands of rearing six young children. Her father and uncle also shared their cramped housing commission home in suburban Victoria Park. The house was filthy, and Catherine ignored the children and her duty to them. They were never given enough to eat.

In the midst of this strife, Catherine turned to David Birnie again. She had been seeing him secretly for two years, and Birnie continued to exercise the almost hypnotic power he had over her. In 1985 Catherine simply walked away from her husband, her children and her home and back into the arms of David Birnie. Later that year she changed her name by deed poll to Birnie. Although the pair never married, Catherine became Birnie's common-law wife.

🪦 🪦 🪦

David Birnie was heavily into kinky sex and routinely used Catherine as his plaything. He had an enormous pornographic video collection, including numerous movies with bondage and torture as the central themes. He injected cocaine into the tip of his penis and found that he could extend his periods of sexual activity for days on end. His brother James, a convicted paedophile, took up lodgings at the Birnies' house in Moorhouse Street, Willagee, after his release from prison. He witnessed first-hand his brother's depravity. 'He has to have sex four or five times a day,' James recalled. 'I saw him use a hypodermic of that stuff you have when they're going to put stitches in your leg. It makes you numb. He put the needle in his penis, then he had sex. David has had many women. He always has someone.'

David Birnie had Catherine, but that was not enough for him. Increasingly, he spoke of the thrill of abducting and raping young women. He told her that he regularly thought about having sex with women who were bound and gagged while she watched. Ever eager to please her lover, Catherine entertained these sick fantasies. Caught in a vortex of obsession and dependence on David, she became at first a willing accomplice, and then an active participant, in abduction and murder.

Mary Frances Neilson, 22, became the couple's first victim. On 6 October 1986 Mary had called in to David Birnie's workplace, an automotive spare parts shop, to inquire about purchasing some new tyres. Birnie told her to go to his Moorhouse Street home later that day. He offered her a bargain price for the tyres but said he would only sell them to her from his home. Mary was a bright girl who was studying psychology at the University of Western Australia. Her parents were away on an extended holiday in England when she called on David Birnie at the car yard. She was last seen leaving the car yard. Her Chrysler Galant sedan was found six days later in a car park opposite Western Australia Police headquarters, dumped there by her killers.

When the unwitting girl arrived at the Birnie house, she was seized at knifepoint, gagged and tied to a bed. David Birnie repeatedly raped the girl while Catherine watched. Occasionally, Catherine participated too and performed fellatio and analingus on David as he raped the young woman. Mary had seen both Catherine and David throughout the ordeal. There is no doubt that she would have been able to identify them and the house where they lived. David and Catherine knew this. And they realised that she had to die.

The couple drove the young woman to remote bushland at Gleneagles National Park on Perth's southern fringes. Birnie raped Mary again, then strangled her with a nylon rope attached to a tree branch. When he twisted the tree branch, the rope tightened around her neck. Mary died slowly in front of Birnie's eyes, then he stabbed her in the chest once. Mary was already dead, but Birnie told Catherine that the stab wound would allow gases and body fluids to escape during the decomposition of the body. David and Catherine dug a shallow grave and placed Mary's tortured body into it.

⚰ ⚰ ⚰

Two weeks later the Birnies got the urge to commit another murder, and when they saw 15-year-old Susannah Candy hitchhiking along the Stuart Highway in Claremont, they knew they had their second victim.

Susannah was a talented student at Hollywood High School who had a bright future. She lived at home with her parents, two brothers and a sister. Her father was an ophthalmic surgeon. The family lived a happy life in the leafy Perth suburb of Nedlands. Susannah's only mistake was getting into the car with Catherine Birnie at the wheel and David sitting next to her. Perhaps she thought that, as the car was driven by a couple, she would be safe. But she was in deep peril. Birnie stuck a knife to her throat and told her not to resist or make a noise. Then they drove back to Moorhouse Street where Susannah was gagged, tied and chained to a bed. Birnie raped Susannah, and afterwards Catherine got into the bed with them and continued the torment. Birnie tried to strangle the young girl, but she struggled and fought so hard that he was forced to defer her murder. He forced tranquilisers into her mouth and made her swallow them. Gradually, the pills took effect and Susannah fell into a deep sleep. She would feel no more pain. Birnie then put a nylon cord around her neck, and implored Catherine to commit murder. Catherine strangled the young girl as her husband watched on. Later she would remark, 'I didn't feel a thing. It was like I expected.'

Susannah Candy was buried near the grave of Mary Neilson at Gleneagles National Park.

⚰ ⚰ ⚰

On 1 November 1986, Noelene Patterson was having a bad day. She had run out of petrol on her way home from work and was hoping someone might stop and assist her. Stranded on Canning Highway in East Fremantle, the 31-year-old woman looked expectantly at the motorists as they drove by. Maybe someone would be kind enough to give her a lift.

When Catherine and David Birnie pulled up in their car, Noelene gladly accepted the offer of a lift home. The couple seemed friendly enough, and she was relieved that her ordeal at the roadside was over. But, once inside the vehicle, Noelene had a knife thrust up against her and her hands and legs tied. She was driven to Moorhouse Street, where she was taken inside the Birnies' house, gagged and secured by Birnie with chains and ropes to a bed.

Noelene Patterson was a beautiful woman. A former flight attendant, she had worked as a hostess on Alan Bond's private jet. Sophisticated and charming, she was a popular member of staff at Nedlands Golf Club, where she had been working for the past year. David Birnie was captivated by her and raped her repeatedly throughout the night without any intention of killing her just yet. Meanwhile, Catherine was enraged with jealousy. She feared that Birnie was falling for his latest victim. She implored him to kill Noelene, but he refused. He kept her tied to the bed for three days, raping her at will. Finally, Catherine held a knife to her own heart and threatened to commit suicide. Birnie knew then that Noelene had to die.

Birnie forced sleeping pills into Noelene's mouth and forced her to swallow them. He strangled her while Catherine watched. Later that evening, they took Noelene's body to the forest and buried it along with the others.

⚰ ⚰ ⚰

Four days later, the Birnies abducted 21-year-old Denise Karen Brown. Denise had been waiting for a bus on the Sterling Highway in Fremantle. She was a trusting girl who enjoyed life. A computer operator, she shared a flat in Nedlands with her boyfriend and another couple. She accepted a lift from the Birnies without hesitation. Again it would seem that Denise felt safe in the company of another woman.

She was taken to Moorhouse Street at knifepoint. Once inside the Birnies' house, she was chained to a bed and raped. The next day the Birnies drove her to north of the city, where they knew they could bury her undisturbed in a remote pine plantation.

On the way to the plantation that afternoon, the Birnies attempted to abduct another girl. Later, the 19-year-old girl told police how she had been approached by the Birnies in their car while she was walking along Pinjara Road, Wanneroo. She had seen a man driving with a woman in the passenger seat. She had looked in to the back seat of the car and seen what she thought was a child slumped over. She now realises that this was Denise Brown.

The young woman had instinctively felt that something was wrong and could not be coaxed into the car. She said:

> I felt uneasy. I didn't recognise the car. There was a man driving and a woman in the front seat of the car. The man kept looking down, not looking at me, and the woman was drinking a can of UDL rum and coke. I thought the fact that she was drinking at that time of the day was strange. He didn't look at me the whole time. It was the woman who did all the talking. She asked me if I needed a lift anywhere. I said, 'No. I only live up the road.'
>
> They continued to sit there and I looked into the back seat where I saw a small person with short brown hair lying across the seat. The person was in a sleeping position and from the haircut, looked like a boy but for some reason I got the feeling it was a girl. I told them again that I did not want a lift because walking was good exercise. The man looked up for the first time and gazed at me before looking away again. By this time more cars had appeared and I started to walk away but they continued to sit in the car. Finally the car started and did another U-turn and drove up Pinjara Road towards the pine plantation. It wasn't until I saw a really good photo of Catherine Birnie that I realised who they were. Somebody must have been looking after me that day.

The Birnies drove on to Gnangara Pine Plantation. They dragged Denise from the car, and Birnie raped her once more, then plunged a knife into her neck while he raped her. Catherine urged her husband to stab Denise again and produced a bigger knife for him to use. He stabbed the young woman repeatedly in the neck and chest. By this time Denise had lost consciousness but was still alive. The couple prepared her grave, placed her into it, then began covering the body when, suddenly, Denise regained consciousness and sat up. Birnie hit her in the back of the head with the blunt edge of an axe. Denise sat up again, but this time Birnie turned the axe around and hit with her all the force he could muster. Denise was finally dead. The Birnies buried the body and left the scene.

⚰ ⚰ ⚰

Five days after the murder of Denise Brown, the Birnies abducted a 16-year-old girl. Held at knifepoint, the young girl was driven to Moorhouse Street, then taken into the Birnies' house and chained to a bed. Birnie raped her repeatedly. The following day, he left the house, leaving the young girl with Catherine. She unchained the girl, got her off the bed and insisted that she telephone her parents to tell them she was all right. While doing so, the girl made a mental note of the Birnies' telephone number. Later that day when Catherine went to the front door to speak to a caller, the girl escaped through the bedroom window. Half-naked and severely distressed, she ran to a nearby shopping centre. She was then driven to Palmyra police station to tell police her astonishing tale. She provided a full description of the assailants, along with their address and telephone number.

Heavily armed police swooped on the Moorhouse Street address and arrested Catherine. Birnie was arrested later that day at the spare parts shop where he worked.

The police had been aware of the disappearances of the four women over the past month. As police had no reason to believe the women could just disappear, they regarded their disappearances as highly suspicious. Detective Sergeant Paul Ferguson had already theorised that the four women were victims of a serial killer. He was further troubled to learn that two of the women had contacted friends and relatives to assure them that they were all right. Two letters from Susannah Candy had been posted to her parents from a Fremantle post office. Both letters urged her parents not to worry about her and told them that she would be home soon. Denise Brown had phoned a girlfriend the day after she had disappeared to assure her that she

was all right. There had been no further communication from any of the
missing women. When Detective Sergeant Ferguson and his colleague
Detective Vince Katich learned that the 16-year-old girl abducted and
imprisoned at the Moorhouse Street address had been forced to phone
her parents and assure them that she was fine, they suspected that
Catherine and David Birnie were responsible for the disappearances of
the four women.

Police interrogated Catherine and David Birnie for hours at police
headquarters. The Birnies maintained that the young girl had gone
to their home willingly. David Birnie acknowledged that he had had
sex with the girl, but he maintained that she had consented. Police
conducted a thorough search of the Birnies' house and established
that the girl had been there. But they could not prove that she had been
abducted and raped by the Birnies. Detective Sergeant Ferguson knew
that he needed a confession. He thought that Catherine might crack
under intense questioning, but she persisted in the story that the girl
had gone to the house of her own volition. After hours of interrogation,
Ferguson tried to bluff David Birnie. He got up and said, 'It's getting dark.
Let's go and dig them up.'

Birnie rose to the bait. 'Okay,' he replied. 'There's four of them.'

When Catherine learned of her husband's confession, she too
dropped her defences. The Birnies agreed to direct police to the site of
the graves. The convoy of forensic vans and police cars travelled north
20 kilometres out of Perth to Gnangara Pine Plantation, off Wanneroo
Road, where the body of Denise Brown lay. The police were shocked
that neither David nor Catherine showed any remorse as they drove
towards the scene. They chatted with the officers, unaware of their
disgust. David Birnie identified the rough track he had used to drive
through the plantation to the spot where he had raped and murdered
Denise Brown.

'Dig there,' he told police. Within minutes they discovered Denise's
body. Forensic staff went to work at the scene while the Birnies directed
police south of Perth to the Gleneagles National Park on the Albany
Highway near Armadale. Birnie directed police into the thick bush, and
some metres from a walking trail, he pointed to a mound of loose earth,
where 22-year-old Mary Neilson was found shortly afterwards. About
ten minutes' walk down the track, Birnie pointed out the shallow grave
of 15-year-old Susannah Candy.

Catherine identified the burial site of the third victim, Noelene Patterson, whom she despised. Catherine seemed proud of her role in the killings and delighted in showing police where she and her husband had disposed of the body. She spat on Noelene's grave, still mindful of her husband's attraction to the beautiful woman.

⚱ ⚱ ⚱

On 12 November 1986, Catherine and David Birnie were brought before a Perth Magistrates Court, charged with four counts of wilful murder. Birnie was still dressed in his work clothes: a pair of blue overalls with a pair of old trainers. Catherine was led into the court barefoot, wearing a pair of jeans and a beige shirt. They stood passively in the dock as the charges were read out. They did not enter any pleas, bail was refused and they were both remanded in custody. When Catherine was asked to provide a suitable date for her next hearing, she stated: 'I'll go when he goes.' It was exactly as she had lived her life.

David Birnie's trial commenced on 10 February 1987 in the Perth Supreme Court. Media reports of the murders hinted at the barbarous nature of the Birnies' crimes. The city of Perth was in shock. A large crowd waited outside the court, and as the prison vans drove past the throng, they chanted for the reintroduction of the death penalty and rocked the vehicles. A huge police presence ensured that the mob remained at bay.

Those in the packed courtroom recall that both Catherine and David Birnie appeared dwarfed by the process. In the refined magnificence of the Supreme Court building, the couple seemed not to fit in. Other court observers remarked that they appeared ordinary. It was difficult to believe that these two could have performed the violent crimes for which they stood accused. The diminutive former apprentice jockey, David Birnie, was led in first by a single police officer. He glanced around the courtroom, blinking, seemingly unsure what the fuss was about. He stood in the dock with his head slightly bowed, awaiting the arrival of the judge. Catherine was then led into the courtroom by a male police officer, with whom she fought as she descended the narrow jarrah stairway. Other officers came to assist and became embroiled in the fight. She spat and swore at the officers until she reached the dock and saw Birnie. At the sight of him, she calmed down and took a seat behind him.

David Birnie pleaded guilty to four counts of murder and one count each of abduction and rape. At least the families of the victims were spared a protracted trial. 'It's the least I could do,' Birnie confided to a police officer. Catherine was not required to enter a plea as she was awaiting a psychiatric report to determine her fitness to stand trial. Catherine appeared in court in her role as supporter of her accused husband. During the proceedings she regularly reached forward from her seat and stroked her husband's hand. After her husband was sentenced, she returned to her feral state and was led from the court, kicking and screaming.

Mr Justice Wallace sentenced Birnie to life imprisonment, the maximum sentence he could hand down. He told the court: 'The law is not strong enough to express the community's horror at this sadistic killer who tortured, raped and murdered four women. In my opinion, David John Birnie is a such a danger to society that he should never be released from prison.'

Birnie, who was accustomed to dominating women, stood shaking in the dock. The door had just closed on his freedom. According to Mr Justice Wallace, Birnie had forever disqualified himself from participating in society. He was then taken from the court to a waiting prison van. He provocatively blew a kiss to the crowd, at which all available police outside the court had to struggle to contain the melee.

Catherine was determined fit to stand trial, and faced the court on 3 March 1987. The psychiatric report declared that she was unable to resist involving herself in Birnie's evil crimes. Her love for him was such that she would do anything for him, no matter how grotesque. As she told police after her arrest: 'I was prepared to follow him to the end of the earth and do anything to see that his desires were satisfied.' The psychiatrist's report stated that this was 'the worst case of personality dependence I have seen in my career'. In the courtroom it was Birnie's turn to provide the emotional support. Throughout the hearing the two chatted quietly together and smiled while the court heard the details of their appalling crimes. Occasionally, Catherine would gently massage Birnie's arms and shoulders. It appeared that the Birnies were transfixed by each other and content for the court's proceedings go on around them.

Catherine offered no defence for her role in the abduction and murder of the four women. It is possible that her action in unchaining the 16-year-old girl abducted by them on 9 November 1985, enabling her to escape from their house, which subsequently led to their capture, was a calculated attempt on her part to stop the killing. After she was arrested, she had told police:

> I think I must have come to a decision sooner or later [that] there had to be an end to the rampage. I had reached the stage when I didn't know what to do. I suppose I came to a decision that I was prepared to give her [the 16-year-old girl] a chance.
>
> I knew that it was a foregone conclusion that David would kill her and probably do it that night. I was just fed up with the killings. I thought if something did not happen soon, it would simply go on and on and never end. Deep and dark in the back of my mind was yet another fear. I had great fear that I would have to look at another killing like that of Denise Brown, the girl he murdered with an axe. I wanted to avoid that at all costs. In the back of my mind I had come to the position where I really did not care if the girl escaped or not. When I found out that the girl had escaped, I felt a twinge of terror run down my spine. I thought to myself, 'David will be furious. What shall I tell him?'

It took four vicious murders for Catherine Birnie to reach the conclusion that she did not want to kill anymore.

Mr Justice Wallace sentenced Catherine to life imprisonment. 'In my opinion,' he told her, 'you should never be released to be with David Birnie.' Taken from the courtroom, she turned to take a last look at the man who had held such power over her.

Catherine Birnie's love for Birnie remains undiminished. She sent thousands of letters to him in his prison cell and he responded just as prodigiously. They sought permission to marry, but the authorities wouldn't allow it. They have not seen each other since Catherine was sentenced for her role in the murders of the four women on 3 March 1987. Requests for contact visits and phone calls have similarly been declined. Perhaps this is the most appropriate sentence that could have been handed out to the Birnies: that they would never see each other again.

David Birnie was not well received by his fellow inmates at Casuarina Prison's maximum-security division. He has felt the wrath of his fellow inmates on numerous occasions. The convicts' code that rapists and child killers will invariably be subjected to acts of intimidation and violence has been enforced on Birnie. He was bashed on many occasions. He briefly saw the light of day in 1993 when police escorted him around the suburbs of Perth in the hope that he would confess to other murders. To this day, police believe that Birnie may have killed on other occasions. He made no admissions and was swiftly returned to his prison cell.

Catherine has had her trials behind bars. Memories may be all she has left. On 22 January 2000, Donald McLaughlin, her first husband and the father of her six children, died suddenly, aged 59, in Busselton, a country town 225 kilometres south of Perth. She sought special leave to attend the funeral, but the application was refused outright. The then Western Australian premier, Richard Court, declared: 'As far as I am concerned the Birnies have forfeited their rights for those type of privileges.'

According to Western Australian law, Catherine and David Birnie were to be eligible for parole in 2007. At the time the two were sentenced, Justice Wallace was unable to mark their files 'never to be released', so they could make an application for parole 20 years after they were first sentenced. Yet the city of Perth remembers the Birnies' crimes all too well.

On 7 October 2005, David Birnie, 54, was found hanged in his protective custody cell at Perth's Casuarina Prison. A coronial inquiry into his death was told Birnie used a length of cord, probably obtained from Casuarina's garment section, to hang himself from an air-conditioning vent in his cell.

Catherine Birnie, 69, is serving a life jail term with a 20-year minimum at Bandyup Women's Prison, located in the rural north-eastern Perth suburb of West Swan. Her application for parole is reviewed every three years and so far, it has always been rejected. It is believed that she will die behind bars for her crimes.

Chapter Ten

THE WALES-KING MURDERS

The brutal bashing murders of Margaret Wales-King and her husband Paul in April 2002 were dubbed by the Melbourne press 'The Society Murders', yet nothing could be further from the truth. Admittedly, Paul and Margaret Wales-King had all of the trappings of high society, but outside of their wealth and comfortable townhouse in the leafy establishment suburb of Armadale, they were just ordinary people beyond reproach.

The Wales-Kings were much more interested in their children and family life with their 11 grandchildren than any glittering fundraising cocktail party where they could be photographed for the social pages in the Sunday papers. Well off, yes. But A-list society? Never.

At the time of his murder, 74-year-old retired investor Paul King was an invalid due to two strokes. He was 68-year-old Margaret Lord's second husband; Margaret had previously been married to airline pilot Brian Wales, with whom she had five children.

When she married Paul King, who was of independent means, the now Margaret Wales-King was substantially wealthy in her own right. She was estimated to be worth in the vicinity of $5 million, which consisted of her home, car, jewellery and antiques, cash, and substantial shareholdings and superannuation. Mrs Wales-King had made out her will, with her husband and five children each getting a sixth of her estate upon her death.

But one of the children wasn't prepared to wait that long. In his warped mind he had been hard done by and it was time to do something about it – no matter the cost.

Although it had been building up in the killer's mind for years, the path to a shallow grave for Margaret Wales-King and Paul King began with a vegetable risotto and soup. That was the meal Margaret's youngest son Matthew Robert Wales – Paul's stepson – made for the couple the night he murdered them in cold blood in the front yard of his house while his wife put his toddler son to bed.

The events of what the press came to call the Society Murders began on the afternoon of 4 April 2002, with Matthew preparing the meal in the kitchen of the $1900-a-month Melbourne house he rented with his wife Maritza and toddler son Domenik on Burke Road, Glen Iris.

While two-year-old Domenik slept, Matthew ran through the events of his life in his head. He thought about the way his mother still treated him like a child, despite the fact he was 34 years old – how she tried to control his life, how she didn't let him grow up and be his own man, how she had never seemed to show him affection, but was always ready to tell him what to do and how to do it.

He thought about the power games she played by holding back family money he believed he was entitled to. In fact, it hadn't been very long since Margaret had sold a flat in Surfers Paradise that had been left to Matthew and his brothers and sisters by their grandfather. Margaret had refused to allow them to see the paperwork for the sale and there had been a large family argument. As was her way after such events, Margaret hadn't spoken to Matthew for a month afterwards. Matthew hated it when she acted like that.

He also thought about the thinly veiled contempt Margaret had for his wife Maritza, the true love of his life, just because she was born in Chile and came from a lower socio-economic background than their family.

He thought about how Margaret acted towards Domenik, as if he was a pet she had to treat nicely but didn't particularly care about. He thought about the way she had kept him separate from his older siblings.

Then, with a spoon, he crushed up a bunch of strong painkillers and blood pressure tablets stolen from his mother-in-law and scraped the resulting powder into a wine glass for later use. Then he went back to stirring the risotto.

After Domenik woke up, Matthew watched his beautiful young son play with some of his many toys for a while, then he went outside and retrieved a solid piece of pine with a round end from his garage and stashed it behind a hedge in the front garden of the house, a yard hidden from street view by a six-foot-high brick wall.

Maritza returned from the shop that she ran – Maritza's Imports, at 1264 High Street, Armadale – at 5.30 pm and took over playing with Domenik while Matthew got busy on a vegetable soup he would be serving that night as an entree.

The small fashion business wasn't going very well – it was $52,000 in the hole after just nine months' trading. Money was tight in the Wales house. There were plans to sell Maritza's Imports and set up a cafe, using Matthew's skills in the kitchen, skills he had developed as a house-husband since having to give up his trained profession as a hairdresser after hurting his hand.

Maritza's Imports had been on the market for six weeks, but as yet there hadn't been any solid interest.

Margaret and Paul arrived at Burke Road at about 6.45 pm, with Margaret driving her silver Mercedes-Benz E320 sedan through the front gate that Matthew had left open for them. Paul, whose most recent stroke had occurred just two months earlier, sat in the passenger seat. He wasn't considered to be safe behind the wheel anymore. In fact, most of Margaret's time these days seemed to be devoted to looking after the man that many had seen as little more than her handbag ever since they had gotten together. It was a far cry from the social butterfly she had been renowned as just a couple of years previously.

Wearing his best attempt at a smile, Matthew greeted his mother and stepfather and walked back inside with them. He went to check the meal while Maritza poured wine for the guests. She spoke to Margaret while Paul and Domenik went into the front room to play with the young boy's toys.

After a while, Matthew decided dinner was ready. Margaret and Maritza took their places at the table while Matthew went to fetch his son and Paul.

Withholding the rage that burned inside him, Matthew silently picked up his son and carried him back to the dining room, where he gave him to Maritza before going to the kitchen to serve up the soup. Into two of the bowls he dispensed the powdered pills he had prepared earlier and carried them out to Margaret and Paul, telling them to start before the entree got cold. He wanted the pills to slow them down so they wouldn't suffer any pain when he carried out the next phase of his plan.

With a million thoughts going through his head, Matthew somehow managed to remain calm through the meal. Margaret presided over the dinner from the head of the table, where she told everyone about Matthew's four older brothers and sisters and what her other grandchildren had been up to.

Matthew couldn't believe how inconsequential the conversation was. Margaret only ever seemed to talk about trivial matters. When it came to the important stuff in Matthew's life – money, his feelings towards Paul, what was happening with his own family – it seemed to be a closed book. Instead, Margaret told everyone that she needed a holiday; she was tired after handling her own financial affairs and caring for Paul, who had started going to a care facility every Monday.

So Margaret talked and the others listened and then, after dinner, they all went to the lounge room for tea. Like any toddler, Domenik was a handful. He played for the amusement of the adults, who went through two bottles of wine – mainly drank by Margaret and Paul.

By 9.30 pm, Domenik had worn himself out. He had sung 'Twinkle, Twinkle, Little Star', talked and showed off his toys, and now it was late for such a little boy. He started turning into trouble, so Maritza decided to give him a bottle and take him to bed. He kissed his grandparents sweetly and went up the stairs to his room with his mother.

Once they were gone, Margaret said that she and Paul should make their way home as well. She helped her husband stand up and they walked outside, with Matthew behind them.

Standing in the front yard, Margaret looked around and told Matthew that he needed to tidy it up. It was, she said, in need of attention.

Her son turned the light off and retrieved the slab of pine he had hidden that afternoon. As his mother walked behind Paul to the car, Matthew used both hands and all of his strength to swing the wood into the back of her neck. He watched as Margaret fell silently to the ground.

Paul hadn't heard a thing. He was still heading towards the car when Matthew hit him. He crashed to the ground as well, landing with his face on the cold concrete pavers. Matthew then continued to hit both of his victims across the back of the neck, each successive blow getting harder and more violent. He didn't stop until he saw blood flowing out onto the ground.

Dropping his weapon, Matthew checked for signs of life. Margaret had no pulse, no breath – just a lot of spilled blood. Paul was the same. He had finally murdered them. He walked around the yard frantically.

It didn't seem real, to have killed them after so much time, so many years, waiting for the day, dreaming about it, acting it out in his head in a constant troubled loop. Now he just felt relief – relief for himself and for his family. His mother would never meddle. He could finally live his own life.

Then Matthew noticed a woman in the upstairs window of the shop across the road. He was concerned that she had seen what had happened. He finally realised there was a good chance he would get caught, but he still didn't really care – the feeling of relief was so strong.

Matthew decided he had to go and find Maritza, but at that same moment she came outside after putting Domenik to bed. She couldn't believe what she saw – the couple she had just had a normal if somewhat uncomfortable meal with were lying on the ground in her front yard covered in blood. Matthew told her to go back inside. She asked what had happened. 'I hit them,' he told her twice.

Maritza looked at her husband. He was sweaty and visibly agitated. There was blood on his tracksuit top. Maritza didn't understand the situation. She ran inside and vomited. Matthew followed her and tried to comfort her but even then, Maritza knew things were different now. She saw the blood on his hands when he made an attempt to hold her. She screamed, asking what had happened, and then she went into their bedroom and looked down from the window. She could see the bodies from there, as well as a light in the window of the shop across the road. Matthew again told her he had hit them, adding that it was a relief. 'I had to,' he said. 'I had to do it.'

Matthew asked Maritza if she hated him. He again tried to hold her. She moved away and asked what he was going to do. 'I'll fix it,' Matthew said, telling her to stay there and not do anything. He then made his way back downstairs while his wife felt her simple world crumble and his young son slept.

Maritza looked back down into the front yard. She saw her husband dragging his mother's body by her feet towards the front fence. He was wearing latex kitchen gloves and dumping her on a patch of grass, where he turned her over so her lifeless body faced the sky. He then dragged his stepfather to the same area, before covering the bodies with a deflated plastic child's wading pool. Maritza vomited again. She didn't want to watch any more.

When Matthew finally returned to the upstairs bedroom, he explained that he was going to do something with his mother's expensive car – he had to get rid of it. Maritza couldn't even look at him. Instead she waited while he left the room, and then she heard the Mercedes' engine start. After she heard the gate shut behind it, she got into bed and began to cry.

Matthew didn't get back for several hours. He asked her if she hated him. All Maritza could do was ask what Matthew was going to do as she held his shaking body while he wept.

Neither Matthew nor Maritza slept that night. They talked until the sun came up. Maritza had begged her husband to phone the authorities and explain what he had done. He asked her to give him time. He wanted to be with her and Domenik. He tried to explain that feeling of relief that had washed over him after he had committed the murders and released himself from his mother's stranglehold. She still couldn't understand. Matthew again told her he would fix the situation.

Just after the sun first started to light up the yard in front of the rented house on Burke Road, Matthew made his way down the stairs again. He found a green sheet in a cupboard and went outside to the bodies. After ripping the sheet in half, he took the pool off the bodies and covered each of his victims' faces with the material. He didn't want to look at his mother or stepfather anymore. He put the pool back over the bodies and thought about what he should do next.

Matthew drove away from the house in his red Nissan Patrol at 7 am. His first stop was an ATM facility at some nearby shops at Tooronga Village, and then he went to a Mobil service station near his house and hired a trailer. At such an early hour, he was only the second customer looking for a trailer that day. He used his real name when he filled out the hire form, but gave the address of a house he and Maritza had lived in previously. He paid for the transaction using his ATM card, and also grabbed a D-shaped metal shackle that he would need to attach the trailer to his four-wheel drive.

When he got back home, Matthew pushed the trailer up to the bodies. But before he could start to move them, he noticed that Domenik was looking through the window of the front room where he had been playing with his toys. Matthew left the bodies where they lay and went to make his son breakfast instead.

Inside, Maritza wouldn't let Matthew touch her. Despite the fact that she looked a mess from a night of crying and worrying, Matthew told her to go to work. It was important to act as if nothing unusual had happened. Work was the last thing Maritza felt like doing, but she reasoned that it might help her calm down – or at least get her mind off the destructive mess she had been cast into.

With breakfast made, Matthew put Domenik in front of the television for the morning children's shows and told his wife he would speak to the police when he thought the time was right. 'I want to spend some more time with you and Dom,' he added.

He then drove to the closet hardware store and bought five more D-shaped shackles, a five-metre length of red and white striped sash cord and six-metre-long lengths of stainless-steel chain.

At the Melbourne Brick Company outlet across the road from Tait Timber and Hardware he got three bricks, after telling an assistant he needed them for a feature in a fireplace.

When he got home, Maritza needed the car to get to work, so Matthew couldn't do anything about the bodies in the front yard – and he had a toddler to look after. The pair played inside for the day, in case Domenik got interested in what was beneath his colourful plastic pool.

When the young boy went for his sleep at lunchtime, Matthew put on another pair of the kitchen latex gloves and took two quilt covers from the linen cupboard.

He went outside and, hidden by the high front fence, removed the pool from the cold and stiff bodies. Matthew found it difficult to manoeuvre his mother into the quilt cover, but he knew he had to do it – he needed to try to fix this mess. He placed Paul inside the other one, and then tied the cotton covers around them with the sash cord.

He tied one of the thick lengths of chain around Paul's neck and across his body. Another of the chain lengths was used to connect the three bricks to one of the shackles, in case he decided to dump the bodies in the water.

Mentally and physically exhausted by now after so long without sleep, Matthew went back inside and called Maritza at the shop, as he had done several times already that day. He told her he was starting to lose it. She didn't particularly want to speak to him about the situation.

Back outside, Matthew finished what he had started and put the bodies into the trailer, then put the deflated pool over them again. He also threw in a sawhorse and some paint tins, then covered the lot in a tarpaulin and pushed the trailer back into the garage.

Before he went to wake up Domenik from his nap, Matthew noticed that blood had dripped through the doona covers and onto the grass where he had tied up the bodies.

The bodies remained in the garage for the night. The next morning, Saturday, 6 April 2002, Matthew dropped Maritza and Domenik at Maritza's Imports in High Street, then went to another hardware shop – Dean's True Value Hardware on Malvern Road – where, according to records, he used his credit card to purchase an industrial cleaner called Liquid Magnet, made especially for cement surfaces, and a mattock.

Ten minutes later he was ordering a load of Surecrop compost to be delivered to his home the next Monday morning. Then he returned to Burke Road and attached the trailer to his Nissan Patrol.

Before he could go about dumping the bodies, though, Maritza rang. She was feeling sick and thought a migraine was coming on. Matthew picked her up and drove her home, where she threw up again and, drowsy from her migraine tablets, went to bed. Domenik followed her lead soon after.

At 12.38 pm, Matthew began working on an alibi by phoning his mother's house and leaving a message for Margaret on the machine.

Before leaving home, he placed various items belonging to the dead couple – Margaret's car keys, some of her jewellery, her mobile phone, which he had broken, her handbag, as well as her and Paul's shoes and his own bloodstained top from the night of the murders – in several black plastic bags. He then drove the trailer holding its lifeless cargo to a service station on Burwood Road, where he pumped out $20 worth of fuel and bought a map. Once again, he used his credit card, leaving further documentation of his travels.

From there he drove to the Maroondah Highway and motored along it, not exactly sure where he was going. Along the way he stopped randomly at public garbage bins and placed the rubbish bags holding the evidence in them as he went.

He eventually decided he should get rid of the bodies in bushland somewhere, so he continued to head east. He stopped at a Bunnings hardware store at Croydon and bought a crowbar and a book called *Guide to Garden Ponds*. Then he was back on the road, driving for a solid three hours until he came across a dirt road that headed into a national park near the small town of Warburton. He went down the track for a while and finally found a quiet, isolated spot to stop. It was as good a place as any, he thought, to bury the bodies. He found a clearing about 20 metres from his car and decided that would be the final resting place of his mother and hated stepfather.

Matthew used the mattock he had purchased to start on the shallow grave. He cut out a rectangle that would be large enough to fit his mother and set about removing the soft soil. After a while the ground got tougher and he had to use the crowbar to go any deeper.

It was around 8 pm and dark by the time he could dig no further. He pulled the corpses to the hole and dropped his mother in first, then dumped Paul's body on top of hers. Again he used the deflated pool to cover the bodies, and then threw the bricks in on top.

Matthew's next job was to fill the hole. Not wanting to turn the car lights on in case he attracted anyone who might be passing by, he had to work by moonlight. What a terrible sight that must have been.

Once he had filled the hole, he trampled the spare dirt on top with his feet, by now eager to get home.

As he found his way back to the road from the dirt track, he saw a big white four-wheel drive coming at him from around a corner. There were two men inside. He pulled a hat down low over his eyes as it passed him. These men would later come forward as witnesses against Matthew.

Along the way home he threw the crowbar onto a nature strip, then made his way back to the scene of his crime. Maritza didn't want to know where he had been.

Matthew started the next day, Sunday, by digging out a garden bed in his front yard and placing the dirt and grass in the hired trailer. When Maritza asked him why he had picked such a hot day to work in the garden, Matthew told her he had to 'go back' and added, 'They need some more dirt.' That was more information than she wanted. She had no idea Matthew had become worried that wild animals would dig up the remains. She left her troubled husband to his work and took Domenik to buy a cake for her nephew James's birthday party.

Matthew kept digging until he had what resembled another shallow grave, where Margaret and Paul had been lying on the grass. He would fill it the next day with the compost that was being delivered. He figured that the digging would have removed any forensic evidence that the bodies had been there.

Next, he scrubbed down the pavers outside the door where he had struck his victims, and the garage floor, using the entire bottle of the Liquid Magnet he had bought. He went as far as to take out the entire contents of the garage and use a powerful hose on the floor. The woman who lived above the shop across the road noticed him doing it and thought it was rather strange behaviour.

After Domenik woke from his lunchtime nap, Matthew and Maritza took him to the party for James. Maritza's whole family, the Pizzaros, were there. It was hard for the two of them to keep up appearances – and it would only get more difficult as time went on and Matthew tried to maintain his facade of innocence.

Maritza found the day especially difficult. She was close to her sister. To not be able to talk to her about the trouble she had been cast into burned her up inside.

That night in bed, the pair of them started to cry. While Maritza wondered what would become of them, what would happen to little Domenik, Matthew told her that the bodies would never be found. Then the phone rang.

Matthew let it go through to the answering machine. It was his oldest sister, Sally Honan. Sally asked if he knew what had happened to their mother and Paul. No-one, she said, had heard from them for days now.

Matthew rang Sally back the next day and told her he had no idea about Margaret and Paul's whereabouts. Sally explained that she was at a holiday house at the beach and asked if he could go around to their mother's house with his other sister, Emma. Matthew told her that would be fine, then rang Emma and told her he was too busy. He suggested she go with their other brother, Damian.

Instead of helping his worried siblings find their mother, Matthew dug the compost that had been delivered into his new garden bed, then set off to the shallow grave with a trailer full of dirt and grass. Maritza didn't work Mondays, so she was free to stay home and look after Domenik.

Matthew made good time getting back to the bush. Along the way he stopped for petrol, and again at a gardening supply shop to buy six hefty river rocks.

When he arrived at the grave, he was relieved to find it hadn't been disturbed. He covered it with the dirt and grass he'd brought and left the rocks on top.

On his way home again, he stopped at a car wash and removed what he hoped was all traces of the dirt from the car and trailer. He also threw away the map. He obviously had no desire to go back to that area of bushland. He then returned the trailer to the service station he had hired it from at around 3 pm.

At home later that afternoon, and feeling slightly better having finally got rid of the bodies, he received another phone call from his sister Sally. She was livid. She knew that Margaret and Paul had been his dinner guests at his house on the Thursday night, and that was the last time they had been seen. She demanded that he come over to Margaret's house at Mercer Road, Armadale, immediately. Matthew knew he had no choice. When he arrived, there were two police cars there as well.

The previous few days had seen several friends and family members trying to get in touch with Margaret Wales-King. At 9 am on the Monday, her concerned children Damian and Emma had arrived at the house with a spare key. A taxi had arrived not long after, looking to take Paul to the care facility he had been attending. Their mother wasn't the sort of woman who would forget to cancel a cab, even if her disappearance was something as innocent as an impromptu holiday. Their concern grew even stronger.

Inside the house they found dirty wineglasses and a bowl with crumbs in it on the kitchen bench. It was most unlike Margaret. Further discounting the holiday theory was the fact she had left behind her mobile phone charger, sunglasses and toothbrush. There were three days' worth of messages on the answering machine. Emma went straight to Malvern police station to report her mother missing.

The officer on duty, Constable Rebecca Jones, wasn't a stranger to missing persons reports. A large proportion of the local population are older residents who are usually found not long after such a report, lost and confused. But the cursory evidence suggested something more serious. Jones asked Emma to provide some recent photos and phone numbers for the police to check.

After that, Emma went back to her mother's house to do whatever she could. She and Damian went through her phone book and diary. They rang hospitals and friends. Nothing came of their inquiries.

That afternoon, Detective Senior Constable Craig Shiell, Sergeant Sharon McCrory and Detective Senior Constable Sheahan arrived at Mercer Street a little after 5 pm. Emma, Damian and Sally were there, and they showed the officers around the house. There were no signs of forced entry. They organised for other officers to ask for information around the neighbourhood.

While they were investigating, friends of Margaret and Paul's arrived – Janet and Fred Roche. They had been trying to get in touch. It turned out they'd had drinks with the couple the afternoon they disappeared. They explained that Margaret had had to ask them to leave so she could have dinner with Matthew. They'd left shortly before 7 pm.

The family couldn't believe it. That's when Sally called Matthew and told him to come right over. In a later statement, Emma told police about Matthew's arrival that day, saying:

> He burst into the front room, his head looked like it was going to explode
> … He looked very emotional and asked, 'What's going on?', acting as
> though he was surprised to see the police and acting as though he
> feared the worst. He then walked himself into the corner of the room we
> were in and held his eyes with his fingers and let out a distraught cry
> and moan.

What surprised the family most about Matthew's reaction was that it seemed an 'absolute overreaction', Emma added. After all, there had been no mention of anything actually happening to Margaret and Paul. None of the family members present looked or acted as if there was a problem. As Emma said, 'For all he knew, Mum and Paul could have been away for the weekend.'

His older sisters started asking Matthew about the night they had dinner together. Matthew gave vague answers about what the missing couple had been wearing and their behaviour. He punctuated his recollections with cries of 'Where's my mama?'

After a while he told them, 'It's all a blank. I can't do this now.'

Emma rang Maritza because she thought Matthew's answers were evasive. But her sister-in-law was not much more help. Maritza eventually asked Emma to send Matthew home because she had a headache.

Meanwhile, Detective Shiell questioned Matthew. He told the policeman that the dinner had finished at 9.45 pm, when he walked Paul and Margaret to their car and waved them goodbye. When asked, Matthew told Shiell he couldn't remember his phone number. He then started crying, saying that he couldn't 'handle this'.

Matthew went home shortly after his emotional outburst. He didn't answer any calls from his siblings that night; their suspicions were aroused. Damian phoned Detective Sheahan shortly before 11 pm and told him that Matthew hadn't been answering his phone, and that he thought he could have something to do with the case. Sheahan sent two officers to check up on the residents of the Burke Road house.

Detectives Hodgson and Nolan pressed the intercom outside the house at 12.15 am. Matthew let them in, and then a tired-looking Maritza joined them all in the kitchen. The officers told Matthew they had been sent around as he hadn't answered his phone. His excuse was that he had taken some painkillers, which had knocked him out. He added that he was 'a bit upset and concerned about my mother, you know'. His behaviour didn't sit right with the officers, with Hodgson making a note: 'Matthew Wales didn't appear to be sincere.'

That night – after it was discovered that neither Paul nor Margaret had accessed their bank account in five days – the case went from a missing persons report to a suspected murder. The official homicide investigation began at 8.45 am on the morning of Tuesday, 9 April 2002. Under the name of Operation Compradore, the six-person crew was led by Detective Sergeant Steve Waddell.

Margaret's children were interviewed again, and a forensics unit investigated her Armadale house. Matthew arrived at the premises at 11.25 am with a handwritten letter in which he put forward notes of what the dinner conversation with his mother and stepfather on 4 April had involved. Waddell found the details included were totally inconsequential.

At lunchtime, Shiell visited Maritza at her shop. Business was so slow she had time to provide him with a five-page statement about the night in question, explaining what they had eaten and drunk and what time the guests had left. Her belief, she said, was that her in-laws had driven home at 9.45 pm, and that Matthew remained in the house and hadn't made any phone calls.

She also described Margaret as something of a snob, but said the extended family mostly got on fine.

The next order of business for Operation Compradore was to take Matthew Wales' statement. Waddell handled this formality himself at Malvern police station. His five-page statement mostly mirrored Maritza's, though he stated that his wife and child had gone outside to see off his mother and stepfather when they left.

He added, 'Their disappearance is totally out of character,' and said that Margaret and Paul seemed 'to be their normal selves' the last he had seen of them.

⚰ ⚰ ⚰

The next day – 10 April – the police brought the media into it. From that point, the case took on a life of its own.

A press conference was called at the Victoria Police Centre, where the head of the Homicide Squad, Detective Inspector Brian Rix, opened proceedings by telling the assembled members of the media that there 'is no real reason' for the disappearance of Paul King and Margaret Wales-King.

Though Margaret's children Prue, Emma and Damian were on hand to put a private face to the public appeal for information, Matthew stayed at home. It was 'not his thing', he told his family.

Still, the press conference brought investigating officers results that very night, when a solicitor named Mark Hester saw the report about 'wealthy couple' Margaret and Paul's disappearance on the 7 pm news. The story on the ABC mentioned their silver Mercedes-Benz. It sounded like the one that had been parked near Mark's Middle Park house for the past few days. He went out to Page Street, near the corner of Armstrong Street, made a note of the number plate and phoned the authorities. By 7.40 pm the car was a crime scene.

Shiell and Waddell were soon there. Shiell surmised that the Mercedes had been parked quickly, judging by the wheels pointing to the right. The seat was also set close to the wheel – much closer than a tall woman like Margaret would have been comfortable with. Still, there were no fingerprints on the steering wheel, indicating that the last driver had worn gloves of some sort.

Some members of the family congregated at the site the next day to try to work out what the car had been doing there, but they could think of no connection between their mother or stepfather and Middle Park. They would spend the next few days combing the area and surrounding suburbs looking for a sign of any sort, but to no avail. Needless to say, Matthew didn't join them.

Around 3.30 pm on the afternoon of 11 April, four detectives from Homicide were at Matthew's house. When he arrived soon afterwards, he let them in and the men started questioning him again. Matthew ran through the same answers he was no doubt used to giving by now – vegetable risotto, wine, no idea where they are, no idea about Middle Park.

While Matthew was telling one detective that out of all his siblings, he got on with Paul King the best, that he 'really liked him', two of the other officers were in the garage. They noticed a strong chemical smell, but couldn't explain it. They wrote down that it smelt of a heavy-duty cleaning product.

After that visit, the detectives split up and spoke to Matthew and Maritza's neighbours. The woman across the road told them she had seen Matthew move everything out of his garage and clean it thoroughly the weekend Margaret and Paul disappeared.

Two of the detectives returned to speak to Matthew the next day. They took his car away for forensic testing, but nothing was found inside it except for a street directory with maps 93 and 94 marked with a piece of paper.

That evening, Waddell and some other officers were back at Burke Road. They asked Matthew if they could look for signs of blood in his garage. Matthew's answer sounded somewhat pre-planned and possibly rehearsed: 'Yes, you have our permission to do whatever you have to do. I understand that we have to be investigated because we were the last people to see Mum and Paul before they disappeared. We will give you as much help as you want.'

Using a forensics product called Luminol that makes blood show up in the dark as a bright blue mark, they found five spots of evidence. The net was tightening around Matthew Wales.

Authorities spent the next fortnight weighing up what evidence they had against the potential suspects. Matthew was a hot topic of conversation. His behaviour was one thing, the blood in the garage another. There had also been open talk from Wales family members that they thought he was involved in some way.

The trickle of new evidence seemed to have dried up, though. Several suspects had been eliminated, but no new ones had been added. The Wales family went to the media asking for public assistance again on 16 April. 'If we can't have them, we want their bodies,' Prue begged.

Her request was granted on 29 April 2002, when 48-year-old Parks Victoria ranger Jon Gwilt was given the job of closing down a dirt road known as Track 3 in the Yarra State Forest, as part of a plan to protect a reservoir in the region that helped supply the water to Melbourne. Looking around the area, he noticed a mound of dirt that looked to have been compacted down. There was also grass growing on top of it, but it didn't look native to the area. It was the same sort of grass one would find in a suburban yard. There was also some rope left on the ground near it.

Closer examination showed the mound to fit the dimensions of a grave, but Jon convinced himself he was making too much of the find and went back about his duties.

Still, the idea nagged at him. Later that morning he was having coffee with a colleague, Alan Caddy. Jon mentioned the mound and the men decided they should investigate it further.

At noon, they started clearing the dirt from the top – hoping to find rubbish or anything other than a dead body. But no such luck. Just 10 centimetres into the freshly turned earth, they came across three bricks joined by a length of metal chain. Then they found a child's plastic pool. They were sure it was just some illegally dumped rubbish until they found some cotton material beneath the plastic and when they lifted it, they were hit with the unmistakable stench of death.

The men reported the find immediately and Senior Constable Wayne Phillips from Warburton police station was there by 1.30 pm. Other officers arrived soon after and for the next 12 hours they removed as much evidence as they could find. They collected insect matter from the bodies, which could tell investigators when the corpses had been dumped. They also took some blue–green chips of paint from the walls of the shallow grave that had obviously been left by whatever tool had been used to dig it.

An autopsy was performed on both bodies in the early hours of the next morning. It was obvious that the bodies had been on the receiving end of some serious violence, with bruising still visible to the neck and face, despite the length of time they had been buried.

The stomachs held mostly rice and vegetables that hadn't been fully digested, which meant the deaths had occurred not long after a meal. But rather distressingly, it was found that the blunt force administered on the victims was most likely not the actual cause of death. It seemed that the blows had merely rendered them unconscious, and death had occurred some time later as a result of asphyxiation, while they were lying on the ground after they had been bashed.

A toxicology report indicated the two victims had also consumed alcohol before their deaths, along with paracetamol and codeine. The female victim also had signs of a medication called atenolol, which was prescribed for people suffering high blood pressure.

The insect evidence proved inconclusive, but the clincher came when the dental records were checked on 1 May and the bodies were formally identified as Paul King and Margaret Wales-King.

Even before the formal identification, though, investigating officers were telling the Wales family that two bodies had been dug up matching the description of Margaret and Paul. Matthew's face lost all of its colour when he received the news. Other than that, he displayed no emotion.

After the detectives left, Maritza unleashed at Matthew. She cried and hit him and demanded he tell the police what had happened, what he had done. It had been 27 days of pain and torment for her. Matthew begged for more time. No doubt knowing his days as a free man were limited, he said he wanted to be with his wife and young son as much as possible.

That night, Matthew and Maritza made a rare appearance at a family meeting with all of his siblings and their partners at his sister Sally's house. As they watched reports of the grisly find in the national park, Matthew remained emotionless, while Emma noticed Maritza growing more irate.

Detective Sergeant Steve Waddell arrived at Sally's house shortly before 8 pm. He was there to tell them that Paul and Margaret had been formally identified by their dental records, and to ask Matthew Wales to accompany him back to Burke Road so he could carry out a search of the premises. He showed Matthew the warrant, and they left.

Among the items found during the search that night were a shovel, a mattock and three D-shaped shackles. Knowing that the bodies had been found in queen-sized quilt covers, investigators took a similar one from the bed, but a search of the linen cupboard turned up no other such items. It seemed strange that the couple only had one quilt cover.

As plans were being made for the funeral, the police examined the evidence seized from Burke Road, and tied it with everything they had noted in the earlier stages of the investigation. Matthew was clearly now the obvious suspect. The press hounded his and Maritza's every move, and the rest of the family's emotions moved from suspicion to shock to outright anger.

Forensic accountants pored over Matthew's finances and bank records. They found he had bought a pool on January 11 that year that was exactly the same as the one covering the bodies. However, there was no such pool at his house when the search warrant had been executed.

One by one, all of the other purchases recorded in the lead-up to dumping the body were ticked off as well – the D-shaped shackles, the mattock, the trailer (which was taken for forensic testing), the Liquid Magnet cleaning product, even the compost.

A private funeral service was held on 8 May. Around 40 members of the Wales and King families were in attendance. Damian Wales offered the eulogy. Outside, the hungry media lay in wait; the press was having a field day with this case. Matthew was even being cast as a suspect in mainstream newspapers.

After the ceremony, the families went back to Emma's home. Matthew and Maritza decided not to attend the wake. Neither did they attend the scattering of Paul and Margaret's ashes on 11 May. They couldn't have even if they wanted to; they were in police custody being questioned.

Like any mother, Maritza was worried about what would happen to her son if both she and Matthew were sent to prison. Maritza had already retained the services of Phillip Dunn QC, whom her solicitor, Paul Galbally, had brought to her. She told them what had happened, and the legal experts worked on a plan and met with the authorities.

At first the police weren't interested in making a deal – they figured it was only a matter of time before they had the married couple locked away themselves. But they eventually came on board. On 11 May, Maritza told the authorities everything she knew about the killings and her husband's subsequent actions. Matthew was arrested that day.

For the first time, Matthew spoke honestly about the murders. He was asked almost 1500 questions in an interview that lasted more than four hours. He answered all of them. He told Detective Sergeant Waddell that there had been 'so much animosity and hurt between my mother and myself'. He said that money was a factor behind the slayings, but more because of the way Margaret used 'her money for power' than simply to obtain funds through her will. 'She used it [her money] against us all the time,' he said.

He also told of the way his mother manipulated him and his siblings, and how he felt she had 'alienated' him from his older brothers and sisters. As an example, he said, 'I walked around my sister's house the other day, and I noticed everybody else's photo was up except for mine.'

He spoke about the actual murders. 'I hit them on the back of the neck with a block of wood,' he said. 'Maritza had nothing to do with this at all. This is me. This is my emotions that went out.'

Matthew was taken to Melbourne Magistrates' Court at 5.30 pm that afternoon. He was denied bail and spent his first night of many to come in custody.

Maritza was charged as being an accessory to the murders but was let out on bail so she could care for her child.

On 18 December 2002, they appeared at Melbourne's Supreme Court before Justice John Coldrey. Matthew pleaded guilty to both counts of murder, while Maritza pleaded guilty to concealing knowledge of the events.

Due to the Christmas break, it was going to take much longer than usual for a sentence to be handed down after all of the evidence had been presented to the court. Matthew and Maritza didn't go back to a packed court for sentencing until 11 April 2003 – exactly 53 weeks after the murders. Justice Coldrey entered at 11 am and spent 80 minutes reading his judgement. He spoke about the facts of the case and the autopsy findings, of the psychological reports and the ways Matthew had lied during the investigation. Eventually he sentenced Maritza to two years in prison, which would be suspended for two years. That meant she was free to look after Domenik, who had by now turned three. But if she committed any serious crimes during that time, she would be sent to jail.

Matthew was sentenced to 30 years in prison. He must serve 24 of those before he is eligible for parole. By the time he is free to walk the streets again, Matthew Wales will be 58 years old. The son he loves will be 26.

Chapter Eleven

PYJAMA GIRL

When a local farmer discovered the charred body of a young woman in a stormwater culvert just off the Albury–Corowa Road in south-western New South Wales, it triggered one of the most intriguing murder mysteries in Australian history. But it would be many years before the killer was caught, and then it was only due to the determination of investigating officers not to give up in their pursuit of the killer.

On 1 September 1934, Tom Griffiths was leading his prize bull home from a cattle show in Albury when he almost stumbled upon the woman's hidden body, clad only in distinct Asian-style crepe yellow pyjamas with a green dragon motif on the top. Griffiths borrowed a bicycle from a passing cyclist and left its owner holding his bull and watching over the body while he cycled to the police station. When the local police inspector, Mr Goodsell, accompanied by a constable and a detective, arrived at the scene, they found that a sack had been placed beneath her body and set alight and as a result the woman's pyjamas had been badly burnt. They also concluded that, due to apparent skid marks on the road near the crime scene, the victim had not been killed where her body was found, but had been driven to the spot in the dead of night and dumped.

When the woman's body was examined at Albury Hospital, it was discovered that a bath towel had been wrapped around her head. Doctors carefully removed the towel to find that the left side of her face had been smashed in by a sort of blunt instrument and that there was a bullet hole in her right temple. The woman appeared to be in her mid- to late 20s, with blonde hair and a full figure. A plaster cast was taken of her teeth, to be photographed and circulated among dentists to help identify the victim should no-one come forward. Despite a lot of publicity about the discovery of the body in local and city newspapers, no-one did.

Forensic experts from Melbourne went to work on the evidence available. The bullet had come from a Webley & Scott .25 calibre and it was matched to all of the guns of registered owners of similar weapons, but this lead came to nothing. Nor did the investigation into where the sack, towel or pyjamas may have come from. Everything led to a dead end.

After a couple of months, the police were satisfied that they had fruitlessly exhausted all avenues of identification, even after continuous publicity in the press and over the radio. In an unprecedented move, they decided to put the body on public display in the hope that someone might recognise the woman who had by now become known as the 'Pyjama Girl'. To jog people's memories the New South Wales Government offered two separate rewards: £200 for information leading to the identity of the Pyjama Girl; and £500 for information leading to the conviction of the person or persons responsible for her death.

At first, the body was displayed at Albury Hospital, where it had been kept on ice since its discovery. Despite numerous leads, this tactic led to nothing. After six weeks, the dead woman was taken to Sydney, where she was placed in a specially built zinc-lined bath filled with formalin, a solution of formaldehyde in water used for preserving organic specimens, at the University of Sydney under the watchful eye of Professor Burkitt, the resident Professor of Anatomy. It was then put on display for all to come and view.

The Pyjama Girl became such an attraction that large queues formed each day for the viewings. Thousands of curious onlookers passed by the embalmed body, and soon it became the main attraction for something to do on the weekend. Leads came thick and fast, but all petered out to nothing until someone suggested that the Pyjama Girl could in fact be a young woman named Linda Platt, whose married name was Agostini.

⚰ ⚰ ⚰

Linda Platt had owned a small shop in Kent, England, with her sister, but after a relationship with a soldier broke up, she sold her share in the business and emigrated to Australia. She settled in Sydney, where she worked as an usher and lived with girlfriends in Darlinghurst.

Linda fell in love with an Italian immigrant named Tony Agostini, who held the lease of the cloakroom at Sydney's flashest restaurant, Romano's. This restaurant was the place to be seen in Sydney in the 1930s, and the tips for cloaking a hat or coat provided a comfortable living. Although it was no secret that Linda had a drinking problem and was troublesome when she had had one too many, Tony Agostini loved her dearly. They were married on 22 April 1930, and moved into an apartment in Kellett Street, Kings Cross, where Linda took up hairdressing in a salon nearby.

A few years later, the Agostinis decided to move to Melbourne. Friends told police that they believed the move was because Linda's drinking had become worse and Tony thought a change of environment might make life easier for them both. Tony had also secured a job in Victoria as a representative of an Italian publication. This was the last their Sydney friends saw of them.

Victorian detectives knocked on Tony Agostini's door in Carlton, a northern Melbourne suburb, almost a year after the discovery of the Pyjama Girl. When questioned about his wife, he informed the detectives that Linda had walked out on him a year earlier and he had not seen or heard from her since. Tony said that, as far as he knew, it was her intention to go and work on the Union Steamship line, where she had worked previously as a ship's hairdresser. He said that sometimes the ships went away for a long time. When the detectives showed Agostini photos of the Pyjama Girl, he said that it wasn't his wife. He was told to report to Russell Street police headquarters the following morning, but when he turned up he was treated with disinterest, as he was on two subsequent occasions when he called in at detectives' requests. Eventually, he stopped calling.

Although investigators kept the file open, the finding of a coronial inquest conducted at Albury on 18 January 1938 before Coroner CW Swiney was that, between 28 August 1934 and 31 August 1934, a woman whose name was unknown and whose partly burned body was found near Albury on 1 September 1934 died from injuries to the skull and brain that were inflicted upon her, but where and by whom he could not say. About the same time, Agostini visited an old friend in Sydney, Gertrude Crawford, who had known both Linda and him when they lived in Kings Cross. He said he hadn't seen Linda in months, and after telling her of the visit by police, Crawford said that she had viewed the body at the University of Sydney but didn't believe it was Linda. Agostini accompanied Crawford to view the body in formalin the following day and confirmed that it definitely wasn't his wife.

⚰ ⚰ ⚰

Over the next seven years, the Pyjama Girl's identity remained a mystery. From time to time someone would 'positively' identify the body in the formalin bath, but it always proved wrong.

During this time, a Macquarie Street heart specialist, Dr T Palmer Benbow, became obsessed with the case. Fancying himself as an amateur sleuth (his name certainly could have come straight out of an Arthur Conan Doyle novel), Benbow set about solving the riddle of the identity of the Pyjama Girl, with bizarre results. After several years of studying every aspect of the case and talking to anyone who had any sort of an opinion, irrespective of where they lived, Benbow became convinced, as were numerous people who had viewed the body, that it was that of Anna Philomena Morgan, who had disappeared in 1933.

In 1939, Dr Benbow's travels led him to an elderly woman, Lucy Collins, who lived just outside of Albury. She told him an unusual story. A few weeks before the discovery of the Pyjama Girl, Lucy Collins was living with a man named Ginger Quin. One freezing morning when Ginger wasn't there, a tearful young woman came to her front door, asking for directions to Sydney Road. Collins invited the distressed young woman inside, sat her down in front of the fire and made her a cup of tea. When Collins went outside to the back of the house to milk the cow (whether the milk was for the tea or not isn't quite clear), she returned to find Quin in the middle of a raging row with the woman. Collins said she witnessed Quin pick up a large piece of wood and repeatedly batter the woman's head with it. Then he wrapped the young woman's bleeding head in a towel, took the body outside, dumped it in the back of his sulky and drove off in the teeming rain.

Benbow's sleuthing led him to believe that the dead woman was Anna Morgan, the illegitimate daughter of a Jeanette Routledge, who claimed that her daughter had left home in 1932, aged 21. Routledge claimed that items of clothing the woman was alleged to have left at

Collins's home belonged to her missing daughter.

With the eminent Dr T Palmer Benbow rubbing his hands together with glee at the prospect of solving Australia's most infamous murder mystery, and with Routledge laying a claim to the body and the £75 in her missing daughter's estate, police started asking questions.

It transpired that Collins was partial to a drink. It was an accepted fact locally that anything that she said couldn't be taken seriously. But Benbow and Routledge would have none of it and applied for delivery of the Pyjama Girl's body to Routledge's home. Police found that there was no substance to the story and the request was refused. The anonymous body remained in its formalin bath at the University of Sydney.

⛢ ⛢ ⛢

In 1940 Italy had entered the Second World War against the Allies in Europe, and Tony Agostini, deemed to be an open supporter of Mussolini, was held in an internment camp in South Australia until he was released in 1944. He immediately headed for Sydney, where he took a job as a waiter at his old haunt, Romano's, which still catered for the privileged and famous. One of Romano's regular customers was the New South Wales Police Commissioner, Bill Mackay, who lunched there almost daily. Agostini was his favourite waiter. Keen to make a name for himself, Mackay was intent on solving all outstanding murder cases, which, of course, included Australia's most famous case of the time, the Pyjama Girl murder.

Mackay assigned a squad of detectives to the case and their fresh inquiries kept coming up with the same name – Linda Agostini. Mackay had the body transferred to police headquarters, where a team of specialists from local mortuaries went to work on it in an endeavour to bring the woman back to life and make her look as she did the day she died. In March 1944, detectives rounded up 16 people who had known Linda Agostini before she left Sydney for Melbourne with her husband. Seven of the acquaintances recognised the face immediately. The others couldn't be certain.

Later that day, Commissioner Mackay telephoned his favourite waiter at Romano's, Tony Agostini, and asked him if he could come down to police headquarters as soon as he had finished his lunch shift to see whether he could identify his missing wife. When Agostini arrived, Mackay explained to him that, even if the body was that of Linda Agostini, he was no way implicated in her murder. To the police commissioner's astonishment, Agostini broke down and confessed to the murder of his wife. 'I have been through hell for ten years,' he said. 'No matter what happens to me now, I am going to tell the truth.'

Agostini then made a full confession. He said that his life with Linda was a hell on earth, and although he loved her very much, her drinking binges, which always resulted in fits of jealous rage and were followed by long periods of deep depression, finally drove him to despair. He had been forced to move eight times since the couple had moved to Melbourne because of her fits of screaming and violence.

Agostini told the investigators that the beginning of what was to become the Pyjama Girl murder mystery began on 27 August 1934, a Sunday night. The couple was living at 589 Swanston Street, Carlton. He was preparing to make a business trip to rural Shepparton the following morning. He had invited his wife along for the drive, but she had refused, adding that he wouldn't be going either. Agostini ignored the remark, as it was not unusual for Linda to fly into a fit of jealous rage on the eve of one of his trips. He awoke early the next morning to find a revolver pressed against his temple with Linda's trembling finger wrapped around the trigger. Agostini claimed that he swung around on the pillow, grasped Linda's arm and forced the gun away from him. A shot rang out and Linda fell dead on the bed, a bullet in her head.

Agostini then alleged that he sat on the bed for some hours, panicking as he looked at his dead wife and wondering what to do. Eventually, he walked downstairs and sat and gathered his thoughts about the best solution to his dilemma. He said he feared that, if he told the truth and no-one believed him, he would be charged with murder. This would become a smear on the reputations of all Italian-Australians.

After considerable thought, Agostini continued, he decided it would be best to dispose of his wife's body and all of the evidence. The following night, he bundled Linda's body into the back seat of his car and headed out into the bush with no specific place in mind to dump it. As he approached Albury, he turned off into a side road and after a few kilometres stopped the car on a culvert, or bush bridge, which is simply a large stormwater pipe beneath the road. Agostini said it was raining as he dragged the body of his wife in the headlights of his car and concealed it as far as he could in the drain. He took a hessian sack from his car, placed it beneath Linda's body, poured a jerry can of petrol over it and set it on fire. Terrified that someone would see the flames or another car would come along, he jumped into his car and fled in the direction he had come. He didn't stop until he had arrived back home to Carlton in the early hours of the morning.

The police commissioner was curious as to what happened to the gun. 'I threw it into the Yarra River,' Agostini confessed, although he wasn't sure exactly where.

The night of his confession, Agostini slept in the police commissioner's office. The next day, he accompanied two detectives to Albury where they were met by senior Victorian detectives and taken to the culvert where the body was found. Agostini re-enacted everything that had taken place that night almost ten years earlier. He was very cooperative with the detectives, who interrogated him on the train back to Melbourne. But there was one important thing they realised Agostini had not mentioned to them: that it was most likely that Linda Agostini had died from multiple injuries to the skull inflicted repeatedly by a blunt instrument, not from the gunshot wound. The distraught husband had mentioned nothing about head wounds.

Agostini was confronted by police with the question of Linda's head wounds. He was quick to explain that, as he was carrying his wife's body downstairs, he fell over and she slipped from his arms and bumped down the stairs, eventually crashing into a flowerpot. He had wrapped Linda's head in a towel as it was bleeding profusely from the wounds incurred, he claimed. But the police would have none of this explanation, and Agostini was charged with the murder of his wife and remanded in custody.

⚰ ⚰ ⚰

At the subsequent inquest into the death of Linda Agostini, which took 19 days, 62 witnesses appeared, including the colourful Dr T Palmer Benbow and his entourage of Jeanette Routledge and a sober Lucy Collins, complete with an array of exhibits they believed would, once and for all, prove the Pyjama Girl to be Anna Philomena Morgan and not Tony Agostini's wife. It was standing room only at the inquest. Despite Dr Benbow's efforts to throw the inquest into bedlam, the coroner decided that, on or about 27 August 1934, Linda Agostini, formerly Linda Platt, died from severe head injuries that were feloniously and maliciously inflicted on her by her husband. Antonio 'Tony' Agostini was committed for trial in the Victorian Supreme Court.

Mr Justice Lowe presided over the trial, which commenced on 19 June 1944. Mr Cussen appeared for the Crown and Mr Fazio acted for Tony Agostini. Agostini's main defence was exactly what he had told police: his life was that of a tormented man who lived in fear of his wife's drunken rages and that he feared one day she might kill him. But, gentle-natured person that he was, he stood by her as he believed if he left her, she would kill herself. Agostini told of a house littered with empty whisky bottles and his wife's persistent accusations of his infidelities with numerous other women. His life was a nightmare.

Despite a determined effort by the prosecution to portray Antonio Agostini as a monster who beat his wife to death, after a 90-minute deliberation, the jury chose to believe the defence and returned a verdict of 'not guilty of murder, but guilty of manslaughter'. In his summing up, Mr Justice Lowe said that he agreed with the verdict and that Antonio Agostini had been tormented to the limits by his wife's erratic behaviour. But he added: 'The weapon you used must have been a heavy one and must have been used with great violence; such conduct constitutes a serious crime.' Having said that, the judge sent the prisoner to jail for six years with hard labour.

At the state's expense, Linda Agostini was finally laid to rest in Melbourne's Preston Cemetery on 13 July 1944 after Antonio Agostini had refused to accept the body for burial. Agostini served three years and nine months of his sentence and was deported back to Italy on board the *Strathnaver* on 21 August 1948, bringing down the final curtain on one of Australia's most puzzling and enduring murder mysteries.

Chapter Twelve

THE SUITCASE MURDERS

Sydney wife killer Edwin Street has been likened to Ned Kelly, yet their crimes had absolutely nothing in common. Kelly and his gang robbed and murdered and went into Australian folklore with the daring final iron-clad shootout at Glenrowan, while Edwin Street murdered helpless women and concealed their bodies.

When it all boils down, the only thing that linked the man's man, Ned Kelly, and the spineless woman-killer Edwin Street, was their final words before their punishment was given. It seems as though both of them went to a horrible fate on the same cliché, but while Ned Kelly's words will be with us forever as a part of our history, Edwin Street's will only be remembered in the annals of despicable crime and their association with Kelly.

On 17 December 1993, a group of teenagers found the half-naked body of 42-year-old Dawn Rebecca Street, a kindly charity worker who dedicated all of her time to caring for people with quadriplegia, partially buried in a large shopping bag in heavy undergrowth about 20 metres from a main road in a North Sydney public park.

It eventuated that the body had been there for almost three weeks. Dawn's de-facto invalid pensioner husband Edwin, 39, reported her missing after she left the boarding house where they lived in Annandale in Sydney's inner west at around 8.30 pm on 29 November, to buy some milk and had not returned.

After the discovery of Dawn's body, Edwin Street, a big brute of an individual of scruffy appearance who resembled a vagrant, made an emotional and somewhat unusually threatening appeal on radio and television to the general public for help to solve the crime. Street said in his appeal: 'Anyone with any information should let somebody know because if I have to come out and do my own little investigation, I will.' The public was left to interpret that as best they could.

Almost three months later, on 23 February 1994, detectives investigating the murder went to the boarding house where Street lived to collect some of his wife's clothes to assist them in their investigations. When they asked Street for a bag to put the clothes in and casually opened a suitcase in Street's bedroom, to their amazement they found the dead body of a young woman. 'That's Linda,' Street told them, as if by way of introduction. 'We had a hell of a fight last night.' The deceased Linda turned out to be 25-year-old Linda Whitton, who had been living with Street for less than a week after knowing him for only for a short time.

Street was placed under arrest and taken downtown for questioning. Starting from the beginning, he told police in a statement that he had snapped when his wife Dawn told him that one of her ex-boyfriends was a better lover than him. Street said he held a pillow over his wife's face, then had a few drinks and went to sleep. When he awoke the following morning, to his dismay he discovered that his wife was dead.

Street told police that he put his wife's body in a bag, which he then put in a suitcase and caught a cab to the park at Berry Island Reserve at Wollstonecraft on Sydney's lower North Shore, where he buried it. When the body was discovered it was in an advanced state of decomposition and no definite cause of death could be established, though the post mortem revealed that there were signs of suffocation.

Street then went on to explain that he'd had a terrible fight with Linda Whitton on the night she had died, after which his partner had committed suicide. Street said that during the 'hell of a fight', Linda produced a big knife and before he could do anything to stop her, she had stabbed herself seven times – including once in the back – before he could wrestle the knife from her. Linda died soon after from the wounds and given the circumstances with his previous partner, he had panicked and hid her body in a suitcase.

Edwin Street was charged with both murders.

Although he maintained that Dawn had suffocated herself and Linda Whitton had committed suicide by stabbing herself to death during an argument, Edwin Street was found guilty of the murders at his trial at the Supreme Court. Presiding Justice Dunford said Street's story about Linda Whitton stabbing herself was 'obviously absurd, as the

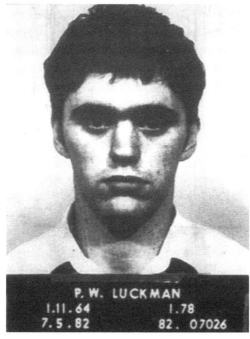

A police mugshot of Paul Luckman. *Chapter 1*

(Below) Paul Luckman shows Detective Sergeant Bob Jackson and Detective Ian Spiers around the 4WD Daihatsu in which he and Robin Reid abducted Terry Ryan and Peter Aston. *Chapter 1*

(Opposite) Robin Reid demonstrates how he and Paul Luckman had to fold their victim's legs up to fit him into the grave before they buried him alive. **Chapter 1**
(Opposite below) Robin Reid points out Peter Aston's gravesite to detectives. **Chapter 1**

(Below) One of the pages from an exercise book that contained bondage photos of young men. **Chapter 1**

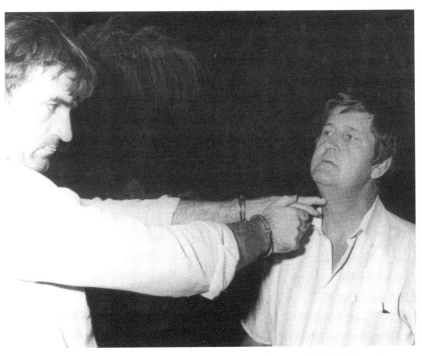

Detective Sergeant Bob Jackson keeps an eye on prisoner Robin Reid as he demonstrates how he stabbed Peter Aston in the throat. *Chapter 1*

Robin Reid has a good laugh to himself as he sits on the grave of the teenage boy he tortured and helped bash to death. *Chapter 1*

A young Paul Denyer before he gained weight and earned the nickname John Candy, after the overweight comedian. But Denyer's crimes were no laughing matter. *Chapter 3*

(Below) An aerial shot of an area where police found a body in what became known as 'the Family murders'. *Chapter 17*

After the remains of three women were found, James Miller led police to four more gravesites, including that of 15-year-old Tanya Kenny. **Chapter 5**

(Opposite) James Miller (centre) took police to the remaining graves of the seven women whom Christopher Worrell had murdered. **Chapter 5**

(Below) Handsome young Christopher Worrell didn't find it hard to entice women to their deaths. **Chapter 5**

Kevin Crump shortly after his capture. **Chapter 15**

(Below) Allan Baker in handcuffs after he was captured following the shootout with police. **Chapter 15**

Kevin Crump arriving at court. *Chapter 15*

(Below) Crump and Baker are led from the courthouse after being charged with the murder of Ian Lamb. *Chapter 15*

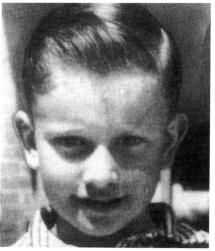

Lottery winners Bazil and Freda Thorne. *Chapter 16*

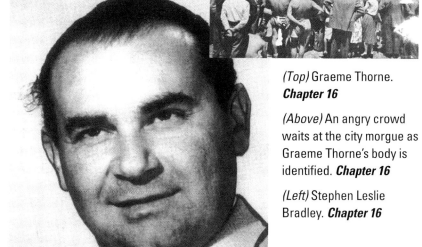

(Top) Graeme Thorne. *Chapter 16*

(Above) An angry crowd waits at the city morgue as Graeme Thorne's body is identified. *Chapter 16*

(Left) Stephen Leslie Bradley. *Chapter 16*

Neddy Smith (left) with his wife, Debra, and Harvey Jones in 1983. Soon after, Smith had killed Jones and buried his body on the foreshore of Botany Bay. **Chapter 19**

(Below) Throughout the 1980s, Neddy Smith was the undisputed boss of the Sydney underworld. The murder of Harvey Jones saw to it that Smith is now behind bars for the rest of his life. **Chapter 19**

(Above) Ivan Milat murdered seven young backpackers and concealed their bodies in bush graves in Belanglo State Forest. He is Australia's most prolific individual serial killer in the modern era. **Chapter 18**

(Left) Mugshot of Matthew Elliott. **Chapter 20**

The car park where, in broad daylight, Janine Balding was abducted by a gang of street kids. Within a few hours she was dead. **Chapter 20**

jury has found' and described the murders of the two women – who were both small and had epilepsy – as brutal. 'I regard the prospects of rehabilitation as only slight and the risks of his re-offending as significant,' the judge said.

At Street's sentencing on 29 June 1995, Justice Dunford said Street had a 'terrifying record of physical violence, particularly toward women'. The judge also said that Street had a number of convictions for carnal knowledge and indecent assault and in 1989 was sentenced to four years' jail for attacking a young woman who rejected his sexual advances.

'Whilst the maximum penalty is intended for the worst category of cases, I regard the quite separate murders of two women some 12 weeks apart as amongst the worst category of cases,' Justice Dunford said.

The judge then imposed the maximum sentence available under the truth-in-sentencing legislation – life in prison without the possibility of parole. As he was led from the court, Street looked around and said, 'Such is life,' the famous last words Ned uttered before he was hanged. Now they also were the last words spoken by Edwin Street before he was led from the court to begin the rest of his life in prison.

Given the nature of his crimes, things were never going to be easy behind bars for Edwin Street, who never showed the slightest remorse for committing the murders. He was despised by the other prisoners, who appropriately nicknamed him 'Suitcase' due to the extraordinary circumstances that had led to the discovery of his second victim's body inside the suitcase in his bedroom.

Over the years, Edwin Street was moved from prison to prison and eventually, for his own protection, wound up in Goulburn Jail's maximum-security wing. Goulburn is the last home for the worst of the worst. Recognised as Australia's coldest city, in winter the temperature at Goulburn reaches as low as minus 7 degrees Celsius, and little has been changed since the jail was built in 1883. Goulburn was a fitting place for the likes of Edwin Street to spend his last years.

In March 2007, Edwin Street was taken from Goulburn Jail to Long Bay Prison Hospital, where he died of bowel cancer soon after. He will be missed only in contempt and for the fact that he and Ned Kelly had the same three words in common ... 'Such is life'.

Chapter Thirteen

THE MURDER OF ANITA COBBY

Textbook sadist and rapist, 18-year-old John Raymond Travers was a psychopathic time bomb with a short fuse waiting for the right moment to explode. It happened in Sydney's outer western suburbs on 2 February 1986, when Travers and his gang extinguished the bright light of Anita Lorraine Cobby in an unprecedented attack that left a nation asking how such a thing could happen. The abduction and murder of Anita Cobby is arguably the most barbaric crime in Australia's history. So gross was the violation to the 26-year-old Sydney Hospital nursing sister that newspapers could only hint at her injuries. Talk-back radio switchboards lit up for weeks with callers demanding the reintroduction of capital punishment.

Travers and his gang, consisting of Michael Murdoch, 18, and Les, 24, Gary, 29, and Michael Murphy, 33, abducted, tortured, raped and murdered Anita Cobby and left her to die concealed in high grass in a paddock in Prospect in Sydney's western suburbs. Even hardened detectives were shocked by the violent nature of the crime. But those who were acquainted with Travers knew what he was capable of. Many other victims had witnessed his cruelty and perversion at first hand.

⚰ ⚰ ⚰

John Travers was the eldest of seven children and grew up in the blue-collar district of Mount Druitt in Sydney's western suburbs. His father, Ken, drove buses and left the family home when Travers was a young boy. His mother, Sharon, struggled to cope with bringing up her children and developed an eating disorder that rendered her morbidly obese. By the time Travers was in his early teens, his mother weighed in excess of 120 kilograms and could not easily move around the modest home. Forced to remain in bed for most of the day, Sharon was unable to attend to her own basic needs, such as going to the toilet or washing herself, let alone tend to her children.

Travers was left to his own devices, which invariably led him to crime. Before he was a teenager, he had been in and out of institutions after being caught for petty crimes, including stealing offences. His first conviction was for possession of marijuana when he was just 12 years of age. He was an alcoholic at 14 and roamed the streets of Sydney's outer west, stealing and robbing to pay for his addiction.

The most disturbing aspect of Travers' personality was his apparent sadism. He kept two bull terriers that he named 'Arse' and 'Cunt'. He regularly tortured the animals by kicking them in the testicles or applying lit cigarettes to their anuses. The tormented creatures became too vicious to control, but they continued to do their owner's bidding and were known to attack people unfortunate enough to be walking past Travers' home. There are numerous stories that recall Travers torturing other animals. His mother remembers him killing kittens for kicks. Others recollect attending a barbeque in Mount Druitt. Travers brought a sheep to the party. Shocked onlookers witnessed him sodomise the beast, and as he prepared to climax, he pulled the sheep's head back and killed it by cutting its throat. The word around the working-class suburb was that Travers regularly engaged in bestiality, and there are reports of him having sex with pigs, sheep and chickens.

Generally, the objects of Travers' attacks would end up dead. Employed briefly in an abattoir, he had learnt how to prepare a carcass for the dinner table. He would often steal pigs, sheep and chickens from nearby farms and cut their throats with a sharp knife. His family thought he was doing the right thing by providing some food for the poverty-stricken household. The reality is that Travers obtained perverse pleasure from killing animals.

In his mid-teens Travers began directing his cruelty towards humans. Often in the company of Michael Murdoch, he used to loiter outside public toilets and bash and rape women and gay men. The victims were too terrified to report the assaults to police.

Michael James Murdoch and Travers were as thick as thieves during their teenage years. Murdoch was the same age as Travers and doted after him. It is thought that the pair had a sexual relationship, but both denied it. Murdoch had been in trouble with the police from an early age, racking up his first criminal conviction for possession of marijuana at 14 years of age. Travers and Murdoch used a home-made tattoo kit on each other and by the time they were both 16 years of age, they were covered in permanent scrawls and childlike pictures. Travers always went one step further: he asked Murdoch to tattoo his face. From then on he had a blue teardrop under his left eye. Travers thought it made him stand out from the rest of the delinquents he knocked about with, but the tattoo would only serve to assist his victims to identify him to police. He also had tattoos on his penis and it is likely that Murdoch put them there.

Travers' reputation was a magnet for many young criminals in the Mount Druitt area and by the time he was 17, he had a motley crew of hangers-on who saw him as the leader of the gang. He was an inveterate coward, but his gang members saw him as a hero, performing crimes against people and property at his whim. Some of the gang members would come and go, but the three Murphy brothers remained constant members of the clique. The oldest was Michael Murphy, known as Mick to the other gang members. A career criminal, he had spent most of his adult life behind bars.

✝ ✝ ✝

Born in 1953, the eldest of the nine Murphy children, Michael Patrick Murphy had fallen into a life of crime as a young boy. Six weeks before the murder of Anita Cobby, Murphy had escaped from Silverwater Jail while serving a 25-year sentence for 33 counts of break, enter and steal and larceny. He had additional time added to his sentence when he had attempted to escape from lawful custody. Just prior to Christmas in 1985, the heavily tattooed Murphy succeeded in escaping from prison with an accomplice in tow. He linked up with Travers, Murdoch and his two brothers, Les and Gary, not long afterwards. He remained on the run until he was captured in July 1986.

Like his older brother, Gary Stephen Murphy was a habitual criminal with a long criminal record stretching back to his youth. He had convictions for receiving, assault, car theft, breaking and entering and escaping lawful custody.

Leslie Joseph Murphy was born in 1962. He was a scrawny boy

who looked harmless enough. However, he had a string of convictions, including for sexual intercourse without consent and car theft. He too had spent much of his adult life behind bars.

Gary considered himself to be a good fighter but often ended up on the floor, nursing a black eye or broken nose after coming off second best in a bar-room fight. Michael was known as a person to avoid, but this had less to do with his tough guy image and more to do with his extensive criminal record, and his reckless attitude to his own safety and the safety of others. Les had a reputation as a loud mouth and would get into fights. His less than imposing physique ensured that he was often at the receiving end of a hiding. The fights he started frequently ended up with Les being dragged away kicking and screaming to avoid further punishment.

On their own, the three Murphy brothers were craven weaklings. When the three were together or were in the company of Travers and Murdoch, they grew strength in numbers to form a violent combination that would lead to murder.

In 1985, Travers had come under the scrutiny of New South Wales Police for raping and assaulting a young woman in Toongabbie, near his home in Mount Druitt. The woman had gone to police and told them of her ordeal. She was able to provide police with a detailed description of the heavily tattooed 18-year-old youth. She recalled her attacker having a teardrop tattoo under his left eye. Travers was cunning enough to know that the police were on his trail, so he fled to Western Australia. With several cohorts, he settled in Mandurah, south of Perth, for a few months while the police continued to search for him. While in Mandurah, Travers started a relationship with a 17-year-old youth. The poor fellow clearly did not know what he was getting himself into. One night, Travers and his gang went to his young lover's home and brutally assaulted and raped him. They took photographs of the young man being bashed, raped and slashed with a knife. Left in agony and covered in blood after the assault, the young man made it to the local police station and provided a detailed statement. Western Australian police arrested two of Travers' gang, but he avoided capture and fled back to Sydney.

⚰ ⚰ ⚰

Twenty-six-year-old Anita Lorraine Cobby was a nurse at Sydney Hospital, attached to the hospital's distinguished microsurgery department. An attractive young woman, she had been a beauty pageant winner and had, at one time, considered a career as a model. She chose to avoid the catwalks and the spotlight, preferring to pursue a career where she could help people in need.

Anita had grown up in the working-class suburb of Blacktown, in the heart of Sydney's western suburbs and just a short drive from Mount Druitt. She was raised in a loving family environment. She had a younger sister, Kathryn, born five years after her. Their mother and father, Grace and Garry Lynch, provided both girls with every support and undying affection. Grace was a registered nurse, and although she was in semi-retirement, she continued to do the odd shift at the local hospital. Garry was a graphic artist who had worked with the Royal Australian Navy until he had retired some years before. The family enjoyed holidays together, boating on the Nepean River.

Anita was a very popular student and was in the best academic group at her local high school. She received good marks in her final year but had yet to determine what she wanted to do with her life. Aged 20, she was encouraged to enter a Miss Australia beauty quest by a family friend. Anita was convinced that the pageant was not simply a beauty contest: it was an opportunity to raise money for what was then called the Spastic Centre. When she agreed to enter, her family threw their support behind her and was regularly seen in the local area, selling raffle tickets and raising funds for people with intellectual disabilities. The Lynch family managed to raise $10,000, and Anita, with her dark hair, broad smile, almond-shaped eyes and infectious laughter, was crowned Miss Western Suburbs Charity Queen. The then premier, Neville Wran, was present at the pageant and was photographed congratulating Anita on her success.

While Anita briefly enjoyed the attention the pageant win had given her, it was clear to her family that she wanted more from life than a career in which she lived by her appearance. She wanted to pursue a career that allowed her to help people. She chose to enrol in nursing and began her training at Sydney Hospital. While she trained at the hospital, she met and fell in love with John Cobby, who had also his sights set on becoming a nurse. John was three years older than Anita but the two seemed to be a perfect fit. Within weeks of their meeting, they fell in love. The romance blossomed, and Anita and John were married in a church ceremony in March 1982. The happy couple were the envy of their friends. They shared interests in music and sports and studied together. With their nursing training completed and still in their youth, they went on an extended overseas working holiday. They spent the next two years travelling around the world, stopping only to live and work in Coffs Harbour on the north coast of New South Wales. They returned to Sydney in 1985.

Anita and John's marriage fell apart shortly afterwards. They maintained their dignity throughout this difficult time. And while the couple remained close friends and communicated regularly by telephone, they were unable to reconcile their differences. Heartbroken, Anita went back to the family home in Blacktown to live. With her experience and qualifications, she had no difficulty finding work. She was offered a position back at her old alma mater, Sydney Hospital, and she quickly accepted it. She sought to overcome her personal problems by working long shifts at the hospital. When she did socialise, she would go out to the movies with some work colleagues. When she returned home by train from the city to the Blacktown railway station, she would give her father a call and he would come and pick her up. Her father had told her that, no matter what time of day or night, he would always be happy to come and collect her from the station and spare her the long walk home.

⚰ ⚰ ⚰

Anita had finished a shift at the hospital at 5.30 pm on Sunday, 2 February 1986. She decided to go with two of her friends and work colleagues to grab a bite at a Lebanese restaurant in Redfern. Her two friends, Lyn Bradshaw and Elaine Bray, accompanied her to the restaurant. They had all been friends since their days as nursing students and enjoyed each other's company. Working together in the wards at Sydney Hospital had made them even closer friends. They shared a couple of bottles of wine, and after their meal, Lyn dropped Anita at Central Station to catch the train home. Anita could have stayed the night at Lyn's home if she had wanted to, but she told Lyn and Elaine that she wanted to go home. They saw Anita walk up the ramp to the busy railway station. They would never see their friend again.

Anita did not contact her father on that night. Garry Lynch would have happily jumped in his car for the short drive to the railway station. He had always told his daughter that she should feel free to call at any time. He knew that she was responsible and could take care of herself in most situations, but he preferred collecting her from the station. He would feel at ease knowing that his daughter was safe. It became a ritual. Anita would call him from the station, and within minutes, he would be in his car and on his way to collect her. But this night he did not receive a call. It appears that Anita decided that she did not want to bother her father. She stepped off the railway platform and onto the darkened streets. As it was a Sunday night, the streets were quiet.

Garry Lynch thought that his daughter might have stayed with friends that night. Sometimes, she did. After a long shift at the hospital, she might stay with one of her workmates, returning to the hospital the following day to commence another long shift. Garry was not worried that he had not heard from his daughter on the evening of 2 February.

The following day, Garry received a telephone call from the duty sister at Sydney Hospital, wondering why Anita had failed to turn up for her shift. When he learned that Anita's workmates were at work and that they too had not heard from her, his concerns grew. He telephoned his wife. Had she heard from Anita? He contacted Anita's husband, John, and asked him if he had seen or heard from her. Then he made a series of increasingly desperate phone calls to places Anita may have been. He continued to draw a blank. By the afternoon, Garry and Grace were beside themselves with worry. With John Cobby providing assistance, they checked hospitals and Anita's long list of friends. Garry reported his daughter missing to the Blacktown Police on the evening of 3 February 1986. A tense atmosphere prevailed at the Lynch home in Blacktown. They waited by the phone for news, any news, of the whereabouts of their daughter.

On Tuesday, 4 February, John Reen contacted police. A farmer with land in Prospect, he had checked his paddocks that morning. John Reen's farm was only a few minutes' drive from Blacktown railway station. Reen recalled that he had been awoken by screaming late on Sunday night. While he was walking through the 'boiler paddock' – so-named because that was where he kept his older stock – he noticed that the cows were crowding in a strange manner. Later, he saw that the cows had remained in that same odd position, encircling a dark object on the ground. He went to investigate and discovered a body of a woman. John Reen told police that it looked like she had been murdered.

Police raced to the scene. What they saw would remain indelibly etched in their memories. The woman had been savaged. She had been dragged through a barbed wire fence, causing deep cuts over her body. She had been punched and kicked repeatedly, and had bruising on her face, shoulders, groin, thighs, legs and breasts. Her throat had been cut twice, almost severing her head from her body.

Garry and Grace Lynch had their worst fears confirmed when Detective Sergeant Ian Kennedy and Detective Constable Garry Heskett knocked on their door later that day. When Detective Kennedy showed Garry and Grace Anita's wedding ring, they knew that police must have found their daughter. Garry accompanied the detectives to the morgue. Sobbing and barely able to stand up, he confirmed the body as Anita's.

⚰ ⚰ ⚰

A task force to investigate Anita Cobby's murder was established at Blacktown police station. Detective Sergeant Graham Rosetta and Detective Constable Kevin Raue joined the task force. Their knowledge of the local area and the criminals who moved within it would be critical to the success of the investigation. The brutality of the murder and the sight of Anita's grieving family provided the experienced investigators with a steely resolve. The task force would not stop until the perpetrators were safely under lock and key.

Media reports of the murder of Anita Cobby omitted certain gruesome details. News editors determined that the extent of the barbaric crime would be too much for the general public to take. Journalists, hardened by years of reporting every type of crime, recoiled at the information passed to them by police. One journalist stated: 'I have covered a lot of shockers in my time. I thought I could not be shocked anymore. But what I heard and saw about the murder of Anita Cobby will go to the grave with me.' While the public had been spared some of the most grievous outrages of Anita's murder, their reaction was swift and uncompromising. Polls taken by radio and television networks indicated that, overwhelmingly, the public favoured the reintroduction of the death penalty for the perpetrators of this awful crime. Two days after Anita's body was found, the New South Wales Government posted a reward of $50,000 for any information that may lead to the conviction of the killers. Within several days, the reward was raised to $100,000.

Due to the apparent random nature of the crime, police had little to go on initially. Anita's body had been stripped naked, and her clothes were not left at the scene. There was little physical evidence available in John Reen's old boiler paddock. Scrupulously, the police commenced the long procedure of checking the whereabouts of local criminals, with particular emphasis on sex criminals. Detectives interviewed Garry and Grace Lynch, John Cobby and Anita's two workmates, Lyn Bradshaw and Elaine Bray. But they still had no direct leads. Had Anita been abducted outside the railway station? At this stage police were unsure.

Several days later, two Blacktown residents, Linda and John McGaughey, came forward and gave police their first break. They told a story of seeing a dark-haired woman being dragged into a car on the night of Sunday, 2 February. They reported that they saw the woman struggling and screaming. The car she had been dragged into had driven away with its lights off. The woman was still screaming as the car drove off. The two witnesses thought the car was a grey Holden Kingswood. Linda and John's brother, Paul, had arrived home shortly afterwards with his girlfriend, Lorraine Busher. Armed with a description of the car, Paul McGaughey and Lorraine had driven around the local area, looking for any sign of the dark-haired girl. They had also driven around Blacktown Station but found nothing. They had then driven around to Reen Road, which Paul knew to be a notorious spot for joy riders. They had seen a parked grey 1970 HJ Holden, but had not examined the vehicle closely as it was not the car Linda and John had told them they had seen earlier that night. Paul and his girlfriend had searched the area for two hours before returning home.

The information provided by the McGaugheys lent support to the theory that Anita had caught the train to Blacktown and had been abducted nearby. A week later, on Sunday, 7 February, police organised a re-enactment of what they understood to be Anita's movements. Police Constable Debbie Wallace, dressed in the type of clothes Anita had worn on the evening she had disappeared, caught the 9.12 pm train from Central Station to Blacktown Station. She got off the train and began the half-hour walk towards the Lynch home. Police watched her every move from a distance in unmarked cars. A number of cars pulled alongside Constable Wallace, and they were interviewed afterwards, but it was determined that these people had nothing to do with Anita's murder.

Now a week into the investigation, police had few leads and little concrete evidence by which to identify Anita's killers. The task force continued to pursue all avenues of inquiry in an attempt to get a break. They could not understand why Anita had not telephoned her father on the evening of 2 February to request a lift as she often did. Perhaps she had walked from Blacktown railway station and hailed a taxi coming past. As a result, all taxi drivers who had been in the Blacktown area on 2 February 1986 were interviewed by police. Nothing came of it. The police grew weary at the tedium of their inquiries, but they remained ever vigilant, knowing that soon they would get a break in the case.

⚑ ⚑ ⚑

Two days later an unidentified man approached the task force with information. He told police that he was aware that three men had stolen a Holden and sprayed it grey. They had taken the mag wheels from the stolen car too and replaced them with standard wheels to avoid detection. The man told police that the three car thieves were John Travers, Michael Murdoch and Les Murphy. All three were known to police and had a reputation for violence. The informant told police that Travers often carried a knife. He was terrified that the information he had given to police may lead to reprisals from Travers and his gang. Clearly, he was terrified of the gang, and of Travers, in particular. Police assured him that they would take all necessary steps to keep the information he had provided confidential.

Travers had already been designated a person of interest by police in the course of their investigation into Anita's murder. While he had no conviction for sex crimes, he was being sought in relation to the rape of the young woman at Toongabbie eight months earlier. Police in the Mount Druitt and Blacktown area had been searching for Travers for months. But he had gone to Western Australia, and police inquiries had failed to make an arrest. Now they had information telling them that Travers was back in Sydney.

The police started searching Sydney looking for Travers and his gang. They concentrated on all the gang's known haunts. With a huge reward on offer, several informants came forward with information indicating where Travers and his gang may be holed up. A huge police contingent executed a raid on a house in Wentworthville, a nearby suburb. Bursting into the modest home, heavily armed detectives arrested Travers and Murdoch. They had been sleeping together in bed. A search of the property revealed a blood-stained knife. Travers told the police that he had used it recently to slaughter a sheep. They arrested Les Murphy in a simultaneous raid on a house in Doonside. A search of that property revealed mag wheels and car seat covers belonging to the 1970 HJ Holden car reported stolen several weeks before. Murphy had placed the wheels and the seat covers on his own car.

The police interviewed Travers, Murdoch and Les Murphy at Blacktown police station. All three admitted that they had stolen the car but denied any knowledge of the murder of Anita Cobby. In spite of the men's denials, the police strongly suspected they were responsible for the murder. Now the task force had to build a case. They hoped that if they presented Travers and his gang with incontrovertible proof of their involvement in Anita's murder, then at least one would crack and provide a detailed confession. Members of the task force interrogated Travers, Murdoch and Les Murphy in regard to the whereabouts of the stolen vehicle. The men all refused to provide any details and claimed to be unaware of where the vehicle was. Police knew that the vehicle was the most crucial piece of physical evidence and hoped it would provide a detailed bank of forensic evidence directly linking Travers and his gang with Anita's murder.

Travers was held in custody, pending further inquiries in relation to the rape of the young woman at Toongabbie and numerous other sex offences in the area for which he was a prime suspect. Murdoch and Les Murphy were charged with car theft and released on bail. The police continued to interrogate Travers, but he maintained that he knew nothing about Anita Cobby's murder. Later, Travers requested to see a visitor and gave police the telephone number of a woman whom he wanted to speak with. Police contacted the woman and questioned her at length about her relationship with Travers.

This woman, who became known as 'Miss X', told police that she was terrified of Travers but that Travers had, for some reason, decided to take her into his trust in the past. As a result she found herself being regaled with the most appalling stories of Travers' crimes. She told police that, eight months earlier, he had told her about the rape of the 17-year-old youth in Western Australia. She said that he had delighted in telling her about the vicious attack and provided every sordid detail. He had even shown her the photographs of Travers and his gang raping, stabbing and bashing the young man. Travers had told her that he wanted to cut the young man's throat while he was being raped. He had tortured and killed so many animals in his life and with such callous disregard that, now, he wanted to feel what it was like to take a human life. 'Miss X' was sickened by Travers' confessions but did not go to police for fear that he may one day seek revenge.

'Miss X' was a former heroin addict. She told police that she was terrified of Travers and his gang, and initially she was so stricken with fear that she refused to assist police with their inquiries. But, when assured of her safety, she agreed to do what the police asked. So she arrived at the police station with a couple of packets of cigarettes for Travers, and was fitted with a recording device and ushered into an interview room where Travers sat waiting. He told her everything, going into minute detail about how he, Murdoch and the three Murphy brothers had abducted Anita Cobby and how they had raped her repeatedly. Travers told 'Miss X' that it was he who had cut Anita's throat in the boiler paddock. 'Miss X' was clearly sickened by what Travers had told her. She told the police that Travers seemed to be proud of his role in Anita's murder.

Meanwhile, Les Murphy and Michael Murdoch had been kept under constant surveillance since their release from police custody two days earlier. After Travers' discussion with 'Miss X', Murdoch was arrested at his mother's home. Les Murphy was found in a suburban home, hiding underneath the blankets of a bed while two women lay beside him. True to form, Murdoch and Murphy refused to accept any responsibility for Anita's murder. They blamed Travers for the crime. They had simply gone along, they said. Travers was the killer. Police told Travers about the statements they had obtained from Les Murphy and Murdoch, pointing the finger directly at him. Travers made a full confession. He gave them all up – Murdoch and Les, Gary and Michael Murphy.

Travers, Murdoch and Les Murphy were all charged with the abduction and murder of Anita Cobby. They appeared at Blacktown Local Court and were remanded in custody. It had been just 22 days since Anita had been murdered. A large group of people gathered outside the courthouse to get a look at the three accused. News of the unspeakable nature of the crime had circulated throughout the community, and there was much talk of the mob taking matters into their own hands. Police were obliged to provide a substantial guard for the trio.

Now the focus of the task force turned to Michael and Gary Murphy. Descriptions of the two wanted brothers were circulated throughout the media. It would only be a matter of time before they were behind bars. The police received information that two men answering the description of Michael and Gary Murphy were living in a townhouse in Glenside, a southern suburb of Sydney. Members of the Tactical Response Group, detectives and uniformed police, as well as the police helicopter, swooped down on the property. They arrested a young woman leaving the townhouse. She told them that the two Murphy brothers had left. The police raided the house in any case. When they marched through the doorway, they found the wanted fugitive, Michael Murphy, calmly watching television. He was arrested without a struggle. Gary Murphy made a futile break for it and ran out the back door, only to be confronted by an army of police. He was so frightened at the prospect of being arrested that he wet his pants. He was photographed being escorted from the Glenside townhouse with urine staining his faded blue jeans.

Both brothers were taken back to Blacktown police station and charged with the murder of Anita Cobby. Again, a large crowd of about 2000 people stood outside Blacktown Local Court and hurled abuse at the accused men. And, again, police were on hand in number to prevent the situation from getting out of hand.

Travers and his four followers faced committal hearings in July 1986. All five pleaded not guilty, but the committal proceedings were merely a formality. On the basis of the evidence police had obtained, including Travers' confession, the magistrate determined that all five had a case to answer. They were remanded in custody until their trial commenced in March 1987.

✝ ✝ ✝

On 16 March 1987, the crowds spilled onto the streets outside the New South Wales Supreme Court. The public was keen to see Travers and his gang face the music. Within minutes of the trial commencing,

Travers changed his plea to guilty. He would throw himself on the mercy of the courts.

Murdoch and the three Murphy brothers continued to plead their innocence. Friends and family of Anita were forced to submit to further injury by sitting through an emotionally exhausting 54-day trial, every minute of which acted as a constant reminder of the torment and violence Anita had suffered. Then, the unthinkable occurred: Mr Justice Maxwell was forced to abort the trial after the court was made aware that Michael Murphy had been identified in the media as an escaped felon. Justice Maxwell determined that this might be prejudicial to Michael Murphy receiving a fair trial. The jury was dismissed and a new trial date was set down for a week later.

When the trial was properly underway, the jury discovered that it was the statements of the five accused that were most damning. The prosecution would present a raft of forensic and circumstantial evidence linking the five accused to Anita's murder. But it was the admissions of Travers' gang that would sway the jury. In the signed statements provided to police, a clear notion of the circumstances of the abduction and subsequent murder of Anita became clear. All five had been directly involved.

Travers and his gang had been drinking at the Doonside Hotel on the afternoon of Sunday, 2 February 1986. Drunk and out of money, they decided to go for a ride in a car that Travers had stolen a week earlier – a 1970 HJ Holden. All five had discussed various illegal methods of obtaining money so they could continue drinking. As they drove along Newton Road, they spotted a woman – Anita Cobby – walking away from them, with her handbag slung over her shoulder.

The gang pulled up alongside Anita, and Travers and Murdoch got out of the car and grabbed her. In spite of her protestations, the men dragged her back into the car and threw her into the back seat. Within seconds of the abduction, the gang ordered Anita to remove her clothes. She refused, and screamed and yelled at her assailants, but they continued relentlessly. Travers and Murdoch started ripping her clothes off and punched her in the face repeatedly. Anita was held hostage in the back seat of the car while they purchased petrol with money stolen from her handbag. After the car left the petrol station, Travers and Murdoch raped Anita at knifepoint while the three Murphy brothers ransacked her handbag in the front seat.

The car stopped in Reen Road, and Anita was thrown from the vehicle into a deep gutter. Travers and Gary and Les Murphy raped her again. Gary Murphy forced Anita to fellate him. All five men dragged Anita into the boiler paddock. They forced her through the barbed wire fence, causing long, deep cuts all over her body. As Anita screamed for mercy, Mick Murphy raped her while Murdoch forced her to give him oral sex. After enduring this unspeakable violence and violation, Anita was then sodomised by Les Murphy. Travers then raped her once again. Murdoch and Gary Murphy attempted to force Anita to fellate them again, but they were interrupted when Michael Murphy stormed in. He raped, bashed and kicked her in an uncontrollable rampage. Les kicked her several more times in the head. And, with their violent urges sated, the five simply walked away, leaving Anita barely breathing and now semi-conscious.

The gang went back to the car and had a casual discussion as to what they should do with their victim. Travers made the point that the woman would be able to identify them all as she had heard them refer to each other by name. He considered that the police would be on to them in days. 'I'm going to go back and kill her,' Travers said. 'She'll never give us up. I'll slit her throat.'

Murdoch and the three Murphy brothers did not object to Travers' suggestion. Indeed, they urged their leader to do the deed. 'Yeah, she'll see us all in the shit,' Murdoch stated. 'Go on, go back and do it.'

Travers calmly climbed the fence and walked back down to where Anita, still semi-conscious, lay. He pulled her head back, made two deep incisions from ear to ear, and then walked away, leaving Anita Cobby to bleed to death in the boiler paddock. As he walked back to the car, the sadistic Travers ruminated on the enormity of what he had done. It was just like killing one of the animals he had slaughtered, he concluded. Now, covered in Anita's blood, he looked down at his hands and smiled. He could not wait to get back to the car and brag about what he had done.

According to Murdoch's statement, Travers got into the back seat of the car and Murdoch asked him what it was like to take a human life. 'It didn't feel like nothing,' Travers told him. 'I didn't feel anything at all.' He provided the gang with vivid details about the murder. They all sat entranced, laughing and asking questions about how their leader had killed the woman. They continued joking about their appalling crime until they arrived at Travers' house where they went inside. Travers was soaked in Anita's blood and the others carried the signs of their involvement in the murder on their faces and hands. They gathered up Anita's clothes and belongings from the car and took them into Travers' backyard. Murdoch set fire to Anita's clothes in an incinerator. The gang sat around drinking beer while the fire disposed of the evidence. Travers went inside to wash up. His mother was lying on the couch. She wondered why he had blood all over him, and he told her he had killed a dog that had tried to attack him. His mother was satisfied with this, and Travers went outside again to join the others. Several days later, Murdoch and Travers took the stolen car to a remote clearing in the bush and set fire to it.

Cowards to the end, Murdoch and the Murphy brothers made unsworn statements from the dock, claiming their innocence. By providing unsworn statements, they could not be cross-examined. Gary Murphy had the temerity to claim that he was not even in the stolen car on the night Anita Cobby was murdered. He had been drinking that day, he said, but he could not remember who he was with. Michael Murphy acknowledged that he was in the car when Anita was abducted, but, he said, he was so appalled by Travers' and Murdoch's behaviour that he did not move out of the car, registering his protest in silence. Gary Murphy found religion in the dock and asked God and the jury to believe that he did not have anything to do with the rape and murder of Anita Cobby.

⚰ ⚰ ⚰

After hearing all the evidence, the jury retired to consider its verdict. After deliberating for nine hours, the jury returned with its verdict on 10 June 1987. Michael Murdoch and Les, Michael and Gary Murphy were all found guilty of the abduction and murder of Anita Cobby. Travers had previously pleaded guilty to his involvement in the matter. Justice Maxwell remanded the gang in custody until 16 June 1987, when he would hand down his sentence.

A packed Supreme Court was hushed while Mr Justice Maxwell sentenced Travers and his gang. He stated:

> *There is no doubt that apart from the humiliation, the degradation and terror inflicted upon this young woman, she was the victim of a*

prolonged and sadistic physical and sexual assault including repeated sexual assaults, anally, orally and vaginally. ... Wild animals are given to pack assaults and killings. ... This is one of, if not the most horrifying physical and sexual assaults I have encountered in my forty-odd years associated with the law. The crime is exacerbated by the fact that the victim almost certainly was made aware, in the end, of her pending death.

Throughout the long trial, the prisoners, albeit to a lesser degree in the case of the prisoner Murdoch, showed no signs of remorse or contrition. Instead they were observed to be laughing with one another and frequently were seen to be sniggering behind their hands.

Justice Maxwell handed out life sentences to all five of Travers' gang. He went on:

The circumstances of the murder of Mrs Anita Lorraine Cobby prompt me to recommend that the official files of each prisoner should clearly be marked 'never to be released'. If the Executive deems it proper in the future to consider their files, then I would echo the advice proffered, in a case in which the facts were not entirely dissimilar, by a former and distinguished Chief Judge at Common Law, that the Executive should grant to the prisoners the same degree of mercy that they bestowed on Anita Lorraine Cobby on the night of 2 February 1986. I do not think the community would expect otherwise.

In May 1989, the High Court found that Leslie Joseph Murphy hadn't received a fair trial as evidence pertaining to his intellectual capacity had been omitted. In August 1990, he was found guilty of the murder of Anita Cobby for the second time and sentenced to life imprisonment again. His papers were not marked 'never to be released' as the September 1989 'truth in sentencing' legislation saw to it that all prisoners sentenced to life imprisonment would stay behind bars forever.

⚰ ⚰ ⚰

Travers and his gang have not had a happy time in prison. The prison code of punishing rapists and those who murder young women has been enforced. Every one of Travers' gang has been attacked and savagely beaten. The gang members have had their opportunity to prove their courage behind bars. Each has failed. They are, after all, cowards.

John Travers was last heard of when he attempted to escape from a New South Wales Corrective Services security van transporting him between prisons. His escape attempt using a cutting implement to get out of the van was foiled when he was spotted by a guard. He was returned to maximum security at Goulburn Prison and remains there, in the state's most notorious prison. Murdoch and the Murphy brothers remain incarcerated in maximum-security wings within New South Wales' prisons.

On 21 February 2019, Michael Murphy became the first of Anita Cobby's killers to die in jail. Murphy, 66, died of advanced liver cancer in Long Bay Jail's hospital. The other four of Anita Cobby's killers, John Raymond Travers, Michael Murdoch, and Les and Gary Murphy, will never be released, no matter the circumstances. All men are destined to die in prison.

Chapter Fourteen

THE CRIMES OF BRUCE BURRELL

While this is not specifically a story of shallow graves, rather a story of suspected very, very deep graves, it is worthy of inclusion in a book of this nature. Rather than give away the gravity of these crimes, best you read on and find out for yourself.

In September 2007, at his trial for a second murder, the jury got it right with the conviction of Bruce Allan Burrell, who, for the first time in our history, had now been found guilty of not one but two murders for which the bodies of his victims have never been found.

Besides the fact that Burrell's victims were both wealthy women, they may well have lived on different planets. The only thing they had in common in life was that they both knew Bruce Burrell. But in death it is possible that they could be very much closer, their bodies perhaps buried in the same grave or secreted together forever in any of the many bottomless mineshafts on Burrell's New South Wales Southern Highlands farm.

Burrell had been a suspect for 10 years in both the women's disappearances.

The beginning of the end for Burrell began on 6 May 1997, when 39-year-old Kerry Whelan, the mother of three and wife of Bernard Whelan, a successful Sydney businessman and CEO of Crown Forklifts, went to a hairdressing appointment in Parramatta and vanished. A surveillance video from where Mrs Whelan had left her car revealed a distinctive two-tone Mitsubishi Pajero with a bull bar leaving the scene a few seconds after she left the car park.

Soon after, a ransom note demanding $US1 million or his wife would die arrived at Mr Whelan's work. The ransom note instructed that within seven days after the money was ready, an advertisement was to be placed in Sydney's *Daily Telegraph*. The ad was to read: 'Anyone who witnessed a white Volkswagen Beetle parked beside the eastern gates of the Sydney Olympic site at 10.30 pm on Tuesday 8.4.97 please call ... then put your home telephone number at the end of the advertisement'.

The Whelan family nanny came forward and told police of an unusual circumstance that had occurred just a month earlier when a former sales employee of Mr Whelan, a Bruce Burrell, had arrived unannounced at the Whelans' rural home during the day and had secretive discussions with Mrs Whelan over a cup of tea. What Mrs Whelan would be doing associating with Burrell was a mystery. Burrell was a 44-year-old balding, portly braggart who was always broke, swigging on a can of VB and smoking a cigarette.

When Burrell had left, Mrs Whelan said to the nanny: 'Can you do me a favour? You never saw him here. Don't tell anybody. Give me a couple of weeks and I'll tell you why. Don't worry. I'm not having an affair.' Police have since proved as close to conclusively as possible that this was definitely the case and that Kerry Whelan had never been unfaithful to her husband, least of all with a lowlife like Bruce Burrell, whom her husband had sacked years earlier because he couldn't be trusted.

Police raided Burrell's farm in the Southern Highlands and found a Mitsubishi Pajero identical in every way to the one in the surveillance video, a typewriter that could have typed the ransom note, two handwritten cryptic lists that could have been the outline of a kidnap plan, empty bottles that contained traces of chloroform, and a map book with the car park where Mrs Whelan parked her car highlighted.

Hundreds of police converged on Burrell's farm looking for Mrs Whelan but apart from some stolen cars and rifles, they found nothing.

They discovered that Burrell was unemployed and desperately broke and couldn't keep up the mortgage payments on his farm. This information would prove to be important later.

It wasn't until police began investigating Mrs Whelan's disappearance that they considered Burrell a suspect in a similar case that had happened two years earlier. Between 1 and 1.30 pm on 30 May 1995, 74-year-old grandmother Dorothy Davis left her house in Sydney's exclusive Lurline Bay and told a builder she was on her way to visit a cancer-stricken friend down the street. She has never been seen since.

The sick friend was Bruce Burrell's wife, who was a nearby neighbour and had been a friend of Mrs Davis for many years. Police believe that when Mrs Davis arrived at the flat, her sick friend was not there. Instead, Bruce Burrell was waiting alone to murder her.

That same afternoon, Burrell made a 'sudden and unexpected trip' to his farm near Goulburn and returned that night, before making the same five-hour round trip again the following day. It would later be concluded that Burrell had murdered Mrs Davis in his apartment; the first trip was to leave Mrs Davis's body at the farm, and the second was to conceal it. But why did Burrell murder the elderly lady? What was his motive?

It seemed that in 1994 Bruce Burrell secretly approached Mrs Davis, a wealthy widow whose husband had left her a lot of money, and borrowed $100,000, which he said was to purchase a unit in the street. He paid Mrs Davis back $10,000 and when she kept asking for the balance, Burrell confided in a friend that 'she had gone as far as saying that she would take legal action to get the money back'. Burrell had allegedly gone to comfort her, to get her to back off from her threats. Soon after, Mrs Davis disappeared. Burrell had never come under suspicion. Until Mrs Whelan's disappearance.

But despite the mountain of circumstantial evidence against Burrell, to charge him with the murder of Kerry Whelan, police desperately needed him to make a mistake. It happened early on 23 May 1997. As police turned his home upside down with the media camped outside his property, Burrell drove to Goulburn, where, seemingly in the belief that calls from public phone boxes weren't traceable, he made a call from the phone box outside the Empire Hotel.

At 9.21 am – the exact same time as Burrell was in the phone box – a call was received at Crown Equipment. A man spoke to a receptionist and asked her to write a message down and give it to Mr Whelan. He said: '*Mrs Whelan is OK. Mr Whelan must call off the police and media today. Tell him, the man with the white Volkswagen*', and hung up.

Only the kidnapper, the police and the Whelan family knew about the white Volkswagen reference from the ad. Phone traces showed the call came from a phone box outside the Empire Hotel at exactly 9.21 am. Burrell told police he had made a call from that phone box but said it was to his lawyers. That was soon disproved. They had their man, but the absence of a victim was going to make proving the case almost impossible.

In the meantime, Burrell was charged with six counts of stealing cars found on his property, including the Pajero. On 22 October, in the Parramatta District Court, he pleaded guilty and was sent to prison for two and a half years. Police now had him where they could keep an eye on him and have the run of his property.

By 31 March 1999, police had finally gathered enough evidence to charge Bruce Burrell with the abduction and murder of Kerry Whelan but the charges were later withdrawn through lack of evidence. In 2002, a coronial inquest found a 'known' person was responsible for the kidnapping and murder of Kerry Whelan and referred the case to the Director of Public Prosecutions.

In August 2005, Burrell went on trial in the New South Wales Supreme Court for kidnap and murder, but after nearly two weeks of deliberation the jury could not reach a unanimous verdict. On March 2006 Burrell was re-tried and on 6 June 2006, after nine days of deliberations, he was found guilty in a unanimous verdict and sentenced to life in prison without the possibility of parole.

Charged with the abduction and murder of Mrs Dorothy Davis, the laws of sub judice meant that mention of Burrell's previous conviction for an almost identical crime was not permitted at the trial or in the press during the trial. But it seems it wasn't necessary. All the evidence pointed to a clear case of murder of an old lady in the pursuit of personal greed. In September 2007, Burrell was also found guilty of the abduction and murder of Mrs Dorothy Davis, and received a further 28 years.

We can only wonder if the details of the Kerry Whelan murder, which was one of Australia's most sensational and publicised trials, had any sway on the jury's decision to find Bruce Burrell guilty of murdering and concealing the body of Dorothy Davis.

But then again, who really cares? Do you? The chances of the same set of circumstances ever happening to an innocent man would surely run into the trillions.

On 4 August 2016, 63-year-old Bruce Burrell died in prison from liver and lung cancer. Until his dying breath, he refused to tell police where they could find the remains of his victims, down which bottomless mine shaft or in which of the countless shallow pits that covered his property. Kerry Whelan and Dorothy Davis's burial sites died with him.

Chapter Fifteen

CRUMP AND BAKER

Late on the morning of 13 November 1973, Constable Brian Neale was patrolling in a police-issue Holden Torana along the highways that converge around Newcastle, about 200 kilometres north of Sydney, when a Holden exceeding the speed limit sped past him. A routine check of the vehicle showed that the car had been reported stolen from the area a fortnight earlier. The vehicle had also been spotted near Narrabri in northern New South Wales, where the body of a 43-year-old farm labourer, Ian James Lamb, had been found. He had been killed by a single shot in the neck.

Constable Neale called for assistance as he followed the vehicle at great speed along the New England Highway, proceeding towards the township of Maitland. Constable Bill Millward and Senior Constable George Jones joined the chase moments later just in time to witness Constable Neale's car being forced off the road by the stolen vehicle. They grew uneasy as they realised they were in pursuit of the type of criminals who would stop at nothing to avoid capture. Constable Millward, who was at the wheel, drew alongside the speeding vehicle. Constable Jones yelled at the driver, ordering him to stop. The driver ignored him and accelerated away. As the police car approached again, the passenger in the stolen vehicle fired his rifle directly at the police car. Millward and Jones's vehicle continued to draw closer and Constable Jones returned fire with his service revolver.

The two cars careered down the road, exchanging gunfire. Constable Millward could see the passenger in the stolen vehicle leaning over the front seat, steadying his grip on the rifle and firing repeatedly in his direction. One shot from the fugitive's rifle blasted through the police car's windscreen and struck Constable Millward in the forehead.

Fortunately, his injury did not prove fatal. But, with blood streaming from a head wound, Millward and Jones were out of the hunt.

By now the police radio was blaring. All squad cars were told to converge on the area to assist with the chase. Next on the scene were Constables Wayne Hore and Ken Snedden. They saw the stolen car lose control and leave the road, spinning counter-clockwise on the grassed surface at the side of the road. The two fugitives jumped from their vehicle and ran into an adjoining paddock, heading towards the Hunter River, firing their rifles as they went. Hore and Snedden returned fire, stopping briefly to level their .38 calibre service revolvers at the two men.

By now all available police were in the area, surrounding where the two men were likely to be and blocking off their escape route across the river. Out of ammunition, Kevin Crump and Allan Baker eventually emerged, wringing wet, from the bamboo swamp at the river's edge and were taken into custody. Four of the officers involved in the chase were later recipients of police bravery awards. Police searched their stolen vehicle and found personal items belonging to Ian Lamb. The itinerate farm worker had few possessions: a kit bag, which contained shaving gear and toiletries; a pair of shorts; and a fleecy-lined coat to ward off the cold at night when he slept in his car while on the road looking for casual farm work.

Back at the police station, Crump and Baker admitted to killing Ian Lamb. But police knew this was not the full extent of their crimes. On 7 November, 33-year-old Virginia Morse had gone missing from a farm at Collarenebri that she tended with her husband, Brian, and their three young children. She had not been seen since Morse had left the farmhouse to work in the fields that morning. Her car had been found dumped outside an old abandoned police station near the farmstead at Mogil Mogil.

⚰ ⚰ ⚰

Allan Baker and Kevin Crump had extensive criminal records. Baker was born in Helensburgh, in Sydney's south, on 16 January 1948. The son of a coalminer and one of six children, he left school at 14 and worked mainly as a labourer and in the artificial jewellery business before resorting to crime for a living. By the time he had met up with Kevin

Crump in jail, he had multiple convictions for breaking and entering and firearms offences.

Kevin Garry Crump was born into a Methodist family at Wingham on the New South Wales North Coast on 1 October 1949. He worked mainly as a labourer before making crime his livelihood and had numerous convictions for larceny and petty crimes. He escaped from Emu Plains Prison and was recaptured in January 1969 and, after serving additional time, was released in 1972. It was in prison that he had met and become friendly with Baker, and they had made a pact to join up when they were both out of prison.

When he was released from jail, Baker went to work as a farmhand at Boggabilla, near Goondiwindi on the New South Wales–Queensland border. Kevin Crump had stolen a Holden car on 30 October near Cessnock in the Hunter Region and driven the 600 kilometres to catch up with his old prison yard acquaintance. Baker told the farmer that he was leaving, and the farmer shrugged his shoulders. Heavy rains had meant there was little work on the farm at the time. In any event, Baker was not the hardest worker he had encountered, so the farmer was happy to see him go. Baker never relished the prospect of gainful employment, and when Crump arrived in the stolen car, they both decided to pursue a life of crime. They would rob and steal for a living. On Saturday, 3 November, Crump and Baker drove to Goondiwindi in the stolen car and purchased a .308 rifle, the perfect weapon to commit robbery in rural Australia.

On the same day, Ian James Lamb, 43, was gathering a few possessions prior to heading out west in search of employment as a farmhand. In the evening, he kissed his elderly mother on the cheek and left his home in Gosford on the New South Wales Central Coast. Mrs Lamb would never see her son alive again. Lamb drove his car as far as Narrabri, 325 kilometres west of his home. Tiring after the long drive, he pulled his car to the side of the road for the night. He had bought a few bottles of beer at the last town. He had a drink and a few cigarettes and went to sleep with the windows down, to allow the cool night breeze to flow through.

Crump and Baker watched Lamb settle down for the night. They were going to rob him and take his meagre possessions. Confessing to the murder, Baker told police:

*We both got out of the car. I got the rifle. I loaded it and I walked over
to the car and I pointed the rifle through the window of the driver's side
and I seen a man asleep on the front seat. Kevin looked in the back to
see if he was by himself and he was. I knocked on the door with both
hands and said, 'Hey you!' The bloke sat up and I pulled the trigger and
shot him.*

*Then for about ten minutes nothing happened. It was deathly
quiet. I was scared. I then went around to the other side of the car,
the passenger's side, and opened the door. Kevin opened the driver's
side while I went through the man's pockets. I got about $20 out of his
pockets. From the glove box I got some cigarettes, wallet, I don't think
there was anything else.*

Crump also made a statement to police in relation to the murder of
Ian Lamb. There was little difference in Crump's version of the events,
but he was desperately trying to convince police that he did not know
Baker was going to murder Lamb. He told Detective Sergeant Bradbury
that he and Baker had been driving around Narrabri when they spotted
Lamb's car. They parked alongside it. He said:

*Allan hopped out of the car with the .308. He went over and knocked on
the door and the driver's side window was down. When he knocked
on the door and the fellow in the car said 'Aahh' and Allan put the gun
through the window and shot him. Just shot him through the neck.*

Crump indicated a point at the centre of his throat where the bullet had
struck Lamb.

Baker and Crump then moved Lamb's body out of the driver's seat.
The dead man's feet had become entangled in the brake and accelerator
pedals, but Baker managed to manoeuvre the body onto the passenger
seat. He then sat behind the wheel and gunned the car into action. He
drove off to an unsealed and remote stretch of road with Crump in tow
in the stolen car. The pair then dragged Lamb's body out of the car and
left it on the roadside. They ransacked Lamb's car, stealing his kit bag,
clothing and cigarettes. Baker already had the $20 in notes and coins
rattling around in his pocket. Finally, they drained Lamb's car of petrol,
pouring what they were able to gather into the tank of their stolen vehicle.

During the police interviews, while readily confessing to the cowardly
murder of Ian Lamb, both men continued to deny any knowledge of the
disappearance of Virginia Morse from her farm at nearby Collarenebri

three days earlier. Nonetheless, police continued to interrogate the pair, hoping that one or the other, or both, would crack under the pressure. After almost 24 hours of constant questioning, Crump finally relented. Detective sergeants Campbell and Doyle asked him once again: 'We are going to ask you a number of questions in relation to the disappearance of a woman named Mrs Virginia Gai Morse from her farm in Banarway on the 7th of November. Do you know anything about this woman's disappearance?'

'Yes,' Crump finally confessed. 'We took her away and shot her.' The detectives breathed a sigh of relief.

When told of his mate's confession, Baker also confessed shortly afterwards. From then on both did their best to implicate the other for the abduction and murder of Virginia Morse. However, what was obvious was that Crump and Baker had planned to abduct and murder Virginia Morse from the outset. This was not a random crime, but rather a calculated and considered plot to deprive Virginia Morse of her liberty and end her life in the most callous and inhumane circumstances.

⚰ ⚰ ⚰

Some years earlier, Allan Baker had worked on the Morse property as a labourer, side by side with Virginia's husband, Brian. Baker had slept under the same roof as Virginia and her three children and had eaten food she had placed on the table. Now Baker and Crump decided to repay this kindness by robbing the farmstead and killing anyone who got in their way. Later, Crump told police that he and Baker had discussed their intentions. It was clear that they always had more than robbery on their minds. Having worked on the farm, Baker was sure to be identified and given up to the police should he leave a witness. He told the detectives: 'We talked about it on the way down from Goondiwindi and Allan said that if there was anyone on the property they would recognise him and that we might have to kill someone.'

Crump also told the detectives that he and Baker had further discussed their intentions while they lay in wait outside the Morses' farm. He said:

> Allan said that if Virginia Morse was there we would take her with us and he thought the youngest kid was there, because he didn't know he was going to school.

When we got to the old police station at Mogil Mogil we put the
petrol in my car and Allan said we would have to get rid of her, but we
would take her away and rape her first. We had guns so we would
shoot her. Allan said that I would have to prove myself and shoot her.

On 6 November, in the very early morning, just three days after the
murder of Ian Lamb, Crump and Baker drove to the Morse property
near Collarenebri. They parked their stolen car on a quiet road,
a short drive from the farm. At dawn they drove to the abandoned
police station at Mogil Mogil, several hundred yards from the Morse
farmstead. They concealed the car from view and kept an eye on
the home. They shared the watch, peering through binoculars at the
early morning activity around the farmstead. They waited while the
Morse family had breakfast. Afterwards, Brian Morse drove his three
children to school in his truck, and then went to work on the property,
leaving his wife on her own. Crump and Baker maintained their vigil,
ensuring that Virginia was alone and vulnerable by the time they
walked into the house.

In Baker's statement, he told Detective Sergeant McDonald how he
and Crump entered the house:

I went to the laundry door and waited near the lounge-room door, not
knowing if anyone was home. I asked Kevin to go around to the back
door and knock and Mrs Morse came to the back door where Kevin
was and I was behind Mrs Morse with a rifle. I said, 'Don't turn around.'
And she did. I took her in the bedroom and tied her up and she asked
me what I wanted and I said I wanted money.

Crump and Baker searched the house, finding about $30 in cash and
a .222 rifle. They then bundled Virginia Morse into her own car and
drove back to the old police station. They threw her, bound and gagged,
into the back of the stolen car, and drove off, leaving her car outside
the old abandoned police station, and headed due north towards the
Queensland border. They had every intention of using her as a hostage,
should police stop them. During the journey, the pair bought beer and
petrol with the money they had stolen from the farmstead. They took
turns in raping Virginia Morse while she pleaded with them to stop.
The young mother could think only of the fact that she would never see
her husband and children again. Baker told detectives: 'We took her
gag off, and she kept on saying, "What's going to happen to me? My

children will be home from school and waiting for me now. I love my children. Please let me go home now." I just told her to shut up.'

Just before they reached the Queensland border, Crump and Baker parked the car in a clearing. They tied Virginia with tow ropes, spread-eagled between two trees, and raped her repeatedly. Then they threw her back into the car and drove a further 100 kilometres over the border. They stopped by Weir River, and parked the car. Both men forced themselves upon Virginia again. Finally, having had their way, they decided to kill her. In his record of interview, Baker recalled the last moments of Virginia Morse's life:

> She wasn't tied to the tree. Her hands were tied in front of her with handkerchiefs. She wasn't crying because I think she was beyond that. She'd been crying most of the time she was gagged and blindfolded. I aimed at her with the .308 and Kevin had the .222 and it was going to be like a firing squad and Kevin pulled the trigger and she fell to the ground before I could pull the trigger of my gun. If he hadn't shot her, I would because we both decided to kill her because we done those terrible things to her and she would have been able to identify me because I used to work for her husband and I knew if she reported me, we would be in a lot of trouble and she just had to be shot.

Crump claimed that he had pulled the trigger of his gun only because Baker had threatened to kill him if he did not kill Virginia. 'I was forced to kill Mrs Morse by Baker,' he told police. 'He wanted me to be in as deep as him. He said he was going to kill me if I didn't. I admit that I was prepared to kidnap Mrs Morse and even to sleep with her but once again, as with Mr Lamb, I did not want any part of her death.' He continued:

> On the day that Mrs Morse died, she was tied up, blindfolded and gagged by Baker. He told me to go down to the tree and pick up a .222. At this time Baker was pointing his rifle at me. He said to go down to the tree. This was where Mrs Morse was sitting. He said if I did not kill her, he would kill me. I was forced to stand in front of Mrs Morse and Baker was saying, 'Go on, go on,' and waving his gun at me. I took aim at her but I just couldn't shoot her. I more or less dropped the gun to the ground and Baker started to wave his gun at me again. He said if I did not kill her, he would shoot me.
>
> I picked up the gun and took aim again. I just stood there for a while and Baker again said if I did not kill Mrs Morse, he would kill me and I believed him. I took aim at her. I fired once. I shot her in the right side

of the nose and killed her. I dropped the gun to the ground and I walked
to a raised portion of the ground about 100 metres from where I was
standing in front of Mrs Morse. I just stood there for a while and I drank
a stubbie of beer. I was dazed. When I came back down, Baker had her
clothes off and he started to drag her towards the river. I said to him,
'Don't drag her, I will help you carry her.'

Both Crump and Baker then carried the dead Mrs Morse to the riverbank
and concealed her body with reeds and bushes so that she could not
be seen.

Crump alleged that he had been forced to murder Mrs Morse in self-
defence. He told detectives that it

... was a choice of either me or Mrs Morse. In fact, a couple of hours
before Mrs Morse died she said to me 'Are you going to kill me?' and
I said 'No' because I had no intention of doing that. The only reason I
took Mrs Morse from her property was because if we had left her at her
home she would have told police that we had robbed her place and we
needed her as a hostage to get away from the farm.

⚰ ⚰ ⚰

Crump and Baker were charged with the murder of Ian James Lamb,
maliciously wounding Constable Millward with intent to prevent
lawful apprehension and shooting at police with intent to prevent lawful
apprehension. Due to the vagaries of criminal law in Australia, the
pair could not be charged with the murder of Virginia Morse in New
South Wales, as this crime had been committed within Queensland
jurisdiction. However, they were charged with conspiracy to murder
Virginia Morse.

At Crump and Baker's trial, a packed public gallery was shocked to
hear of the callousness the pair had displayed during their short-lived
crime spree. When their statements telling of the appalling crimes
committed upon Virginia Morse were read out, a hush fell across the
courtroom. One crime reporter recalled:

Once the appalling nature of their crimes started to sink in, gentle,
pained sobbing broke out around the room. I looked across at Mr Morse
and he had his head in his hands. Then I looked back at the dock and
saw Crump and Baker grinning at each other. Not only did they show

no remorse, they clearly derived some perverse amusement from their crimes.

So heinous was the evidence of some of the atrocities committed upon Virginia Morse as she begged for her life that it had to be told to a closed court and, to this day, has never been published.

Both Crump and Baker offered the coward's defence: they gave statements from the dock, to avoid cross-examination by the prosecution. Both argued that they had not committed murder and appealed for leniency. Baker told the court from the dock:

> *I am not guilty of murder or conspiracy to murder. I did not mean to shoot the man in the car. The gun was a scare weapon. All I meant to do was tie the man up and rob him. When I went over to the car and knocked on the door, I said 'Hey you!' and the guy in the car sat up suddenly and made a noise and I jumped backwards and the gun went off. I didn't know I shot the man until Kevin Crump told me.*
>
> *I know we are responsible for the death of Mrs Morse. I cannot forget it and I know we should be punished for that. We didn't actually agree to kill her until the day that we actually did it. When the police were questioning me about Mrs Morse, I felt so bad about it, I just agreed to everything.*

Baker appeared to be alleging that the statements he had made to police were done so under duress. Oddly, he seemed to believe that the fact that he had not conspired to murder Virginia Morse on New South Wales soil offered him some circumstance of mitigation.

Crump, too, tried to worm his way out of his role in the crimes. He told the court:

> *I did not kill Mr Lamb. I agreed to rob him. I knew Baker had a gun. I never thought he would use it. In fact I never intended to do any harm to Mr Lamb except tie him up and rob him. I never had a gun myself and I never even touched Mr Lamb before he was shot. I thought the presence of a gun would make Mr Lamb all the more willing to hand over his valuables and not make any trouble, and I repeat that I definitely did not think Baker would kill Mr Lamb.*
>
> *As far as the death of Mrs Morse is concerned, there was no agreement between me and Baker to do so. I was forced to kill Mrs Morse because he wanted me in it as deep as him. He said he was going to kill me if I didn't.*

The jury took just under two hours to return with a verdict of guilty on all counts. Baker stared emotionlessly at the jury. Crump averted his eyes, looking at the floor, his body shaking gently in the dock. When sentencing the pair, Mr Justice Taylor locked Crump and Baker away for life. With his steely gaze, he told the pair:

> You have outraged all accepted standards of the behaviour of men. The description of 'men' ill becomes you. You would be more aptly described as animals and obscene animals at that. I believe that you should spend the rest of your lives in jail and there you should die. If ever there was a case where life imprisonment should mean what it says – imprisonment for the whole of your lives – this is it.

Crump and Baker were led away to prison to begin their life sentences.

🛉 🛉 🛉

Initially housed in Katingal, the maximum-security wing of Long Bay Jail, Crump and Baker achieved further notoriety by living there as lovers. A news crew filmed them in jail in what many perceived to be 'soft' circumstances. The ensuing howls of outrage from the general public ensured that Crump and Baker's love nest was disturbed. The two were separated and are now serving their sentences apart.

Kevin Crump had his life sentence redetermined to 30 years and was eligible for parole in 2003. He applied for a fixed non-parole period on his sentence under the 'truth in sentencing' amendments to the *Crimes Act* in 1990. Subsequently, the New South Wales ALP Government led by Premier Bob Carr amended the *Crimes Act* in 2001 to prevent criminals with their files marked 'never to be released' from having a non-parole period fixed to their sentence. The loophole had been closed but not before Crump made his application for a re-determination of his sentence. But he will never walk free. Any person or authority that attempts to release him from prison would do well to recall Mr Justice Taylor's remarks in sentencing Crump and Baker in 1974:

> If in future some application is made that you be released on the grounds of clemency or mercy, then I would venture to suggest to those who are entrusted with the task of determining whether you are entitled to it or not, that the measure of your entitlement to either should be the clemency and mercy you extended to this woman when she begged you for her life. You are never to be released.

However, in the unlikely event that Crump is ever granted parole, he will be taken directly from a New South Wales prison and extradited to Queensland, where he will face the outstanding charge of the murder of Virginia Morse. He was only ever charged with conspiracy to murder in New South Wales.

On Friday, 1 June 2001, shortly after Premier Bob Carr had brought about legislation to the effect that anyone recommended by their sentencing judge 'never to be released' from prison stay in jail for the rest of their lives no matter what, the following letter from Brian Morse, the husband of Virginia Morse, appeared in the *Sydney Morning Herald*:

> *I am the husband of Virginia Morse, who was abducted and murdered in 1973. I have spent nearly 11 years of my life fighting to keep the perpetrators of this heinous crime in jail for life.*
>
> *I welcomed last week's decision by the Premier that nine of this State's most infamous criminals – including Allan Baker and Kevin Crump, who were convicted of my wife's murder – would be, in Bob Carr's words, 'cemented in their prison cells' until they were on their deathbeds.*
>
> *Subsequently, I was deeply concerned to read in the Herald not one but two opinion pieces questioning the Premier's promise. Mr Justice Taylor sentenced both Baker and Crump to life imprisonment back in 1974.*
>
> *However, 'truth in sentencing legislation' introduced by the New South Wales Government in 1989 has meant that even though these two criminals had their papers marked 'never to be released', Baker and Crump have had the opportunity to come before the Court seeking to have their sentences redetermined.*
>
> *Indeed, Crump went to court in 1997 to have his sentence redetermined and, until the law is changed, is now eligible for parole in November 2003. This decision outraged the whole of NSW. Very soon after this the Government passed legislation to try to stop Baker getting the same judgment.*
>
> *Truth in sentencing legislation was changed so Justice Taylor's original sentence 'never to be released' had to be taken into account. After enduring six court appeals and having to bare my soul through the media, as well as fronting the Parliament on numerous occasions, I was gratified last week when the Supreme Court's Justice James refused to redetermine Baker's sentence.*
>
> *Now, through the efforts of Bob Carr and Ms Kerry Chikarovski*

(leader of the New South Wales Liberal Opposition) – and because of pressure from the general public – I can be confident that these two obscene animals will spend the rest of their days in jail contemplating their terrible crime.

When the Government, with the support of the Opposition, passes the proposed legislation, I and my family might at last be able to get on with our lives, and be able to remember Virginia as a vibrant but ordinary wife, mother and friend, who loved life and her family.

The proposed legislation – tabled in Parliament on Wednesday – will also stop the murderers of Anita Cobby and Janine Balding from having their sentences redetermined. It is essential these perpetrators are denied the right to appeal their sentences. If the truth in sentencing legislation was not changed, they would have the right to appeal every three years. After all, they have nothing to lose and everything to gain.

As one of their victims, I find it is impossible to have any regard for the welfare of these prisoners or to offer them 'options' as other contributors to this page have suggested. The public is fully supportive of this legislation and the political powers are doing their job in giving a voice to ordinary people such as myself who have had to endure unspeakable pain and loss.

The Parliament has the powers to make rules governing inmates and it certainly has the power to change these rules. I thank the media for keeping this issue before the public and thank, too, all the individuals and organisations who have helped me through this ordeal. People I do not even know have written letters of support, letters to ministers and to Parliament and petitions with thousands of signatures on them.

All this has been instrumental in getting us to the point where we are today.

On 15 June 2002, Allan Baker's attempt to have his sentence redetermined was rejected by the New South Wales Court of Appeals. Baker had appealed the New South Wales Supreme Court, finding that he was ineligible for sentence re-determination. The New South Wales Court of Appeals found that Mr Justice James had not erred in his finding that there was no reason to justify a review of the original sentence. Baker can apply to the New South Wales Supreme Court to grant a re-determination of his sentence every two years. As with his accomplice, Crump, should he walk from prison he would be extradited to Queensland to face a charge for the murder of Virginia Morse.

But, try as they may to take their place among the community, there is little doubt that Kevin Crump or Allan Baker will never see the light of day outside of prison walls. And the citizens of Australia will be grateful for that.

Chapter Sixteen

THE GRAEME THORNE KIDNAPPING

Most countries have a famous kidnapping. On 10 July 1973, in Rome, John Paul Getty III, grandson of oil billionaire and renowned miser J Paul Getty, was kidnapped and a ransom of $17 million was demanded over the telephone for his safe return. Not one willing to part with his hard-earned money in a hurry, his grandfather refused to pay any ransom 'on principle'.

In November 1973, an envelope containing a lock of hair and a human ear was delivered to a daily newspaper. The note attached said: 'This is Paul's ear. If we don't get some money within 10 days, then the other ear will arrive. In other words, he will arrive in little bits.' Still reluctant to part with the ransom, Getty senior negotiated a deal and got his grandson back for about $2 million. He was found alive in southern Italy shortly after the ransom was paid. His kidnappers were never caught.

America's most famous case of kidnapping and 'crime of the century' occurred in 1932. The baby son of the world's greatest living hero, Charles A Lindberg, was abducted from Lindbergh's New Jersey home by an intruder using a crude, home-made ladder to gain entry to a second-storey bedroom. A ransom note was left on the windowsill. The demand was paid, but the child was found dead in the woods near the house 73 days later. Two years later, 35-year-old Bronx carpenter Bruno Richard Hauptmann was tried, found guilty and executed, despite vehemently protesting his innocence to the bitter end.

In 1960, four-year-old Eric Peugeot, son of the Paris automobile millionaire Raymond Peugeot, was kidnapped from the playground of a fashionable golf course outside Paris. His kidnappers demanded $35,000 – about the equivalent of a round of drinks to mega-rich Peugeot – for the boy's safe return. The ransom was promptly paid and the boy was returned, unharmed, a short time later. His kidnappers were arrested in 1962 and each sentenced to 20 years in jail.

Unlike the more notorious cases from around the world, Australia's most famous kidnapping wasn't of a member of a rich and famous family. It was also Australia's first-ever kidnapping. Child kidnappings only ever happened on the other side of the world, two or three weeks away by propellered aeroplane in America or Europe, not in Australia where children were king and could swim, fish and bushwalk in absolute safety and the only predators were the sharks and magpies protecting their young. Yet, due to the circumstances surrounding the case and the extraordinary scientific detection utilised for those archaic times, the Graeme Thorne kidnapping was one of Australia's best-known crimes at the time, a crime that became famous around the world.

⚰ ⚰ ⚰

On Wednesday, 1 June 1960, amid much fanfare, ticket number 3932 was drawn out of a huge barrel at the State Lottery Office in Barrack Street in the heart of Sydney. It was the winning number of the 10th Opera House Lottery, so named because the proceeds were used to help pay for the construction of what was to become one of the world's most recognised landmarks – the Sydney Opera House – to be situated on the foreshore of Sydney Harbour at Bennelong Point. The first prize was worth £100,000, a considerable windfall when it is considered that, in today's money, it would convert to approximately $5 million. At £3 a ticket, or about 20 per cent of the average weekly wage of the time, it took a while for the lottery to fill and its draw was eagerly awaited by the ticketholders.

The lucky owner of ticket number 3932 was travelling salesman Bazil Thorne, who was in the north-west of New South Wales when news of his good fortune reached him. He was so elated he cut his business trip short and drove home immediately to enjoy the moment with his wife and young family. Bazil and Freda Thorne, with their two children, Graeme, eight, and Belinda, three, lived in a two-bedroom, ground-floor apartment in Edward Street, Bondi, only a couple of minutes' walk to another famous Australian landmark – Bondi Beach. But the money changed little in their lifestyle. Although the Thornes were what

Australians refer to as 'battlers', they persisted in their daily routine as if nothing had happened, although they could now pay cash for the flashest of houses and cars, and could take an extended trip around the world and have plenty left over.

In a business partnership with his father, 37-year-old Bazil Thorne had worked hard enough to send his son, Graeme, to nearby Scots College, one of Sydney's more expensive schools with an outstanding reputation for exemplary education and sports. Graeme loved the beach, football and riding his bike, and the fortune his parents had won made little difference to him. At 8.30 am each weekday morning, he walked up the street in his grey school uniform, turned right into Wellington Street and sat on his school case on the corner of O'Brien Street where Phyllis Smith, a friend of the Thornes, would pull up at the kerb and Graeme would hop in the back seat with her two sons, who were also students at Scots.

But, on Thursday, 7 July 1960, Graeme Thorne walked out of home as usual and disappeared. It was just 36 days after the lottery win. When Mrs Smith arrived at the O'Brien Street corner at 8.35 am and couldn't see Graeme, one of her sons looked in at the nearby grocery store where Graeme sometimes brought potato crisps and waited, but he wasn't there. Concerned, but not overly worried at this stage, Mrs Smith waited a short while, then drove around to the boy's home and spoke to Mrs Thorne, who was convinced that Graeme would turn up somewhere shortly, although it wasn't like him to go astray. Mrs Smith drove to Scots College, but Graeme had not been seen there either. She left her sons at the college and returned to the Thorne apartment. Now very worried, Mrs Thorne rang Sergeant Larry O'Shea at the nearby Bondi police station, and within minutes he was knocking at the front door. Sergeant O'Shea was taking notes when the phone rang and Mrs Thorne answered.

'Is that you, Mrs Thorne?' a man's voice with a thick European accent asked. 'Is your husband there?'

'What do you want my husband for?' Freda Thorne asked, sensing that something was wrong.

'I have your son, Mrs Thorne,' the voice replied.

Mrs Thorne was speechless. Sergeant O'Shea took the phone from her and pretended to be Bazil Thorne. 'What can I do for you?' the sergeant asked.

'I have got your boy,' the man said. 'I want £25,000 before five o'clock this afternoon.'

Unaware that the Thornes were winners of the Opera House lottery, Sergeant O'Shea asked in disbelief: 'How do you think I'm going to get that kind of money?'

'You have plenty of time before five o'clock,' the man replied. 'If you don't get the money, I'll feed the boy to the sharks.'

'How will I contact you?' Sergeant O'Shea asked.

'I will get in touch with you later on,' the caller said and hung up. It was then that Mrs Thorne told the police officer of their recent lottery win, and he understood immediately why someone would want to take their boy. Thus, the events of Australia's first-ever kidnapping were set in motion. It was the little boy of an ordinary Australian family who had been plucked from obscurity and become naively vulnerable by their good fortune.

Instead of keeping the kidnapping under wraps for the time being until negotiations could be made with the kidnapper, a ransom paid and, with luck, the boy returned unharmed, Detective Inspector Bert Windsor, the acting chief of the Criminal Investigation Bureau, chose to call an immediate press conference. That afternoon, every newspaper in the country carried the story on the front page in huge print. And even though they weren't made aware that the caller's voice was that of a European, the newspapers couldn't help but compare the Graeme Thorne kidnapping with that of four-year-old Eric Peugeot, grandson of car millionaire Jean-Pierre Peugeot, who had been kidnapped two months earlier in Paris and was returned unharmed after the ransom had been paid. Eric Peugeot's kidnappers were still at large at the time that Graeme went missing.

To a man, the nation was dumbfounded. This could happen in America or Europe, yes, but not here. It just didn't happen. Australia was so unprepared for a kidnapping that, like all of the other states, the New South Wales *Crimes Act* didn't even carry a provision for the crime. The nearest listed offence was 'abduction', which commonly referred to the abduction of a woman for the purpose of marriage or carnal knowledge. It carried a maximum penalty of 14 years' imprisonment. But it was only a matter of time before there would be a catalyst that would introduce laws for kidnapping. Tragically, for the Thorne family, their missing boy would be it.

⚰ ⚰ ⚰

Police launched a search operation on a scale the likes of which Australia had never seen before. Within hours of the kidnapping, every house and flat in the vicinity of the Thornes' home was searched. Every possible hideout was checked; motels, boarding houses, weekenders and even boats on moorings around Sydney Harbour came under scrutiny. Known criminals across the country were questioned. Officers on leave were called back to duty to help with the search. Bazil Thorne told detectives to offer the entire £100,000 in return for his son, but they declined as they expected that all it would attract were tricksters and conmen and would inhibit the real search.

Although under heavy sedation, Mrs Thorne recalled that, a short time after the lottery win, a man with a heavy European accent and wearing dark glasses had knocked on her door and asked for a Mr Bognor, a name she didn't recognise. The man then asked her if her phone number was 307113, which was correct, although it was not listed in the telephone directory. Mrs Thorne suggested that the man ask the lady living in the flat above. It was later revealed that the phone number was given to the mysterious caller with the European accent by an employee at the State Lottery Office. In 1960 in Sydney, there was no secrecy attached to the name, address or telephone number of a lottery winner.

When the kidnapper had not rung back by 5.00 pm on 7 July as he said he would, the New South Wales Police Commissioner, CJ Delaney, made a personal appeal for the return of Graeme Thorne on the evening television news. The following day, television stations across the nation screened news flashes with photos of the missing boy. Bazil Thorne appeared on television briefly and said: 'If the person who has my son is a father ... all I can say is, for God's sake, send him back to me in one piece.'

The following day at 6.00 pm, Graeme Thorne's empty school case was found a few yards in from the Wakehurst Parkway, a busy highway that runs through several miles of bushland on the outskirts of Sydney. Although it wasn't relevant at the time, but would be of significance in the future, this location is on the way to the oceanside suburb of Seaforth, about 10 kilometres from the heart of Sydney as the crow flies. The school case with the name 'Graeme Thorne' on it was found by an elderly man collecting bottles who, fortunately, had seen the television coverage of the kidnapping, immediately recognised the importance of his discovery and contacted police. Within hours, hundreds of police, assisted by army units, helicopters and tracker dogs, were combing the rugged bushland area for further clues. That night Commissioner Delaney again appeared on television with an appeal to the kidnapper: 'Please let us know if the boy is safe.'

On Saturday night, police arranged with the Bank of New South Wales for a special withdrawal of £25,000 pounds from Bazil Thorne's account, just in case the kidnapper should get in touch with them again. When they had heard nothing by Sunday, 10 July, Mr Thorne went on television and offered all or part of the £25,000 in cash for any information leading to the return of his son. Sitting alongside Mr Thorne was the Reverend Clive Goodwin of St Mark's Church of England in Sydney's Darling Point, who said he was acting as intermediary and promised anyone who came forward that there would be no interference from the police. All the announcement did was attract all the heartless conmen in search of a quick buck, about whom the police had warned Mr Thorne. One such call that sounded genuine was from a woman saying she was acting as a go-between. Police were reluctant to allow Mr Thorne and Reverend Goodwin to connect with the woman without their assistance and only allowed the connection to go ahead if they were allowed to shadow Reverend Goodwin as he made the money drop and collected the information.

The police followed the reverend to Sydney's outer western suburbs at the foot of the Blue Mountains, where he was instructed to hand over an envelope addressed to a Mr Day containing £100 to the owner of a fish and chip shop. The reverend delivered the envelope as instructed, but there was no money inside it. A woman collected it and disappeared before police could catch her.

On Monday, after an exhausting weekend, the hundreds of searchers were rewarded for their efforts. Graeme Thorne's school cap, raincoat, lunch bag – with an apple still inside it – and maths books were found about a kilometre from where the school case was found on the opposite side of the highway. But was Graeme Thorne still alive? That was the question that was on Australia's lips. It would be quite some time before they knew the answer.

ðŸšª ðŸšª ðŸšª

On 16 August 1960, five weeks after Graeme Thorne had gone missing, his body was discovered under an overhanging ledge of rock in the scrub on a vacant block of land only 15 metres from an occupied house in Grandview Grove, Seaforth. His hands and feet were tied with rope. A silk scarf had been knotted tightly around his neck. He was wrapped in a checkered car rug and still wore his Scots College blazer. The boy had died of either a fractured skull or strangulation – or both. The body was discovered by two young boys who had been aware of the bundle under the rock ledge for a couple of weeks and had fantasised that it was a dead body but, unaware of the Graeme Thorne kidnapping, had never told anyone. While taking an older friend to their nearby bushland adventure 'fort', the boys mentioned the bundle and the friend told his parents, who made the terrible discovery that night by torchlight.

The main line of inquiry pursued by police was related to a car seen near the corner on the morning Graeme disappeared. A young man came forward when the story first broke and reported seeing an iridescent blue 1955 Ford Customline at the scene of the abduction. It might have been anyone's car, but police were reaching for any possible lead as they had so little to go on. Dozens of police moved into the Department of Motor Transport for the weekend and started on the daunting task of checking through 260,000 Ford index cards. Today it would take minutes to come up with the 5000 owners of 1955 iridescent blue Ford Customlines registered in New South Wales. For the investigators of 1960 it was going to take weeks. Then each vehicle would have to be traced and each owner located and physically questioned. To speed up the process, police appealed numerous times through the media to members of the public to come forward if they knew of anyone with an iridescent blue Ford Customline who had been acting suspiciously.

William and Kathleen Telford of 26 Moore Street, Clontarf, the suburb next to Seaforth, where Graeme Thorne's body was found, had a neighbour, Stephen Bradley, who drove that model car, but he and his wife seemed such nice people that the Telfords had never bothered to contact police. They hadn't thought any more of it, even when the Bradleys moved out of their house the day that Graeme Thorne disappeared and over the following weeks representatives from finance companies came around knocking on their door, asking if they had any idea where their neighbours (the Bradleys) had moved to. But when Graeme Thorne's body was found in the next suburb, they had a good think about the circumstances and rang the police. The Telfords told detectives that, one week prior to the Thorne kidnapping, Mr Bradley had been leaving home at the unusual time of around six o'clock each morning. They also said that he was Hungarian and had a strong European accent.

Eight days after Graeme Thorne's body was found, two detectives called upon Stephen Leslie Bradley where he worked as an electroplater at a small factory in the inner-city suburb of Darlinghurst. A thick-set, olive-skinned man of average height and in his mid-30s, Bradley was cooperative and pleasant. Born in Budapest, he had arrived in Australia ten years earlier. He had changed his name by deed poll from Istvan Baranyay.

Bradley remembered 7 July well: it was the day he had moved house. His wife and children left by taxi for the airport about 10.00 am. They were going on a holiday in sunny Queensland in northern Australia. The removalists arrived about an hour later. Bradley left at the same time as the removalists, soon after lunch. When he drove off with the removal van, that was the first time the Ford Customline was out of the garage all day. Bradley was now living in an apartment in Osborne Road in the nearby seaside suburb of Manly.

The day following the interview with Bradley at the factory, his wife Magda booked a one-way passage for herself and her 13-year-old son, Peter – by a previous marriage – to London on the ocean liner *Himalaya*. Four days later, Bradley booked a passage for himself and their two other children, Helen, seven, and Robert, eight, on the same ship. The next day the *Himalaya*, with the Bradleys on board, passed through the heads of Sydney Harbour.

The following Sunday's newspapers published a description of Bradley's missing 1955 iridescent blue Ford Customline, and police received a call from a local used car dealer who had purchased it on 20 September from an auction. Police impounded the car and took scrapings from the boot. They also took possession of a vacuum cleaner that was among the household items Bradley had sold to a city furniture auctioneer. The results of the tests of the boot scrapings and the contents of the vacuum cleaner made Bradley a hot suspect. But with Bradley and his family on the *Himalaya* to London via Aden, in

Ceylon (now Sri Lanka), from where there was a direct flight back to Hungary and no extradition treaty, it wasn't going to be easy for police to get their hands on him. They would have to act quickly.

The master of the *Himalaya* was asked by cable to keep the suspected fugitive under surveillance. When the oceanliner berthed at Colombo on 10 October, Bradley was called into the purser's office and confronted by officers of the Ceylon Police Harbour Patrol. Protesting his innocence, Bradley was taken to the shore lock-up. Mrs Bradley was most upset. It was just not possible for Stephen to do such a thing, she said. Nevertheless, she continued the voyage to London with her children.

The antiquated *Australian Fugitive Offenders Act* of 1881 enabled easy extradition within the British Empire, but now that Ceylon was an independent nation and the treaty was invalid, police had to establish a prima facie case to a Ceylonese court to justify an extradition order on Bradley. Ceylon was also in political turmoil at the time and anything but friendly to the British Empire or any nation that was a part of it. With the results of the tests on the boot scrapings and what they had found in the vacuum cleaner, along with the circumstantial evidence they had gathered, police hoped they had a strong enough case. With a briefcase packed with the evidence, detective sergeants Brian Doyle and Jack Bateman arrived in Colombo to have their case heard before a sometimes hostile court.

'Colombo police had refused point-blank to pull Bradley off the *Himalaya* although we said we wanted him for murder,' Doyle said. 'That is why we had to get him taken off the boat by customs officials. The authorities were very unfriendly.'

After a lengthy hearing, the extradition order was granted. Considering themselves lucky to get out of Colombo with their lives, let alone with their prisoner, Doyle and Bateman arrived back in Sydney on 19 November with Bradley in handcuffs. Sydney Airport was packed with reporters and hundreds of curious citizens who wanted a look at Bradley. But they were to be disappointed as the prisoner was whisked out the back way in an unmarked car and taken to Central police station for questioning.

🔒 🔒 🔒

Australia's trial of the century opened at the Sydney Central Criminal Court on 20 March 1961. The public gallery was packed, and hundreds of disgruntled men and women who had camped out the front of the court overnight were turned away. The case was far from cut and dried. While the police were confident they had their man and had built up a strong case, much of the evidence was circumstantial and they were by no means guaranteed of a conviction. Bradley, neatly dressed in a blue suit, pleaded not guilty.

In his opening address, the Crown Prosecutor, WJ Knight, urged the jury to be impartial. From the outset, he made it clear that, if he got a conviction, it would be for murder and not for the lesser charge of manslaughter. He said:

> The prosecution will prove to you that Stephen Bradley kidnapped and deliberately murdered Graeme Thorne and that the boy did not die by accident when he became asphyxiated while in the boot of the accused's car. There are lots of questions that are unanswered that would indicate that Mr Bradley deliberately and willfully murdered the lad. Would Graeme have sat impassively in the car while Bradley paid the bridge toll or when he got out of the car to make the phone call to Mrs Thorne? Did not Bradley's movements on the day of the kidnapping and in the days that followed suggest flight? I suggest to you that Bradley deliberately murdered Graeme Thorne by delivering a blow to the head shortly before or after he put him in his car after kidnapping him.

From then on, step by step, the prosecution built up a strong case against the accused. The prosecution called on a specialist from the New South Wales Department of Health. He said that he had been asked whether there was a flow of air in the Ford Customline or whether Graeme had died of asphyxiation. He said about half the air in the boot changed every hour. He and another officer had fixed an apparatus that carried a tube away from the boot of the car to face masks. They breathed through these face masks for seven hours with doors and windows of the car and garage locked. 'Neither my colleague nor I suffered any ill-effect,' he said, indicating that Graeme Thorne had been killed by the blow to the head rather than asphyxiation.

Then the prosecution delivered one forensic bombshell after another. A team of eight scientific experts had examined Graeme

Thorne's clothing and the car rug that was wrapped around his body. From the mould on Graeme's shoes, it was decided that the body had been where it was found in the bushes for most of the time after the boy was murdered. The Australian Mining Museum had established that the pinkish substance found on Graeme's clothing was a lime stock mortar. Detectives had concluded that at some stage Graeme's body had been lying beneath a house or in a garage.

Dr Joyce Vickery of the National Herbarium at Sydney's Botanic Gardens reported that vegetation fragments on Graeme' clothing came from two types of cypress bush. Two detectives carrying samples of the cypress sprigs, soil and mortar trudged around the streets of Seaforth and finally called at 28 Moore Street, Clontarf, the Bradleys' second-last address. Jackpot! They matched the soil from the rug, the shrubs and the pink mortar. They were all there.

Police forensic experts reported that hair found on the car rug, in the boot of the Ford Customline and in the bag of the vacuum cleaner were all from a single source – a Pekinese dog. The Bradleys owned a Pekinese dog named Cherry. The dog was now a vital piece of evidence. But where was Cherry? A Clontarf resident remembered that a vet had called at the Bradleys' in a Volkswagen. Police looked up the vets in the pink pages of the local telephone directory. They found a vet at Rushcutters Bay on the other side of Sydney Harbour who picked up animals in a Volkswagen. And they were holding the Bradleys' dog, a Pekinese named Cherry, for shipment to London. Hairs from Cherry matched the hairs found on the rug in which Graeme Thorne's body was wrapped.

A real estate agent told police that he had shown the Bradleys several houses that were for sale on 24 June. One had been in Grandview Grove, Seaforth, next to the vacant lot where Graeme's body was found. Detectives rummaging in the garden of the flats in Osborne Road, Manly, the Bradleys' last-known address, uncovered a number of discarded 35-millimetre film negatives among the weeds. The film, which was crumpled and torn and had been lying out in the weather, was carefully cleaned, printed and enlarged to be shown in court. One photo was of Mrs Bradley and her children sitting on a car rug with the same pattern as the one found around Graeme. Other frames showed Stephen Bradley himself.

The court was told that on the morning of Monday, 21 November

1960, 16 men, all looking somewhat alike, stood in a line-up. Mrs Thorne was asked to identify the inquiry agent who called at her apartment looking for Mr Bognor. She stopped at Stephen Leslie Bradley. 'Please place your hand on him,' the policeman asked.

'No,' Mrs Thorne replied. 'I will not put my hand near him.'

Amid heckles and hissing from the public gallery, which Justice Clancy ordered stopped immediately or he would have the court cleared, Stephen Bradley finally took the stand. He was extremely confident and articulate. He said he was never at 79 Edward Street, Bondi. He had nothing to do with taking Graeme Thorne away. He said that on 7 July he got up at 7.30 am and finished packing. He had sat and read the papers in the car, annoyed with his wife for going off early to Surfers Paradise, leaving him to do the packing. A taxi had collected Mrs Bradley and the children to take them to the city airport terminal in time for the 11.45 am flight to Coolangatta. The removalists arrived shortly after. Bradley said his wife had been in a concentration camp during the war. He was part-Jewish and had been a prisoner of the Gestapo for five months in 1944.

Knight, the Crown Prosecutor, suggested that the Bradleys had argued over the kidnapping of the boy. He also suggested that Magda had taken a taxi to the city to avoid being associated with the Ford Customline and that Bradley could have gone over to Bondi and arrived back comfortably in time for the removalists at 10.00 am.

The defence called Magda Bradley, 41, to the stand. She had flown in from London a few days before. She wore a black outfit and a turban-type hat. She was asked to show the Auschwitz concentration camp number, A-11-663, tattooed on her arm.

She said the car rug displayed in the court was very similar to the rug she had possessed but was more worn, and that they had lost the rug some time ago. She denied having seen the scarf that was found around Graeme Thorne's neck. Knight lost no time in endeavouring to implicate Magda Bradley. 'I put it to you that you knew your husband could not drive you to the airport terminal because you knew your husband was somewhere in the Bondi area at the time,' he said to her.

Mrs Bradley replied: 'No sir, I am sorry sir, you are very wrong.' She said she had not been aware that detectives had called on her husband at his work on 24 August.

'You say it is just a coincidence that the very next day you went and booked yourself a passage to London,' asked Mr Knight.

'I am very sorry. It must be a coincidence,' replied Mrs Bradley.

In his summing up for Bradley, Mr Vizzard, Bradley's counsel, emphasised that most of the evidence was circumstantial. Even the police line-up in which Bradley was pointed out had little validity in view of photographs of Bradley that had already appeared in the press.

The jury filed out, and then returned to the courtroom to have the medical report on Graeme's death read out again. They appeared to want confirmation of whether the crime committed amounted to manslaughter or murder. The expression that a 'good force' would have been needed to fracture Graeme's skull helped them to decide. It ruled out an earlier claim that, while still in the boot, Graeme had struck his head on the rim of the spare tyre. Again the jury withdrew.

It was evening. Home-going office workers swelled the crowds already gathered outside the court. In the corridors, television cameras and reporters waited for any news. The tension mounted as the hours ticked away.

The jury returned at ten to eight. 'Guilty,' said the foreman. The gallery in the courthouse and the thousands waiting outside the court erupted.

'Hang the bastard,' they yelled. 'Feed him to the sharks.'

Bradley remained emotionless, his hands on the dock rail. The Thornes, who were in court throughout the entire proceedings, remained stoically calm, their faces pale and drawn. Bradley was asked if he had anything to say. He said: 'Yes, I have a few things to say. I have never had the opportunity before this trial to say anything.' He said he had never been given a chance because of prejudice. He admitted that the jury had done its best under the circumstances, but that they had been influenced by powerful emotions.

Mr Justice Clancy delivered his sentence almost immediately: 'Stephen Leslie Bradley, the sentence of this court is that you are sentenced to penal servitude for life.' The crowd roared its approval.

⚰ ⚰ ⚰

Bradley's subsequent appeal to the full court of the Supreme Court of New South Wales was unanimously rejected. Magda Bradley divorced her husband in 1965 and went to live in Europe.

Bazil, Freda and Belinda Thorne moved out of Bondi into a house in nearby Rose Bay. Unable to get over the death of his boy, Bazil Thorne died suddenly in 1978.

Life in prison for Bradley, one of Australia's most hated men, was far from pleasant. Despised by the other prisoners and subjected to repeated brutal bashings, he was put in protective custody for his own good. Despite the fact that many reporters and investigators considered that Magda Bradley had been party to the kidnapping of Graeme Thorne and when it all went wrong she didn't want to know about it, she was never implicated by Bradley in any way. On 6 October 1968, while playing tennis with other protected prisoners, he dropped dead of a heart attack. He was 43 years of age.

No case of a similar nature has ever been perpetrated in Australia since. As a direct result of the Thorne kidnapping, lottery ticket purchasers are now given the option to remain anonymous.

Chapter Seventeen

THE ADELAIDE 'FAMILY' MURDERS

Easygoing Adelaide, the capital of South Australia with its population of around 1.3 million, is small compared to most of the other capital cities of Australia. Rich in culture and beauty, Adelaide and its surrounding districts are responsible for some of the finest wines in Australia. Throughout Adelaide, seemingly on every corner, are houses of worship of all denominations. For this reason, Adelaide is referred to as the 'city of churches'. And they have never had to canvas for business – South Australians are notoriously reverent.

But there is an inexplicable dark side to Adelaide. In the annals of Australia's most horrific crimes, easygoing Adelaide's sinister past makes other cities look like Camelot. Consider this list of Adelaide's appalling track record of carnage in modern times:

1958: Rupert Max Stuart rapes and murders nine-year-old Mary Olive Hattam at Thevenard.

1966: The three Beaumont children, aged four, seven and nine, are abducted from Glenelg Beach and never seen again.

1971: In South Australia's worst mass murder, ten members of the Bartholomew family, comprising eight children and two women, are shot to death by a man at Hope Forest.

1972: Adelaide University law lecturer Dr George Duncan, a gay man, is thrown into the Torrens River and drowns. Two Adelaide vice squad detectives are eventually charged with manslaughter.

1973: Schoolgirl Joanne Ratcliffe, 11, and Kirsty Gordon, four, disappear from Adelaide Oval while attending a football match, and are never seen again.

1976–1977: Seven women aged between 15 and 26 go missing in and around Adelaide over a 51-day period from Christmas 1976. Their skeletal remains are discovered in the Truro district of the Adelaide foothills several years later in what becomes known as the 'mass murders of Truro'. James Miller is sentenced to life imprisonment for his part in the murders.

1979: David Szach murders his lover, lawyer Derrance Stevenson, and conceals his body in a freezer in Parkside.

1979–1983: During this period, in what would become known as the 'Adelaide Family murders', five men are abducted, drugged, held captive, sexually assaulted, hideously mutilated and murdered.

1984: Sexual sadist Bevan von Einem is tried for the horrific torture and murder of a 15-year-old youth. Later, von Einem is charged with numerous other horrendous crimes relating to the 'Family murders'.

1994: A letter bomb kills Sergeant Geoff Bowen at the Adelaide offices of the National Crime Authority.

1999: Eight decomposing bodies are found in casks filled with acid in a bank vault in rural Snowtown. This find leads to the discovery of two other bodies buried in backyards in suburban Adelaide. Two murders that took place in Lower Light and Kersbrook in 1997 are connected to the same case. Four men are charged with multiple murder.

Of all these cases there are four that are deep-etched into the annals of Australia's most notorious crimes. They are: the mass murders of Truro; the Snowtown serial murders; the missing Beaumont children; and the Adelaide Family murders. The mystery of the missing Beaumont children and the Family murders may be linked by the sinister activities of the same monster.

⚰ ⚰ ⚰

On 26 January 1966, the Beaumont children – Jane, nine, Arnna, seven, and four-year-old Grant – disappeared from South Australia's Glenelg Beach at about 11.15 am while on an outing alone. Their disappearance made headlines all around Australia.

On that morning the weather was fine and the forecast was for a hot and steamy day, ideal conditions for a day at the beach. The Beaumonts were an average Australian family living at suburban Somerton Park, not far from the beach, and the children's father, a travelling salesman, had decided against joining his children at the beach for the day. Instead he chose to call on a client. It was a decision that would prove fateful.

At 10.00 am the children took the bus to the beach, which was only a few minutes' ride away. The eldest girl, Jane, was considered old enough and responsible enough to mind her two siblings. She assured her mother, Nancy, that they would be home on the midday bus. They caught the bus at the stop just 100 metres from their front door. The bus driver confirmed later that he dropped them at Glenelg Beach five minutes later.

When the children didn't arrive home, their mother wasn't unduly concerned. Children simply didn't go missing in suburban Adelaide, especially from a crowded beach area. She concluded that they must have decided to walk home, had spent their bus fare money on sweets, and that she would hear the usual ruckus as they ran in the front door at any minute.

When Jim Beaumont arrived home in the mid-afternoon and his children still weren't home, he went looking for them. When they still hadn't been sighted four hours later, he notified police, and a massive search was launched. By morning their photographs were being circulated to every newspaper across the country, telling of every parent's worst nightmare.

The police were left with three possibilities: the children had run away; they had drowned in the surf; or they had been abducted and were being held for ransom. The only ray of hope was the sighting of the children in the company of a tall blond or light-brown-haired young man in blue swimming trunks. Then, another witness came forward and said that he had seen the children with the same young blond man in a park opposite the beach, then walking away with him behind the Glenelg Hotel. The local postman came forward and said that he had seen the trio walking up Jetty Road away from the beach and towards their home at about 3.00 pm. They were laughing and holding hands. The police received hundreds of calls about possible sightings of the Beaumont children, but they all proved fruitless. The Beaumont children had vanished without a trace and have never been seen since.

But there would be a glimmer of hope, albeit a horrific one, of discovering the fate of the Beaumont children. It would occur many years in the future at the committal hearing of one of the most evil murderers in Australia's history.

🚪 🚪 🚪

At around midnight on a chilly autumn night in May 1972 on the banks of the Torrens River, which flows through the heart of Adelaide and was a known 'pick-up' area frequented at night by gay men, Adelaide University lecturer Dr George Duncan and Roger James were attacked by four men, bashed and thrown in the river and left for dead. Duncan, a frail man with just one lung as a result of juvenile tuberculosis, was drowned. Severe bruising beneath his armpits indicated that he had been man-handled and thrown into the freezing river by a number of people. Roger James escaped with a broken ankle. He had been saved by a tall young blond man in his mid-20s who just happened to be passing by at the time. He was Bevan Spencer von Einem, a name that would be of enormous significance in the time to come.

Dr George Duncan's death was treated as murder, and within days the spotlight fell on three senior Vice Squad detectives who were alleged to have gone to the Torrens River that night in search of 'poofters' to bash after they had attended a drunken send-off for one of their comrades. Witnesses said that the detectives were accompanied by a tall civilian whose name never came to light. The three detectives were called upon to give evidence at a coronial inquest into Dr Duncan's death, but all refused to answer any of the incriminating questions put to them and were immediately suspended from duty.

A subsequent police inquiry failed to find sufficient evidence to recommend prosecution of the three police officers. The public was outraged, and while the whole matter stank of a cover-up, there was little that could be done and the incident was forgotten ... for the time being.

🚪 🚪 🚪

In June 1979, while Adelaide's citizens were trying to come to terms with the murders of seven young women in the mass murders of Truro, the hideously mutilated body of 17-year-old Alan Barnes was found on the banks of the South Para reservoir, north-east of Adelaide, after he had been reported missing seven days earlier. His 'fresh' corpse indicated that he had died the day before he was discovered, and a post-mortem revealed that he had died of massive blood loss from ghastly injuries inflicted upon his anus by a large blunt instrument while he was still alive.

Two months later, police were called to investigate what looked like human body parts found in plastic bags that had floated to rest on the banks of the Port River at Port Adelaide. The body parts turned out to be the dissected remains of 25-year-old Neil Muir, neatly cut into many pieces, placed in the garbage bags and thrown into the river.

In June 1982, the skeletal remains of 14-year-old Peter Stogneff, who had gone missing 10 months earlier, were found at Middle Beach, north of Adelaide, cut into three pieces as if by a surgical saw.

On 27 February 1982, 18-year-old Mark Langley disappeared while walking near the Torrens River. Nine days later, his mutilated body was found in scrub in the Adelaide foothills. Among the mutilations to his body was a wound that went from his navel to his pubic region, which appeared to have been cut with a surgical instrument. The hair around the wound had been shaved as it would have been if performed in a surgical operation. The post-mortem revealed that part of Mark's small bowel was missing and that he had died from a massive loss of blood from gross injuries to his anus.

By now the zealous press was convinced that the murders were the work of a group of surreptitious Adelaide men in very high places throughout the community – politicians, judges, religious leaders and the like – who paid handsomely for kidnapped young men whom they drugged and kept alive for their pleasure. When the victim was no longer of any use to them, the procurers disposed of the bodies. The press christened this unconfirmed clandestine group 'the Family', and from then on the case was referred to in the national press as the 'Adelaide Family murders'.

Working on the now obvious assumption that the murders were the work of the same individual(s) and that the person(s) they wished to talk to most of all was gay, South Australian Police Major Crime Squad detectives infiltrated the vast South Australian gay scene. Through their secret contacts, detectives came up with a short-list of possible suspects. One such person of interest was a tall, blond, meticulously groomed 37-year-old accountant named Bevan Spencer von Einem. Openly gay, von Einem was well known to police as a frequenter of gay pick-up spots or 'beats', as they were more commonly known. Von Einem also had a reputation of being particularly fond of young boys, which was scorned by the gay community.

Von Einem was brought in and questioned at length about the Barnes and Langley killings. He vigorously denied any knowledge of the murders other than what he had read in the papers and the rumours he had heard circulating about the specific injuries to the victims. Police had no choice but to let him go.

⚰ ⚰ ⚰

On 23 July 1983, a fifth victim turned up. Seven weeks earlier, 15-year-old Richard Kelvin was abducted a short distance from his North Adelaide home, and his body was found by an amateur geologist off a track near One Tree Hill in the Adelaide foothills. The boy was wearing a Channel Nine T-shirt, jeans and sneakers – the clothes he had on when he left his parents' home on 5 June. Richard had gone to a bus stop only 200 metres from his home that afternoon to catch a bus to see a friend. Several neighbours reported hearing calls for help in the afternoon, and police were convinced that Richard had been kidnapped.

No real attempt had been made to conceal the teenager's body. Police weren't surprised that the post-mortem revealed that Richard had grotesque wounds to the anus similar to those of the other victims. The post-mortem also revealed that he had been heavily drugged and kept alive for up to five weeks before he was murdered. Richard's body was found to contain traces of four different drugs.

Police rounded up the usual suspects once again, and this time von Einem aroused their suspicions by not protesting as vehemently to their questioning as he had previously. Task force detectives decided to search von Einem's house and to give him and his clothing a thorough scientific once-over. It paid off in spades. In von Einem's possession they found three of the drugs taken from the dead boy's body and found von Einem's hair in the deceased's clothing.

Von Einem was charged with the murder of Richard Kelvin. At his trial he pleaded not guilty, and although he was faced with undeniable evidence that he had been in Kelvin's company, he denied ever having known the boy. Then, in a complete turnaround, von Einem said that he had picked up Richard Kelvin one time when he was hitchhiking and had dropped him off near his home. The jury was not impressed and found him guilty of murder. Bevan Spencer von Einem was sentenced to life imprisonment with a non-parole period of 24 years, which was later increased to 36 years on appeal by the Crown, a record for South Australia.

But that was not to be the end of it ... not by a long shot.

🛡 🛡 🛡

The detectives who had worked on the Kelvin case were convinced that von Einem, possibly alone but most likely with others, was responsible for the deaths of the other youths, Alan Barnes, Neil Muir, Peter Stogneff and Mark Langley, or at least knew who was. And they had very good reason to be. Apart from the fact that most of the other victims had suffered identical anal injuries to those suffered by Kelvin and had died in similar circumstances, the detectives' informants told them it was common knowledge within the gay community that von Einem regularly picked up young hitchhikers, drugged them, and then sexually abused them. The detectives worked tirelessly on new leads and new witnesses, and after four years they visited von Einem in Adelaide's Yatala Prison, where he was being held for his own safety in the protective custody division. They charged him with the murders of Alan Barnes and Mark Langley.

At von Einem's committal hearing held in 1990, the Crown chose to pursue a committal along the lines that 'similar fact evidence' was admissible, and alleged that if von Einem was guilty of the Kelvin murder, then he must also be guilty of the murders of Barnes and Langley as they were identical in every fashion. Furthermore, the Crown alleged, it had circumstantial evidence that could support this allegation. Magistrate David Gurry allowed Crown Prosecutor Brian Murray QC to proceed along these lines. It would prove to be a disastrous ploy. And if the packed public gallery thought it had heard stories of unbelievable horror as the evidence unfolded of how the boys had died from the injuries inflicted upon them, then they must have thought the Crown had saved the most shocking allegations for last. If what the public gallery was about to hear was true, Bevan Spencer von Einem would go down in history as one of the world's most sadistic monsters.

The Crown Prosecutor called 22 witnesses, who included former hitchhikers and associates of von Einem. The police had left no stone unturned in their efforts to nail the person whom they believed to be one of the most heinous killers in Australian history. The first prosecution witness would only give testimony under an alias of 'Mr B' for his own protection, and his name was withheld from publication by court order. 'Mr B' claimed that he believed von Einem had killed ten young people, including five children who had disappeared 24 years earlier.

'Mr B' denied that he was a 'perpetual liar' and that a reward for the unsolved murders of several Adelaide teenagers, which stood at $250,000, had anything to do with his giving information to police. In an angry outburst, he claimed that consideration for relatives of the deceased was part of the reason he was telling what he knew of von Einem's activities. 'I have given a lot of consideration to the relatives of the kids. They deserve to know what's really happened,' he told the court.

'Mr B' was a former friend of von Einem. He said he had evidence that linked von Einem with the five Family murders, and also with the disappearances of the three Beaumont children in 1966 and the 1973 disappearance of schoolgirls Joanne Ratcliffe and Kirsty Gordon from Adelaide Oval. The public gallery was stunned. They couldn't believe what they were hearing.

For four days, 'Mr B' testified that he and von Einem picked up young boys who were hitchhiking and drugged and raped them. On the night that Alan Barnes had died, he and von Einem went looking for hitchhikers after meeting on the banks of the Torrens River. He said that they gave Alan Barnes a lift and gave him alcoholic drinks containing a very strong sedative called Rohypnol, which they knew when mixed with alcohol would induce unconsciousness. The trio then went to a cafe, where Barnes showed signs of being affected by the drug – he looked like he was going to pass out. Von Einem had gone away and made a phone call, and when he came back he said he had rung a friend and arranged to meet him at the Torrens River. They had met up with a man known only as 'Mr R'. Von Einem had gone for a walk with 'Mr R' and had come back ten minutes later, asking if 'Mr B' wanted to come with them while they 'performed some surgery' on the now unconscious Barnes. Von Einem had also said that they intended to take videos of what happened, then kill Barnes and throw his body from a bridge. 'Mr B' told the hushed courtroom that he had declined the offer, and von Einem, 'Mr R' and Barnes had driven off.

'Mr B' said that he had seen von Einem a few days later, who said that the youth had died and that 'Mr R' was concerned about what 'Mr B' knew about what had happened. Von Einem then warned him that if he said anything to anyone about what he had seen, he would be implicated in the murder as well. 'Mr B' then explained that, since that night, his life had been a mess and he lived under the constant threats of an 'Adelaide businessman'.

'Mr B' also said that von Einem had told him he had picked up the Beaumont children at Glenelg Beach on 26 January 1966. Von Einem had told him how he went to the beach regularly to have a perve on people in the showers and had picked up three children, performed some 'brilliant surgery on them' and 'connected them up', but one had died. He said that he had dumped the children's bodies at Moana or Myponga, south of Adelaide. Further, 'Mr B' said that von Einem had told him that he had picked up two children at a football match and killed them. Although von Einem didn't mention any names, it seemed apparent that he was talking about Joanne Ratcliffe and Kirsty Gordon, who had gone missing from Adelaide Oval in 1973. 'Mr B' said that von Einem didn't elaborate any further.

Finally, 'Mr B' alleged that an Adelaide trader whom he said could have helped kill Alan Barnes was in court while he was giving his evidence. 'You've got no idea what I've had to go through … coming here … facing crap like [the Adelaide trader] sitting in the body of the court,' he said during his testimony.

Magistrate Gurry immediately suppressed the name of the Adelaide trader whom 'Mr B' claimed could have helped kill Alan Barnes. The man's counsel said the trader categorically denied being with von Einem and Barnes the night Barnes was last seen alive. The trader was not called as a Crown witness. The trader's counsel said that his business of 20 years would be ruined if he was identified and also challenged the claim of 'Mr B' that the trader was in the public gallery listening to evidence.

Another prosecution witness, Garry Wayne Place, an insurance worker in his 30s, testified that he had come forward late in 1989 as he had 'had enough' after 11 years of being threatened by telephone if he talked. Place said that the last anonymous call was about a week earlier and the caller told him to 'keep your mouth shut or you and your wife will get it'. He told the court that Alan Barnes had introduced him to von Einem one Saturday at an Adelaide hotel about a week before his murder. Barnes had also introduced him to three other people with von Einem – a doctor whose name sounded like Goodard, a man called Mario, and a woman. There had been talk of a party that night where there would be 'women, drugs, booze – anything you like'. Later that week Place and Barnes had gone to a hotel where von Einem had told him (Place) that if he provided sex, he would get 'drugs, women, anything' and the same things would be provided if he brought along some young boys.

Place told the court that the first threatening telephone call came on the night he learned that Alan Barnes had been murdered. A muffled male voice had said something like: 'Keep your mouth shut or you're going to get it', and there had been about 20 other calls that night.

If the parents of the missing children were hoping that von Einem would admit guilt and tell police where the remains of their children were, then they were sadly mistaken. Von Einem vigorously denied any involvement in the abductions of the children and lashed out at 'Mr B', claiming that he was merely out for a portion of the $250,000 reward on offer. But the circumstantial evidence against him appeared to be overwhelming. After two months of hearings, on 11 May 1990, Bevan Spencer von Einem was committed to stand trial in the South Australian Supreme Court on charges of murdering Alan Barnes and Mark Langley.

⚰ ⚰ ⚰

Immediately after von Einem was committed to stand trial, his counsel lodged an interjection to have the trial put on permanent stay of proceedings because, the lawyer argued, it would be impossible for his client to receive a fair hearing because of the amount of public animosity towards him and the over-exposure of the committal hearing in the newspapers. The interjection failed. The trial judge, Justice Duggan, chose to throw it out. But there were other matters about the forthcoming trial that worried the judge. At a pre-trial hearing he ruled that the 'similar fact evidence', so successfully used in the committal hearing by the Crown Prosecutor, was inadmissible. This ruling rendered the evidence led at the committal all but useless.

The Crown had to resort to different tactics. It would present two separate trials for the murders of Barnes and Langley. But a couple of days later, the Crown withdrew the murder charge against Langley, considering that it could build a stronger case by trying von Einem on the Barnes murder alone, the case for which it had the strongest evidence. Then came the biggest blow. After lengthy consideration, Justice Duggan ruled that evidence from the von Einem trial and conviction for the murder of Richard Kelvin was disallowed. Justice Duggan also ruled inadmissible any evidence about von Einem's alleged involvement with hitchhikers and his purported associates. The Crown case was in tatters because, if it went to court without their evidence, it didn't have a prayer of gaining a conviction. To their disgust, on 1 February 1991, the Crown had no choice but to enter a *nolle prosequi* (unwilling to pursue) on the second charge of the murder of Alan Barnes.

To the detectives who had worked tirelessly on the case for years, this was a bitter pill to swallow. To the parents of Alan Barnes and the other young men who were inhumanely violated and died ghastly deaths at the hands of suspected respectable citizens, it meant that their nightmare of wondering would go on. To many Australians, there is little doubt that 'the Family' of paedophiles did, and possibly still does, exist in South Australia. It is also believed by many that there are more victims as yet unaccounted for – transient hitchhikers from other states and young tourists, perhaps. These same believers are convinced, too, that the tall, blond, meticulously groomed accountant with the aristocratic name of Bevan Spencer von Einem knows where the bodies are buried and who the guilty parties are. But as he does his time in Yatala Prison, he keeps his dark secrets to himself.

Footnote: Two of the three detectives who allegedly threw Dr George Duncan in the River Torrens in May 1972, and left him to drown, were eventually brought to trial in 1987 in the South Australian Supreme Court, charged with manslaughter. After a three-week trial, both were found not guilty.

Chapter Eighteen

IVAN MILAT: THE BACKPACKER MURDERS

On 26 March 1996, 51-year old Ivan Robert Marko Milat was led into the New South Wales Supreme Court to face seven counts of murder and one count of attempted murder. He walked confidently into the courtroom with two police officers by his side. With his hair thinning and his skin white from his stay behind bars while on remand, Milat looked as fit and muscular as the day he was arrested almost two years earlier. His piercing blue eyes looked across at the jury as the charges were read out. Counsel for the Prosecution, Mark Tedeschi QC, began his opening address, referring to a raft of physical evidence directly linking Milat to the murders of seven young backpackers whose bodies had been found in shallow graves deep in the Belanglo State Forest, 130 kilometres south of Sydney.

New South Wales Police had executed a search warrant on Milat's home on 22 May 1994, after he had been taken into custody on suspicion of having abducted and killed the seven young men and women. The search revealed items of clothing and camping equipment belonging to the victims in Milat's home. Police also located parts of a Ruger .22 rifle in a crawl space between Milat's house and his garage. Ballistics studies later determined that this was the gun used in the murders of two of the victims found at Belanglo. Police also found Milat's huge personal arsenal, including a loaded automatic pistol, two shotguns, a rifle, cross bows, a bowie knife with a 12-inch blade and a long, curved sword with a razor-sharp cutting edge.

Milat's trial lasted three months, taking evidence from more than 140 witnesses. Milat's defence relied heavily on implications that his brothers Richard and Walter had been involved in the murders. When Ivan Milat took the stand, he denied any involvement in the killings and expressed his belief that police – 'to make me look bad' – had planted the evidence found in his Eaglevale home in Sydney's outer south-western suburbs. But the case against him was watertight, and after three days of deliberation, the jury returned with a verdict of guilty on all counts. Mr Justice David Hunt sentenced Milat to a term of imprisonment for his natural life for the crimes. Milat was never to be released from jail under any circumstances. He would spend his jail time in a cell in New South Wales' 'super-max' prison at Goulburn Jail. The maximum-security facility, a jail within the jail, houses 50 of the worst criminals in the state. There was no hope of escape and Ivan Milat would die behind bars.

⚰ ⚰ ⚰

The bodies of Caroline Clarke, 22, Joanne Walters, 22, Deborah Everist, 19, James Gibson, 19, Simone Schmidl, 21, Gabor Neugebauer, 21, and Anja Habschied, 20, were found in remote bushland in Belanglo State Forest. All seven met their deaths in indescribable terror. They had been abducted, molested and tortured before their agony ended in death at the hands of Ivan Milat. An English traveller, Paul Onions, had escaped his clutches. Onions had accepted a lift from Milat, but just two kilometres before Milat's silver Nissan Patrol 4WD turned into Belanglo, Onions became aware of Milat's intentions and leapt from the vehicle. Milat brazenly fired shots from a handgun as Onions fled along the Hume Highway, but Onions managed to flag down a passing motorist who drove him to the safety of a police station. Paul Onions would later become the prosecution's star witness, and his evidence contributed significantly to Milat's conviction.

Police suspect that Milat killed on many other occasions. On 6 July 2002, a coronial inquest found that he remained a major suspect in the disappearance of three young women in the Newcastle area. The New South Wales State Coroner, John Abernathy, spent a year investigating the disappearances of Leanne Goodall, 20, Robyn Hickie, 18, and Amanda Robinson, 14. He determined that the three girls had been abducted and murdered by a person or persons unknown. In his 60-page report, the State Coroner said that Ivan Milat was of major interest to the investigation. He based his conclusions on Milat's convictions for the backpacker murders and that the inquest had obtained evidence that he had been in the Newcastle area in and around the time the three girls had disappeared. As a road worker, Milat had worked in Newcastle and at the neighbouring beachside town of Swansea in 1978 and 1979 when the girls had gone missing.

Milat gave evidence at the inquest into the deaths of the three women. Under a huge police convoy, he was transported from Goulburn Jail to the Toronto Local Court near Newcastle. In the witness stand, he denied that he had been in the area at the time. He offered some soulless words of comfort to the victims' families. But it was hard to take him seriously. An unidentified woman gave evidence at the inquest, stating that she had seen Milat at a home in the Lower Hunter Valley, near Newcastle, around the time the three women went missing. Counsel assisting the State Coroner, Patrick Saidi, questioned the woman about what he was doing in the area. The woman stated she had seen Milat in Department of Roads clothing and that she was aware that he worked on the roads. Told by Mr Saidi that Milat had given evidence that he had never visited the area, she replied, 'Well, he did.' The Department of Roads employment records, which may have confirmed Milat's presence in the area at the time, had been destroyed. Nevertheless, Mr Abernathy found: 'One cannot discount the involvement of Ivan Milat in any of the disappearances, particularly that of Leanne Goodall.'

Outside the courthouse, Leanne Goodall's mother told reporters that she was particularly horrified at the thought of Milat's involvement in her daughter's disappearance. 'He was such a wicked, evil man,' she said. 'And to just look at him when he was in court terrifies you.'

In 1987 a skeleton of a female backpacker was found in bushland near Taree in the northern part of New South Wales. Milat was believed to be working in the area for the Department of Roads at the time. He is also a suspect in the disappearance of Alan Fox and Anneke Adriaansen. The couple, who had recently become engaged to be married, went missing while hitchhiking between Sydney and the New South Wales North Coast in January 1979. And in January 1988, the body of Peter Letcher, 18, was found in the Kanagara Boyd National Park near Oberon, 160 kilometres west of Sydney. He had disappeared while hitchhiking on 14 November 1987, in an area where Milat was due to commence work resurfacing roads. Peter Letcher had been shot five times in the head with a .22 rifle and his head had been wrapped in material in an identical fashion to that of Belanglo victim Caroline Clarke. Letcher had gone missing on the weekend before Milat's road crew was due to start work nearby. In the minds of investigating police, there is little doubt that Peter Letcher's murder was the evil handiwork of Ivan Milat.

Milat's elder brother Boris told Sydney crime reporters Mark Whittaker and Les Kennedy, 'Everywhere he's worked, people have disappeared. I know where he's been. If Ivan done those [the Belanglo] murders, I reckon he's done a lot more.' Boris Milat speculated that his brother may have killed as many as 28 people. But Ivan Milat remained tight-lipped and refused to assist police with their inquiries.

⚰ ⚰ ⚰

Ivan Robert Marko Milat was born in Sydney on 27 December 1945, the son of Yugoslav parents. He had nine brothers and four sisters. Milat was the fourth born and was raised on the family's spartan property in Moorebank, near Liverpool. His younger sister Margaret died in a car accident in 1971 when she was just 16 years of age. For the most part, he revelled in what was then a semi-rural environment on Sydney's south-western fringes. He was a no-hoper at school. The only thing that gave him any special delight was killing rabbits and other creatures with an air rifle his father had given him. He used to shock his fellow students with stories of torturing and killing animals with knives.

At 17 years of age, Milat notched up his first criminal conviction for stealing and was placed on probation. Later that year, he was brought before the courts again on charges of breaking and entering. This time he was sent to a juvenile institution for six months. Two years after his release, he found his way into trouble again when he was charged with two counts of breaking, entering and stealing. He was sentenced to 18 months' jail. He spent one month in Long Bay Jail before being transferred to the minimum-security prison at Emu Plains, near Penrith, in western Sydney.

In 1965, Milat was convicted of car theft and was sentenced to two years' imprisonment with hard labour. He got a taste of what life for a career criminal had in store: he spent two months of his sentence at the notorious Grafton Prison. Grafton could break a man. Prisoners were beaten on arrival and faced savage attacks from guards for even the most minor infraction of the rules, such as looking a guard in the eye. Now a habitual criminal, in April 1967 he was charged with multiple counts of larceny and car theft. This time he was sentenced to three years' imprisonment, with an 18-month non-parole period. Again Milat was dispatched to Grafton Jail and was subjected to regular beatings by prison guards.

Released in 1969, Milat continued to escalate his criminal activity and began a series of armed robberies with his brother Michael and other accomplices. Milat and his gang would rob suburban milk bars and grocery stores and leave with little more than a few dollars each time. But the effect on their victims, simple shopkeepers trying to eke out a living in their corner stores, was terrifying. Often beaten and staring down the barrel of a shotgun, the shopkeepers were forced to hand over their meagre takings.

Milat and his accomplices graduated to bank robberies shortly afterwards. Ivan was charged with an armed hold-up at a bank in Canley Heights. He and his cohorts left the bank with a mere $360 in cash.

In April 1971, an indication of Milat's more sinister criminal intent surfaced when he was charged with the rape of two girls whom he had picked up in Liverpool. The girls had left a psychiatric hospital earlier that day and were hitchhiking to Melbourne. Both were in a fragile condition when Milat chanced across them. As they were keen to get to Melbourne, they put up with the strange man and his acrid body odour as he chatted to them throughout the drive. Milat's demeanour became more menacing as the drive progressed. Pulling off the Hume Highway onto a dirt track and into bushlands in the Southern Highlands, he allegedly turned to the girls and said, 'I'm going to have sex with both of you. If you don't, I'm going to kill you.' The two girls told of how they tried to calm the man by volunteering to have sex with him. One of the girls allegedly told him, 'If I have sex with you, will you sort of drop us somewhere and we'll let the whole thing go?' Milat had sex with one of the young women, who alleged later that she endured the ordeal in order to save both her and her friend's life. Afterwards, Milat calmly returned to his car and drove the young girls south along the Hume Highway. He stopped at a service station at Goulburn, 180 kilometres south of Sydney. As he went inside to pay for his petrol, one of the girls got out of the car and raised the alarm. Milat quickly jumped back into his car and drove off, heading north back towards Sydney. The two girls reported the nightmarish story to police, and Milat was later charged with rape.

The prospect of facing the rape and robbery charges and a possible return to Grafton did not appeal to Milat, so he fled to New Zealand while on bail, leaving his brother Michael and another accomplice to face the music for the armed robbery. Michael received a long jail sentence for participating in the bank job.

Three years later, Milat returned to Australia. Little is known of the time he spent across the Tasman. However, there is evidence to indicate that he travelled and worked under the pseudonym 'Bill'. He would use this alias in years to come when picking up hitchhikers along the Hume Highway. The court found that there was insufficient evidence to convict Milat for armed robbery and the charges were dismissed. He defended the rape charges by saying that the two girls had consented to his advances. He was found not guilty and walked away a free man.

Ivan Milat had a taste of gainful employment when he joined the Department of Roads as a labourer. The young, powerfully built man proved to be an excellent worker and became a leading hand working with road crews that travelled throughout the state, resurfacing New South Wales' highways and main roads. Milat and the road crews spent hundreds of working hours surfacing the new Hume Highway, which was under construction from Liverpool to Campbelltown and beyond, 55 kilometres from the centre of Sydney.

⚰ ⚰ ⚰

On Saturday, 19 September 1992, two orienteering enthusiasts were preparing to commence the long trek into Belanglo State Forest. Ken Seily and Keith Caldwell were looking forward to a day among the stunning scenery in New South Wales' Southern Highlands. Seily and Caldwell had just passed their fourth checkpoint, near the ominously named 'Executioner's Drop', a sheer cliff face in the Belanglo State Forest. Stopping for a brief rest, Caldwell detected a sharp odour he thought was that of a dead animal. They examined the area and found the remnants of a black T-shirt. With their nerves jangling, they examined the mound more closely. Both recoiled in horror when they saw the heel of a shoe protruding from a stack of branches and leaves.

Police arrived at the scene later that day and cordoned off the area. The following day, two police constables, Roger Gough and Suzanne Roberts, found a second body less than 40 metres from the first makeshift grave. Between the two burial sites police found a campfire made with house bricks. Forensic evidence established the identity of the victims as Caroline Clark and Joanne Walters, both 22, who had been two British backpackers travelling around Australia on a working holiday. They had last been seen leaving a hostel in Kings Cross in December 1989. They had told their friends that they were going to hitchhike to Melbourne to see if they could find work there. An extensive police search of the area did not reveal any more bodies in Belanglo. It would not be until 5 October 1993 when more bodies would be found.

An autopsy revealed that Joanne Walters had been stabbed brutally in the chest, neck and back 14 times. Five of the stab wounds were so vicious that they had severed her spine and broken two ribs. There were no defensive wounds to Joanne's hands or arms, indicating that she had possibly been tied up while her attacker rained down blows with the knife. The depth of the wounds indicated that a bowie knife or a similar type of knife had been used. The zip on Joanne's jeans had been undone, indicating the possibility of sexual assault, but the top button was still done up.

Caroline Clarke had been stabbed just below her neck once with the same knife used on Joanne Walters. Caroline had been shot ten times in the head. Her autopsy revealed four complete bullets and other bullet fragments fired from a .22 calibre firearm. From the entry wounds to Caroline's head ballistics experts would later determine that she had been shot from three different angles. It appeared that she had been tied to a tree and her head used for target practice, her killer turning her head several times before continuing the ghastly deed.

The police sought the assistance of a forensic psychiatrist, Dr Rod Milton, in a bid to understand better the type of person, or persons, who could have committed such terrible crimes. Milton, who had extensive experience in profiling serial killers in Australia, had assisted police in the hunt for the notorious 'Granny Killer', who stalked and killed elderly women in Sydney's North Shore suburbs in 1989 and 1990. Milton's work assisted police to find the perpetrator, John Wayne Glover, a pie salesman who had developed a pathological hatred of older women after vexed relationships with both his mother and mother-in-law.

After examining the scene of the two murders at Belanglo, Milton prepared what proved to be an astonishingly accurate profile of the killer. He believed that the killer would be aged in his thirties, was employed or had been employed in an outdoor job, was involved in a personal relationship with a woman but found this arrangement unsatisfactory. The killer, Milton speculated, would live on the outskirts of the city and was hostile towards police. He also theorised that the killer may not have acted alone. He believed that, if more than one killer had been involved, they could be brothers, with the older dominant sibling overseeing the activities of deferential younger brother. If this were the case, the two brothers would share an obsession with firearms of all types and may have committed sexually motivated crimes together in the past.

Two years prior to the discovery of the bodies of Caroline Clark and Joanne Walters, police were handed information that a person was abducting hitchhikers along the Hume Highway. Crucially, this evidence was ignored until all seven bodies were found in Belanglo State Forest.

⚰ ⚰ ⚰

On 25 January 1990, a year before the disappearance of Simone Schmidl, and 11 months before Anja Habschied and Gabor Neugebauer went missing, English tourist Paul Onions was on the outskirts of Sydney, looking for a lift. The former British navy man and air-conditioning engineer was travelling around Australia. He had spent too long in Sydney and was running out of money. He was going to hitchhike to Mildura in the hope of finding some work there, possibly picking fruit. Leaving a convenience store at Liverpool on the outskirts of Sydney, he was approached by a heavily set man sporting a bushy moustache that reminded Onions of Australian Test fast bowler Dennis Lillee. Onions quickly accepted the offer of a lift. The friendly man, who introduced himself as Bill, told Onions that he was going to Canberra and could get him well on his way.

After an hour and a half on the road, the friendly Bill turned nasty. Following Milat's trial and conviction, Australian *60 Minutes* reporter Charles Wooley and producer Steve Barrett flew to England for an exclusive interview with Paul Onions. He recalled his scrape with death at the hands of Milat in graphic detail:

After about an hour and a half, after we had passed through the township of Mittagong, his speech became aggressive and instead of being a friendly kind of guy he changed all of a sudden. He started checking me out and asking what I'd done for work and things like that.

And then he started complaining about all the people who live in Australia and saying things like there's too many immigrants in this country and going on about the Asians. Although I found it a bit odd, I just agreed with him. I felt a little bit uneasy.

Then he started slowing down a little bit and looking in the rear vision mirrors. He explained that he lost radio reception this far out of town and he wanted to play some tapes that were under the driver's seat. I found this a bit odd because there were tapes on the seat between us.

Then he pulled over to the side of the road and got out and started messing round with the seat. I was a bit nervous and I thought I'd just get out and stretch my legs and try to suss things out.

Milat, who was rummaging around under the driver's seat, was furious that Onions had climbed out of his Nissan Patrol. He ordered him to get back into the car. Moments later, his fears were confirmed when he found himself staring down the barrel of a revolver. He could see the copper-head bullets in the gun's cylinders and realised he was in trouble. Milat told him that he was being robbed, but when he saw Milat produce a length of rope he became truly terrified. He said:

Next thing he had produced a coil of rope and when I saw it I thought, that's it, I'm getting out of here. With that I undid my seatbelt, opened the door, jumped out and ran up the road for my life against the traffic on the highway.

Milat chased after Onions, firing several shots from the handgun in his direction. Frantically, Onions tried to flag down passing cars careering down the Hume Highway, but none would stop. Milat caught up to Onions and grabbed him roughly by his shirt. Again he broke free and ran into the middle of the road, this time determined that someone would stop for him. He recalled:

I turned round and faced the traffic and when the next vehicle, a family van, came across over the rise I put both my hands out in front for it to stop. And as soon as it did I pulled around to the side and opened the sliding door on the passenger side and got in and locked it. There were two women and five children inside and they were all yelling at me to get out and I was saying, 'He's got a gun, he's got a gun.'

The person who stopped for Onions was Joanne Berry, who was travelling with her sister, Gai, and their five children to Canberra. Berry quickly summed up the situation. She could see Milat walking back to his vehicle in the distance, and it was obvious that whatever he had done had scared the young man out of his wits. Berry drove Onions to nearby Berrima police station, but as it was closed she drove the young Englishman a further 10 kilometres to Bowral police station. At Bowral, police took a detailed report of the incident from Onions. He was able to provide a thorough description of his assailant and of his vehicle. A constable, Janet Nicholson, took notes in a notepad while a senior police officer took a formal statement from him. Onions was shown photographs of missing persons and was told by the senior police officer that he had been reckless in hitchhiking in the first place. Berry also provided a brief statement to police, but she told them that she had only seen Onions' assailant returning to his car and did not see his face.

Having had all his possessions taken from him, Onions was given $20 by police and sent on his way. He returned to Sydney that night by train. Inexplicably, Onion's report was lost by the local police. Tragically, three more lives would be taken after the attempted abduction of Paul Onions.

⚰ ⚰ ⚰

On Tuesday, 5 October 1993, a local man, Bruce Pryor, was in Belanglo State Forest collecting firewood when he came across human remains partially buried under a pile of branches and leaves near a fire road known as the Morrice Creek Fire Trail. Pryor, who had attended a community meeting organised by police to get information in relation to the murders of Caroline Clarke and Joanne Walters, instinctively knew that he had found the body of another victim. Detectives were called to the scene and shortly afterwards another body was found. The two bodies were later identified by dental records as Deborah Everist and James Gibson, two friends who had been hitchhiking their way about eastern Australia. They had last been seen on 30 December 1989 on the Hume Highway, looking for a lift to Melbourne.

Deborah Everist had been stabbed in the spine and had numerous fractures to the skull. A pair of pantyhose and a black bra were found nearby. The bra had been slashed with a knife. Detectives believed that the bra and pantyhose had been used to restrain Deborah. James Gibson had multiple stab wounds to his spine, breastbone and chest. As with the previous victims, one stab wound had penetrated James's mid-thoracic spine, slicing upwards, effectively paralysing him. The zip on James's trousers was open but, as with Joanne Walters, the top button remained closed.

With four bodies found in Belanglo, New South Wales Police quickly established a task force, which became known as Task Force Air, under the command of one of Australia's most noted detectives, Commander Clive Small. Small appointed Detective Rod Lynch to coordinate the task force's investigation from Sydney. Small remained close by to the murder scenes, taking up temporary residence in Bowral. The most immediate task Small faced was to oversee a search of Belanglo to determine if any more bodies lay within it.

On 31 October 1993, the body of German hitchhiker Simone Schmidl was found. The now familiar site of branches and foliage over the body alerted searchers to her partially clothed body. She had been stabbed numerous times in the chest. Again there was the characteristic downward stab wound in her upper back, severing her spinal cord.

Two days later the bodies of Anja Habschied and Gabor Neugebauer were found. The two German backpackers had disappeared while hitchhiking along the Hume Highway south of Sydney on Boxing Day, 1991. It took three police officers to lift the heavy log off Gabor's body. The young man had been gagged and probably died of strangulation. There were six bullet wounds to his skull, and again the zip on his jeans was undone but the top button was done up. Anja Habschied had been decapitated and her clothing had been pulled up above her chest. Forensic specialists determined that her head had been removed with a long, sharp instrument such as a sword. It appeared that she had been forced into a kneeling position, and then beheaded.

Most of the seven victims had been paralysed by a knife to the spine. All had been tortured and in all probability sexually assaulted. Members of Task Force Air, led by Commander Small, realised that all seven victims had died at the hands of a serial killer or killers. Experienced investigators believed the killings were all linked but that they may have been the work of a couple or group. Investigators in the task force believed it unlikely that just one man could have tied up his victims single-handedly. The huge log thrown onto the body of Gabor Neugebauer almost certainly had to be lifted by more than man.

🪦 🪦 🪦

By mid-1994, Task Force Air had arrived at a list of 2000 persons of interest. There were 40 detectives attached to the task force, and they worked around the clock, following up every piece of information that came across their desks. But the report from Paul Onions of his attempted abduction by the beefy man known as Bill, with the flowing moustache, remained buried in the burgeoning files relating to the murders. The task force was receiving information from around the world. Meticulously, they scoured every piece of it, looking for a break in the case.

A woman had come forward stating that she knew a man named Ivan Milat who lived near Belanglo, had plenty of guns and drove a silver Nissan Patrol. Another Milat, Ivan's eldest brother, Alex, had provided a detailed statement saying that he had seen two women being taken into Belanglo State Forest. Detectives decided to pay Ivan Milat a visit.

Two detectives turned up at a worksite that was the last-known address for Ivan Milat. They learned that Ivan's brother Richard also worked there. Scanning through employment records and punch clock cards, they found that Richard had been working on the days that the backpackers had disappeared, but that Ivan had not been working on any of these days. Ivan's workmates often referred to him as Bill, a nickname that appeared to be in frequent use. And Ivan had a flowing moustache some years ago but had since shaved it off. Digging further, detectives discovered that Ivan Milat now owned a red Holden Jackaroo, but some years earlier had owned and driven a silver Nissan Patrol. They also found that he had a substantial criminal record, but that most of his convictions were for stealing and car theft and he had not been in any trouble with the police for some time. What most attracted the interest of the detectives was that Milat had been charged with rape in 1971. Although he was later acquitted, statements from the two girls indicated that they had been hitchhiking south of Sydney and had been offered a lift by Milat. They alleged that he drove them further south and off the Hume Highway into remote bushland where he tied them up. He was alleged to have raped one of the girls.

Ivan Milat had just become a suspect in the 'backpacker murders'.

At the same time, Task Force Air was pursuing another lead. Workers at a concrete manufacturing company had come forward and spoken to police about one of their work mates, Paul Miller. Miller was a drunk and a habitual marijuana smoker. He was off with the pixies most of the time and the silly things he said to his workmates in the lunchroom at the factory weren't taken too seriously. But when the bodies of Joanne Walters and Caroline Clarke were discovered in 1992, Miller told some of his coworkers some startling information. He said: 'There's more bodies out there. They haven't found the two Germans yet. Oh yeah, I know who killed those two Germans.'

Later, the notoriously unstable Miller said: 'Stabbing a woman is like cutting a loaf of bread.' He also told workmates: 'You could pick up anybody on that road and you'd never find them again. You'd never find out who did it either.' A cursory check into Paul Miller revealed his identity as Richard Milat, one of Ivan's younger brothers. Police began to concentrate the investigation on the Milats, and on Ivan in particular.

⚰ ⚰ ⚰

A year earlier, Paul Onions had tried to contact the task force. Now residing in Birmingham, England, Onions had heard of the discovery of the seven bodies in Belanglo State Forest. He still had nightmares about his journey south of Sydney in Bill's Nissan Patrol and he knew he was lucky to have survived. He wondered why police had not contacted him. After a conversation with an Australian friend, he decided to go to police and tell them his story again. He wandered down to his local police station in England and told a detective what had happened to him. The detective contacted the Australian Embassy in London, and Onions was put in touch with a detective from Task Force Air. He told the story of his attempted abduction near Belanglo and of the man named Bill with the flowing moustache. The detective took all the information down and filed it in among the reams of paperwork already attached to the investigation.

It was not until 13 April 1994, when Detective Paul Gordon was trawling through the extensive reports attached to the investigation, that Onion's report was taken seriously. Detective Gordon read the report with increasing interest. He thought Paul Onions was the witness the task force was looking for. Onions had a clear recollection of the man and his vehicle. Detective Gordon passed the report directly to Commander Small. Small was angry and disappointed that the report had been disregarded. He requested a copy of the original report, filed at Bowral police station. His frustration grew when he was told that the original report, including the statements from Paul Onions and Joanne Berry, had been lost. Luckily, Constable Janet Nicholson had kept her notebook containing the detail of Onions' statement. Now Commander Small knew that Task Force Air was closing in on Ivan Milat.

Paul Onions was flown to Australia at the request of the task force ten days later. Onions took detectives from the shop in Liverpool down south towards Belanglo. His evidence was unfailing. Detectives stopped the car where Milat had stopped his silver Nissan Patrol four years earlier. They told Onions that they were just two kilometres from the entrance to Belanglo State Forest. Onions then understood just how close he had come to death. He returned to task force headquarters and identified Ivan Milat from a video line-up of 13 men.

⚰ ⚰ ⚰

It was time for Task Force Air to act. In dawn raids on 22 May 1994, more than 300 police officers hit Ivan Milat's home in Eaglevale, the homes of his brothers Richard, Walter and Bill, a property owned by two of the Milat brothers in the Southern Highlands and the home of Alex Milat, who lived in Queensland. Ivan Milat was sleeping soundly at 6.30 am with his girlfriend, Challinder Hughes. They were both awoken by the phone ringing. Detective Wayne Gordon told Milat that there were 50 heavily armed police waiting outside for him, and that there was no chance of escape and he and anyone in the house with him should walk calmly out the door one at a time. Milat put down the telephone. Police heard the signs of scurrying inside the home. Detective Gordon called Milat again, who told Gordon that he thought one of his workmates was playing a prank. The police negotiator assured him the matter was serious. Edgy and nervous, police waited outside for Milat to appear. They thought he might try to make a run for it. Minutes later Milat walked out of the front door and was handcuffed by police without a struggle.

The raids provided police with a treasure trove of evidence.

Milat's arsenal was discovered. The dismantled Ruger .22 was found. Ominously, police found a drinking bottle belonging to Simone Schmidl. The canteen had the name 'Simi' etched on to it. Caroline Clarke's camera was there too. A photograph of Milat's girlfriend was found in which she was wearing a Benneton windcheater that had belonged to Caroline Clarke. Two sleeping bags that belonged to Simone Schmidl and Deborah Everist were also found.

Meanwhile, in the raids of the other Milat properties, police found a huge amount of ammunition, and weapons including shotguns, rifles and crossbows. There were knives and camping gear that belonged to the victims. At the home of Milat's mother, Margaret, a long, curved cavalry sword was found. Police believed that this was the weapon used to decapitate Anja Habschied.

Ivan Milat played dumb throughout the police interviews. He pretended he was deaf on occasions. But the police remained patient. They knew that the evidence they had obtained during the raids on Milat's home would come up trumps. They were going to charge him with armed robbery in relation to the Paul Onions matter in any case. Milat wasn't going anywhere. He was ultimately charged with seven counts of murder and one count of attempted murder.

However, Task Force Air was not finished yet. They continued to investigate the possibility that other family members, notably Richard and Walter Milat, had been involved. They tried to get proof of their involvement. Wiretaps and other electronic surveillance devices were put in place after Ivan Milat's arrest in the hope that one of his brothers would slip up. If they had anything to say about their involvement, they didn't let on. No charges have ever been laid against any other member of the Milat family in relation to the backpacker murders. Eventually, Richard and Walter were charged with several firearms offences, but neither received custodial sentences.

As Ivan Milat waited in the dock, Justice David Hunt told the jury:

> It is sufficient here to record that each of the victims was attacked savagely and cruelly, with force which was unusual and vastly more than was necessary to cause death, and for some of psychological gratification. Each of two of the victims was shot a number of times in the head. A third was decapitated in circumstances which establish that she would have been alive at the time. The stab wounds to each of the other three would have caused paralysis, two of them having

had their spinal cords completely severed. The multiple stab wounds to each of the other three would have been likely to have penetrated their hearts. There are signs that two of them were strangled. All but one appears to have been sexually interfered with before or after death.

Ivan Milat was found guilty of seven counts of murder and one count of attempted murder on Saturday, 27 July 1996. Asked by Justice Hunt if he had anything to say, Milat replied: 'I'm not guilty of it. That's all I have to say.'

Soon afterwards, Milat was transferred to Maitland Prison in the Hunter Valley, north of Sydney, to begin his life sentence. The new arrivals at the prison stood in a corridor, Ivan Milat among them, awaiting the issue of blankets and clothing. A burly, heavily tattooed inmate approached the group. 'Where's Milat?' he demanded. Silently, the group turned to Milat. The prisoner threw a series of lightning punches connecting heavily to Milat's jaw and cheek. Milat dropped like a stone. 'Welcome to Maitland, cunt,' the inmate commented.

Milat conspired to escape the walls of Maitland Prison with convicted drug dealer George Savvas on 17 May 1997. Both were dispatched to solitary confinement. Savvas committed suicide by hanging himself with bed sheets shortly afterwards.

On 26 February 1998, the New South Wales Court of Appeal unanimously rejected Milat's appeal and ordered him to spend the remainder of his life behind bars. In becoming one of the worst of the worst residents at Goulburn Jail's 'super-max' facility, Milat could do little but stare at the walls. On 27 October 2019, Ivan Milat died from oesophagus and stomach cancer at 4:07 am within the hospital wing at Long Bay Correctional Centre. He was 74 years old.

Chapter Nineteen

NEDDY SMITH AND THE BONES OF HARVEY JONES

When wannabe gangster Harvey François Jones disappeared on the evening of 15 July 1983, no-one except his dear old mum seemed to be all that surprised. After all, the last person Jones was allegedly seen in the company of was Neddy Smith, who, at the time, was the undisputed king of the Sydney underworld.

And the fact that Jones was reputed to be carrying a large parcel of cash only fuelled the clandestine scuttlebutt that Neddy had seen his old drinking mate off and helped himself to the loot. But suspect as they may, no-one was saying much – at least not out loud. Not even the police. Such was the fear that Neddy had etched into the carnivorous world of organised crime in Sydney in the early 1980s that he ruled with fists of tungsten and a smoking gun.

Neddy Smith was 'the man'. He had been given the 'green light' from the crooked cops in the New South Wales police force. This was an honour never before bestowed upon a criminal, and it meant that Neddy could do as he pleased, providing he didn't kill a police officer. Bank robberies, SP betting, narcotics trafficking, extortion, murder – you name it – and naturally enough, the bent cops had to get their whack of the earnings.

Neddy Smith and Harvey Jones were an odd alliance. A thin man almost two metres tall, 29-year-old Jones covered himself in crass imitation jewellery and was a gangster groupie and a notorious pest. He was also an obnoxious drunk, and over the years he had rubbed lots of hard men up the wrong way. He only managed to stay alive through the heavy company he kept, such as Neddy Smith.

Harvey Jones always carried a 'Dirty Harry' .44 Smith and Wesson magnum handgun and was partial to producing and shooting it wherever he happened to be imbibing at the time, terrorising other patrons and staff. Seeing as he did this with regular monotony and usually in Neddy's company, Jones relied heavily on his fearsome mate to get him out of trouble when the proprietor of the establishment invariably complained to the police.

Harvey Jones's claim to gangster fame was that he dealt in drugs, sold used cars on Parramatta Road, collected debts with the help of his big gun and managed a brothel at Homebush in Sydney's inner west. He always had large amounts of money in his pocket and didn't mind spending it. Jones had always aspired to be a gangster.

In the mid 1970s he was a 62-kilogram firefighter who lived with his mother and told his sceptical workmates of his after-hours escapades with the likes of 'George' (George Freeman), 'Len' (Lenny 'Mr Big' McPherson) and 'Abe' (Abraham Saffron), and how he used to do 'contract hits' for them. The tall, skinny Jones, with his mop of long, curly hair, drove an extras-laden Ford Cortina with 'Love Bandit' painted along the side. He supplemented his meagre income by selling marijuana, stealing from the fires that he attended in his job and breaking and entering shops and houses on the weekends and at night.

Sacked from the fire brigade, Jones took up hooning off prostitutes. With the money he earned he opened a car yard at the newly established Upper Wentworth Centre at Homebush. Other car dealers moved into the centre, and business boomed enough for Jones to indulge in an extravagant nightlife around the Sydney nightclubs with an entourage of prostitutes and low-life hangers-on.

By 1980, the now very affluent Jones was also managing the Upper Wentworth brothel and driving a metallic green Porsche Targa when he was pinched for his part in a $450,000 gold bar robbery from Transurety Australia. Fourteen gold bars weighing 50 ounces each had gone missing from the company's safe.

Neddy first met Jones in Long Bay Jail when Neddy was in for a parole violation and Jones was on remand for the stolen bullion charge and another of harbouring an escaped prisoner. The next time they caught up was at Stars Disco in Bondi in the early 1980s when Jones, out on bail after being committed for trial, jumped the bar, held a gun to the barman's head and demanded that Neddy be served before shooting a few holes in the ceiling. Neddy allegedly arranged a $14,000 bribe to be paid to a prominent detective to make any possible charges over the incident go away.

In his 1993 autobiography, *Neddy*, Smith claims that he became friendly with Jones and they would often go out on the drink together. According to Neddy, the night would always end up in a fight, with him having to do all the fighting because Jones couldn't hold his hands in the air. Smith claimed that he was forever getting Jones out of trouble after Jones produced his gun and shot at something or another in public places. After a while Neddy made it no secret that he was tiring of his gun-slinging mate. There were also persistent rumours that Jones might be gay, and that wasn't Neddy's pound of steak.

In 1981 Jones had been committed to stand trial on the bullion charge. According to Jones's elderly mother, in whom Jones was said to confide everything, her son was arranging to pay a senior detective $60,000 through Neddy to have the charges dropped.

In mid-1983, as the court case loomed, Jones was seen to be rounding up as much cash as he could to pay the bribe. While still working as manager at the Upper Wentworth brothel on a supposed wage of $2000 a week, he was also pawning jewellery, borrowing money from friends, selling sports cars and dealing in any commodity that might produce a buck.

One of the last people to see Jones alive was Brian Rowe, the owner of the Upper Wentworth, who said that he saw Jones at the Homebush Hotel about 6.00 pm on the night of 15 July 1983. Jones told Rowe that the previous evening he and an associate had been thrown out of a bar in North Sydney, so they had gone back and shot the place up. Jones was carrying a large amount of money and said that he was on his way into town to meet some detectives to have a charge against him dropped. Whether it was for the previous night's effort or the bullion charges wasn't made clear.

From there Jones vanished. Smith didn't deny that he had an appointment to meet Jones that night but claimed that Jones never turned up. But when Harvey Jones did turn up many years later, Neddy Smith had a lot of explaining to do.

⚰ ⚰ ⚰

Arthur Stanley 'Neddy' Smith was born in the inner-Sydney working-class suburb of Redfern on 27 November 1944. The name 'Neddy' was bestowed upon him by his uncle Dick for no particular reason. He was the second of six children in a fatherless family. His father was a United States serviceman who had left shortly after Neddy was conceived.

By 13 he had had enough of Cleveland Street Boys High School and decided on a life of crime. Between 1959 and 1961 young Neddy was in and out of institutions for stealing, assault and breaking and entering. In May 1963, he was sentenced to six years in jail on 13 counts of breaking, entering and stealing. In jail he learned to be as tough as nails. Early in 1967 he came out of jail, more than 180 centimetres tall, weighing 100 kilograms and with the ferocious reputation of a man who wouldn't take a backward step and could fight like a threshing machine.

After being convicted in June 1967 of the violent rape of a 20-year-old Petersham woman, Neddy and Robert Arthur 'Bobby' Chapman were sentenced to 12 years in prison with a minimum term of seven years. When sentencing the two men, Mr Justice Reynolds said that the woman had been raped in circumstances of 'appalling depravity'. The judge told Neddy that his action of 'spitting on the woman when raping her indicated a warped and perverted mind'. Neddy served eight years in Long Bay, Parramatta and Grafton – regarded as the most brutal jails in New South Wales. He was tougher than ever when he was released in March 1975.

In November 1976, Neddy was arrested by Detective Sergeant Roger Rogerson of the Armed Hold-up Squad and charged with two counts of shooting with intent to murder, assault with attempt to rob, attempted armed robbery and possessing an unlicensed pistol. But at Rogerson's instigation, he and Neddy struck a deal and it was found that there was no case to answer on all charges, except that of possession of an unlicensed pistol. So the charges were dropped, and eventually Neddy's conviction on the pistol charge was quashed on appeal. More importantly, Neddy was now Rogerson's underworld confidante.

⚰ ⚰ ⚰

It was only a matter of time before Neddy got into the lucrative narcotics trade, first as an enforcer and then as a dealer. By early 1977 his financial situation had improved dramatically. He bought a house in Henry Street in the inner-western suburb of Sydenham and turned it into an electronic fortress surrounded by three-metre walls, security doors and windows, and closed-circuit television surveillance cameras. While those close to him maintained that the paranoiac security was to protect his family, drug squad detectives thought differently. They believed that it was to prevent him from being robbed of a valuable substance – pure heroin. Big bags of it. In 1978 Neddy's tapped telephone conversations confirmed the police's suspicions and revealed startling information about a heroin smuggling ring that was responsible for shifting up to 11.3 kilograms of the drug every month. This was one of the biggest operations in the country and represented about 15 per cent of the 1978 heroin consumption in New South Wales.

The *Age* Tapes Royal Commission report by Mr Justice Stewart into the heroin ring said:

> By listening to Smith's conversations it was learnt that Smith was organising and financing heroin importation from Thailand. The names of a Bangkok bar owner, William (Bill) Sinclair, a Manly hairdresser, Warren Fellows, and Paul Hayward, a well-known Newtown Rugby League football star as well as others involved were mentioned and details of the importation were discussed.
>
> NSW police passed on the information to Thai authorities and Sinclair, Fellows and Hayward were arrested in Bangkok and charged with possession of 8.4 kilograms of the highest quality No 4 Dragon Pearl heroin, worth about $3 million retail on the streets of Sydney.
>
> All three were convicted and given long gaol sentences. Bill Sinclair vehemently maintained his innocence and on appeal was granted a new trial. On 24 January, 1983, he was acquitted and returned to Australia.

It was later revealed that the most active courier, 26-year-old Warren Fellows, was paid $60,000 per trip to bring suitcases with as much as 13 kilograms of Thai heroin through Australian Customs.

Police raided Neddy's fortress in Sydenham on 12 October 1978, the day after the arrest of Sinclair, Fellows and Hayward in Bangkok, and found $39,360 in cash and a receipt for a safety deposit box at the Marrickville branch of the ANZ Bank. In the box they found $90,100 in cash, $10,000 worth of diamonds and a short manual on 'how to get a container past customs'. Neddy and his de facto wife, Debra Joy Bell, were charged with possession of money unlawfully obtained.

Drug squad detectives raided homes all over Sydney in the following weeks and recovered hundreds of thousands of dollars in cash and vast amounts of heroin. Neddy's stepbrother, Edwin 'Teddy' Smith, was one of the villains arrested and was found to be in possession of 1.5 kilograms of high-grade heroin. Teddy pleaded guilty and was sentenced to ten years in the slammer. Charged with having 'goods in custody' (the sum of $39,360), Neddy got six months. As this was also a parole violation, he was also expected to finish off the four years outstanding from the 1967 rape sentencing. It was during this term in Long Bay Jail that he met Harvey Jones.

Neddy was released in October 1980, two years earlier than expected, by means of a succession of appeals to the High Court by his highly paid legal advisers. Out of the 'can', he teamed up with Warren Lanfranchi, a heroin dealer and thief he had met in prison. By mid-1981, Lanfranchi was having problems with the police. They wanted to speak to him about several bank robberies and the attempted murder of a police officer. Lanfranchi had aimed a handgun at a traffic officer's face and pulled the trigger but the gun had misfired. The police do not like people who try to kill their fellow officers, particularly heroin dealers such as Lanfranchi. They wanted him to pay for what he had done. It would be Neddy Smith who would give the police what they wanted.

Lanfranchi, 22, didn't want to go back to prison and had made it known that, if cornered by police, he would shoot it out. But there was an easier way: Neddy allegedly offered Detective Sergeant Roger Rogerson $50,000 on Lanfranchi's behalf to have the investigations dropped. Rogerson agreed to discuss the matter and a meeting was arranged with Lanfranchi at a secret spot. On the afternoon of Saturday, 27 June 1981, Neddy drove Lanfranchi in a green BMW to a narrow lane called Dangar Place in Chippendale, just a few minutes' drive from the heart of Sydney. According to his girlfriend, Sallie-Anne Huckstepp, Lanfranchi had $10,000 in $50 notes stuffed down the front of his trousers and was unarmed when he left home for the meeting. At 2.50 pm Neddy parked the BMW near the entrance to Dangar Place and watched as Lanfranchi walked with his hands above his head down the lane towards Rogerson, about 40 metres away. What Lanfranchi didn't know was that Rogerson was not alone. The laneway was surrounded by 18 heavily armed police.

According to Rogerson's statement, Lanfranchi said to him as they finally met face to face: 'I can't do any more jail. Are we going to do business?'

'There is no business. We are here to arrest you for the attempted murder of a police officer,' replied Rogerson.

Realising that he had walked into a trap, Lanfranchi allegedly produced a gun from the front of his trousers and aimed it at Rogerson, who also drew a gun and shot Lanfranchi twice, in the neck and the heart, killing him instantly. Lanfranchi had not fired a shot. The gun found lying beside Lanfranchi's body was more than 20 years old and had a defective firing mechanism. It had no fingerprints on it. And there was no sign of the alleged $10,000 that Lanfranchi's girlfriend said he had concealed down the front of his pants.

At the coronial inquiry in November 1981 into the shooting of Warren Lanfranchi, thanks largely to evidence given by Neddy Smith, it was found that Detective Sergeant Roger Rogerson had protected himself 'while endeavouring to effect an arrest'. Acting for the Lanfranchi family, Ian Barker QC said that it was open to conjecture as to 'whether the deceased did in fact have a gun at the material time'. As Smith would later testify in court, it was soon after he had delivered Lanfranchi that crooked police decided to give him the 'green light'. Naturally, the crooked police wanted their whack. The only condition to the 'green light' was that Neddy wasn't allowed to kill or harm a police officer. Apart from that, it was open slather.

Meanwhile, as Neddy was endearing himself to the police by carrying out armed hold-ups and sometimes being driven away from crime scenes in a police car, things weren't looking good on the heroin charge of a couple of years earlier. His stepbrother, Teddy, had had enough of being in jail and had cut a deal with the federal police. He would tell them everything he knew about Neddy's alleged heroin dealing in exchange for remissions on his jail term and immunity from further prosecution.

At the 1980 Woodward Royal Commission into drug trafficking in New South Wales, Teddy Smith sang like Pavarotti and became the first hood ever to spill the beans on organised crime in New South Wales. He told the Commission that he had been inside Neddy's Sydenham fortress when he took delivery of a suitcase containing 30 one-pound bags of pure heroin. Teddy claimed that Neddy started dancing around the room saying, 'I'm rich, I'm rich.' Further, he claimed that by using an ordinary domestic blender to remove the lumps, Neddy adulterated 13 ounces of pure No. 4 Golden Dragon Pearl heroin with three ounces of Glucodin powder to make up one-pound packets, which he sold in sealed plastic bags. Packaging the three-ounce shares of pure heroin into one- and two-ounce packets, he sold them to friendly dealers without telling his partners.

Teddy also alleged to the Commission that during mid-1978 he made three deliveries a day of half-pound and one-pound packets of heroin for Neddy, to cars parked in Sydney's eastern suburbs. Driving past the assigned car at slow speed, he dropped the package into the vehicle's back window, which was wound down a few inches. At the peak of the operation, Neddy employed 14 people and was moving up to 25 pounds of heroin a month. And Neddy was rich. Very rich. His stable of cars included a BMW, a Mercedes and a Porsche, and he owned the fortress at Sydenham, a half-share in a $17,000 speedboat and extensive jewellery, which included a $32,000 diamond ring. According to Teddy, Neddy had once told him that, while there were millionaires in the world who had it in assets, 'he would be one of the only ones who had it in cash'.

On the strength of his stepbrother's evidence, Neddy was charged with conspiracy to supply heroin. On the second day of his trial in May 1980, the prime witness, Teddy, had a sudden change of heart and admitted to the court that he had deliberately given false evidence and that everything he had said about Neddy's involvement in the heroin trade was fabricated. He said that Neddy was in fact a choir boy who was misunderstood. The prosecution could not believe what it was hearing. Judge Alistair Muir instructed the jury that, on the grounds of lack of evidence, Neddy had to be acquitted. But change of heart or not, the non-parole period of Edwin William Teddy Smith's ten-year sentence for heroin possession was reduced considerably, to run from his arrest on 27 October 1978 to 26 August 1982. When he was eventually released from prison, Teddy Smith left town in a hurry.

⚰ ⚰ ⚰

When Harvey Jones went missing in 1983, his mother was frantic and rang the police, who conducted an investigation. Given Jones's track record and the company he kept, it was little wonder they had great difficulty finding anyone to cooperate.

In his 1993 autobiography, *Neddy*, Neddy casually explains away the disappearance of Harvey Jones. He claims that an irate detective had rung him on the morning of 15 July and told him that Jones and an associate, a particularly unpleasant piece of work named 'Bob the Basher', had been thrown out of a disco the previous evening and had gone back later and put two shots into the ceiling before being ejected again. The detective was concerned because these events had occurred on his 'turf' and the disco owners paid him protection money to ensure that these kinds of things never happened. Smith claims that he then rang Jones, and after giving him a blast for about ten minutes, he said that he would telephone the detective to see what he wanted to do about it. Smith claims to have calmed the detective, then rang Jones back and said that he could get him off the hook, asking Jones how much money he could get his hands on straightaway. Jones said that he could come up with $30,000 on short notice. Smith claims to have rung the detective back and persuaded him to accept this amount, which he would have to him that night. He rang Jones back and arranged to meet him at the Star Hotel in inner-city Alexandria early that evening. According to Smith, Jones never turned up.

Not so, according to a statement to police by Bob the Basher, who claimed that he saw Jones earlier in the night and that Jones had had a bag of money to give Smith. The Basher also claimed that he saw Smith meet Jones outside the Star Hotel a little later, and then walk in. The Basher saw Smith emerge alone from the Star Hotel about an hour later. He had not seen or heard of Harvey Jones since. When police presented Neddy with this statement, Neddy handed it back, saying that it was rubbish. Allegedly, he was asked to sign a formal letter of denial of the statement, but he never did so, saying instead that his detective friends had vouched for him.

Three days after Harvey Jones disappeared, Neddy was taped talking to a detective about a bludger he knew who was missing. He told former detective sergeant Ron Daly, who was being recorded by Australian Federal Police:

> *I gotta find the bludger. His mother's cryin'. No-one can find him. If I can't find him it's no good for business.*

Listen, mate, he's an imbecile. But, ah, his mum rang me and ah, apparently he's, ah, pissed off or somethin'. His mother's worried sick about him. Bloody idiot hasn't even rang her. Mate, I don't really, I don't want to help the cunt but his mother is a nice old lady ... she's about 60 and he worries the Christ out of her. If I were her, I'd hit him over the head with a house brick.

In his book Neddy claims that Jones's mother kept ringing him, crying, and asking if he could come to see her as she was too old to travel to his home. Neddy says that he went to her house and took his wife, Debra, with him to see if she could do something to help Harvey's mother, who was terribly upset. Smith says that he and his wife stayed a few hours, offering consolation, then left, promising to keep in touch. But they never did.

⚰ ⚰ ⚰

During the next four years, thanks to the 'green light', Neddy's charmed existence continued. He became the highest-profile gangster in the history of organised crime in Australia. Throughout the 1980s, under the protection of the 'green light', he and his gang netted more than $600,000 from armed robberies, operated one of the biggest SP betting networks in Australia and imported and distributed millions of dollars worth of drugs. It was the era of the infamous New South Wales 'Gang Wars', when opposed underworld factions fought it out, sometimes in the streets, for control of the lucrative drug trade. It seemed as if, every day, someone was shot. Usually, Neddy managed to get a mention in the press somewhere, and as luck would have it, he emerged from it all unscathed.

Neddy's luck held out again on the morning of 2 April 1986. As he was leaving the Iron Duke Hotel in the inner-Sydney working-class suburb of Waterloo and was walking to his car, a Holden sedan burst from behind a line of trees, mounted the footpath and ran into him, slamming him against a wall. It is likely that anyone else would have been killed. But not the tungsten-tough Neddy. The badly battered gangster dragged himself back to the hotel, where he was consoled by the proprietor until an ambulance arrived to take him to hospital. Diagnosed with six broken ribs, a broken leg and suspected fractures of the spine, a heavily plastered and bandaged Neddy was interviewed by television news crews and photographed by the press the following day as he was eased into a car in front of the hospital, after defying the doctor's orders and discharging himself.

The next day, on crutches, Neddy arrived at Channel Nine by helicopter and appeared nationally on the current affairs show *Willesee*. He described himself as an 'average knockabout bloke' whose reputation as an underworld figure and enforcer was a fabrication of the media and was totally undeserved. He told the interviewer Ray Martin that he knew the driver of the car that had run him over. He said: 'This man is in close with the police. The police and certain crooks want me out of the way so they have teamed up. I have trod on quite a few toes.' Furthermore, Neddy said, he was an invalid pensioner who had suffered from Parkinson's disease for six years and he provided for his wife and family by the pension, gambling, borrowing from friends and sometimes stealing things off the back of trucks. He admitted that at one stage he had been a 'debt collector and stand-over man', but he had never had to 'thump anyone'. He maintained that he was broke and 'didn't have two bob to rub together'.

On 26 April 1986, Terrence Edwin Ball, a 41-year-old Sydney pensioner, was charged with the attempted hit-and-run murder of Neddy Smith. At Ball's trial, Neddy failed to identify him as the man who had tried to run him over and the charge was dismissed.

After more press than even the high-profile Neddy could take, he decided to move his wife, Debra, and their three young children to the New South Wales city of Newcastle, about 200 kilometres north of Sydney. The Smiths' transport of a Rolls Royce or Mercedes-Benz would change every couple of months. It was routine for a car to pick up Neddy on Monday mornings and return him to Newcastle on Friday nights to spend the weekend around the pool with his family.

⚰ ⚰ ⚰

On 30 October 1987, Neddy Smith did something very out of character. In a drunken frenzy, he committed murder in a public place and in front of approximately 70 witnesses. It should never have happened. Over a minor traffic altercation, Neddy stabbed another motorist to death in busy Coogee Bay Road and fled. Only hours later he was picked up by police and charged with murder. Then, amid howls of protest from the

State Opposition, on 2 December 1987, he was granted bail of $50,000 on the murder charge after being formally refused twice at earlier hearings. Bail was granted on the grounds that Neddy hadn't had a conviction in eight years, was the father of three children and was suffering from the advanced stages of Parkinson's disease.

On 21 December 1988, police spotted Neddy and a couple of men casing the Botany Municipal Chambers in South Sydney. The fact that the $160,000 Christmas payroll was due to arrive the next morning was no coincidence. The following day, at dawn, armed police took up positions in the council building, the nearby fire station and other locations. After the payroll vans arrived, Armed Hold-up Squad detectives approached a white Holden panel van parked nearby and told its occupants to come out with their hands in the air. Neddy, Glen Roderick Flack, 32, and Richard John Harris, 27, emerged from the van, wearing green sweaters and white gloves. A search of the van revealed a loaded .357 magnum pistol, a sawn-off 12-gauge shotgun, two black balaclavas, a walkie-talkie and a carry bag.

There was no bail for Neddy this time. At his trial, on 9 September 1989, he pleaded guilty to all of the charges relating to the bungled robbery attempt and was given a prison term of 13 years. But that was only the half of it – he still had his murder trial to come.

The murder trial began on 20 February 1990. The court was told by Mark Tedeschi QC for the Crown that, on the day of the alleged murder, Neddy had spent most of the day drinking with a friend and was on his way along Coogee Bay Road to the Coogee Sports Club at about 9.00 pm. For some unknown reason, the Honda (owned by Neddy's wife but driven by his friend) stopped in the line of traffic, Tedeschi said. A tow truck could not pass and its driver, Thomas Millane, flashed his lights a couple of times.

The Crown alleged that Smith and his companion got out of their car and began fighting with Millane and his passenger, 34-year-old Ronnie Flavell. Millane heard Flavell's call for help before seeing his friend lying on his back over the bonnet of a car parked nearby, the jury heard. Neddy Smith was standing over Flavell, and Millane saw what he thought was Smith punching Flavell with his free hand. But, as he pulled Smith away, Millane noticed a bloodied knife in Smith's hand. The jury heard that Smith threatened Millane with the knife before jumping back into his car and driving away. Ronnie Flavell died in surgery shortly after in Prince of Wales Hospital, Randwick.

Neddy was found guilty of murder, and on 16 March 1990, Mr Justice McInerney sentenced him to life imprisonment. But because the killing took place in 1987, prior to the 1989 truth-in-sentencing legislation, which meant that a life sentence meant exactly that, Neddy's life sentence could be reduced to a fixed term on appeal and he could hold out hopes of being released some day.

⚰ ⚰ ⚰

For a crook as smart as Neddy Smith, he must have spent a lot of long lonely hours in his prison cell, wondering how he had wound up back in the joint. His rat cunning and superior criminal ability to negotiate between all of the warring factions of the Sydney underworld had seen him rise to the top of his profession without a conviction in nearly a decade. Everything had been running like clockwork. He had wreaked fear and havoc wherever he went. Neddy was 'the man'. A real tough guy. But his winning streak seemed to have ended. It was now that he decided he had had enough of life behind bars and didn't want to die there. He realised that the only way to have a chance of ever getting out of jail alive, to die in his own bed surrounded by his family, was to rat on his alleged former business associates in the hope that the authorities would show him leniency.

In mid-1992 Neddy began talking to Independent Commission Against Corruption (ICAC) agents, who came to his prison cell to see what he had to offer. Under the deal they eventually offered him, he would be immune from prosecution for any previous offence (except murder) that he admitted being party to, and with normal remissions, the best possible result he could expect was a reduction in his sentence of six years to serve. But with his track record, that seemed unlikely. Nonetheless, a splinter of hope was better than none at all. Neddy weighed up the options and went against what he so often preached – he turned dog.

As he sat in the witness box day after day at the 1992 ICAC hearings, which flowed over into 1993, Neddy's face could have been carved out of granite. It was expressionless as he gave evidence in a voice that showed total disregard for discipline or reprimand. It was a face hardened by a life in the streets and prison. Neddy Smith – underworld boss, gunman, rapist, heroin dealer, armed robber, murderer and now

Crown informer – was dobbing in the cops. Council assisting the ICAC, Barry Toomey QC, nursed his most prized stool pigeon through his evidence, which, if proven, would bring the New South Wales Police to its knees. Neddy was already the most notorious criminal in the country. Now he looked like becoming the most important informer in the nation's history. Although in command intellectually, he was unable to control the continual shaking down the right side of his body and his right arm, the only noticeable signs of the advanced stages of Parkinson's disease that had been ravaging his huge frame for a decade.

In true gangland tradition, Neddy had refused to inform on any of his underworld mates. But he didn't bat an eyelid as he gave up the cops whom he had allegedly done business with over the years in murder, bribery, drug trafficking, armed robberies, extortion and corruption at every level. According to Neddy, the cops ran the lot, and by giving them all up, he had absolutely nothing to lose and everything to gain. After all, he was already doing life for murder and an additional 13 years for attempted armed robbery. He named dozens of corrupt police officers and told of the vast sums of money they earned from heroin trafficking. He told the Commission how he had stood by and watched as Roger Rogerson gunned down an unarmed Warren Lanfranchi in 1981 and police took a bundle of money from the dead man's trousers. He told a stunned audience how he had earned the 'green light' by lying to a coronial inquest about the circumstances surrounding the death of Lanfranchi and how detectives organised armed robberies, then picked up the robbers and drove them away from the scene. For weeks he sang like a nightingale, and Australia hung on his every word. When he had finished, he was promised nothing and taken back to his cell at Long Bay Jail for the long wait to see whether, one day, his treachery would pay off.

⚰ ⚰ ⚰

In 1994, Neddy Smith made a fatal mistake. He spoke frankly in jail to his cellmate, who had been wired by the police, of the fact that he had murdered Harvey Jones and how his driver had buried the body in sand near Botany Bay. Smith's boasts were substantiated at 7.15 am on 23 March 1995 when a Thomas Coburn was searching the beach beside Foreshore Drive, Botany, for coins washed up by the tide. However, on this occasion, he found something quite different from loose change. First, Coburn saw teeth, and then eye sockets peering out at him from the beach. When he scraped away the sand with a stick, he revealed the skull and the skeletal remains of a body – that of Harvey Jones. If skulls could smile, then there was little doubt that this one would have grinned from ear to ear at being unearthed after all those years. Harvey Jones had come back to say hello to his old drinking mate.

In 1995, Neddy was charged with seven murders from the good old days. At his committal hearing in September 1996, the charges of murdering drug dealers Barry Croft, Barry McCann, Danny Chubb and Bruce Sandery were dropped, so the charges against Neddy were reduced to three, being the murders of Warren Lanfranchi's prostitute and drug-addict girlfriend Sallie-Anne Huckstepp, drug dealer Lewton Shu and Harvey Jones.

At Neddy's eight-week trial for Jones's murder, which ended on 9 September 1998, it was alleged that Jones went missing from the Star Hotel in Alexandria on 15 July 1983, where he had gone to meet Smith and give him a large sum of money to pay off a bribe to police. Smith was alleged to have picked up Jones, taken him to Botany Bay, shot him dead, taken his money and ordered his driver to bury the body. The hushed court listened to the damning 1994 tape recorded by his cellmate, a petty criminal code-named 'Mr Brown', of Smith telling of the killing of Harvey Jones:

> When I got him he said, 'I'd die for you.' I said, 'You're about to, ya fuckin' mug' ... Blew his heart out with a big .357.

Neddy's driver, code-named 'Mr Green', told the court that he had witnessed the killing and buried the body at Smith's behest. Mr Green told the jury of eight women and four men that he had met Jones and Smith at the Star Hotel in Alexandria between 7.00 and 7.30 pm and driven them to Botany Bay. He said he kept a lookout near a walkway to the beach while the two men walked off along the beach, and then he heard shots. Mr Green said he went to where the shots had come from to find Jones lying dead on the sand, with Smith standing over him with a gun in his hand. 'He had a gun – it was a big one,' Mr Green told the court. 'I came down near where the body was and he [Smith] said to dig a hole. It was a pretty deep hole.' Mr Green said that he used a shovel that was nearby to dig the hole. 'He [Smith] had crazy eyes,' Mr Green reminisced. 'That's all I remember, his eyes.'

It took the jury six days to return a guilty verdict. In sentencing Smith, Justice Carolyn Simpson said:

> The killing was committed for at least three reasons. One, for monetary gain. Two, to protect and preserve the prisoner's own criminal empire; and three, because Jones had become a nuisance and a pest to the prisoner.
>
> The prisoner's criminal record, as I have stated it, alone disentitles the prisoner to any claim for leniency. Arthur Stanley Smith, you are sentenced to penal servitude for life. You will die in prison.

⚰ ⚰ ⚰

Although he is destined to die behind bars, Neddy Smith still has countless enemies, but perhaps the main one is time itself. The Parkinson's disease that has ravaged his huge frame for decades is now so bad that Neddy was barely audible at times while giving evidence as his head rolled about uncontrollably. One of his associates, who has observed the progress of Neddy's Parkinson's disease (which Neddy calls 'me shakes'), told a reporter that 'he'll never live it out'. There is no shortage of people who hope that this is true.

In 1996 Neddy Smith's life was portrayed in the award-winning television series *Blue Murder*. The show also portrayed the life and times of corrupt detective Roger Rogerson and all of the old gang of everyone's favourite corrupt cops, hitmen, drug dealers and assorted cutthroats who inhabited Neddy's world.

Since being found guilty of the murder of Harvey Jones, Neddy was tried and exonerated for the murder of Warren Lanfranchi's girlfriend, Sallie-Anne Huckstepp. On 14 June 2000, an appeal for a re-trial of the murder of Harvey Jones was dismissed. Neddy Smith, Australia's once most notorious gangster, will die behind bars. In all of this, one thing is certain: the infamy that Harvey Jones so desperately craved in life, he most certainly achieved in death.

At the time of writing Neddy Smith is 75 years old and is incarcerated in a special section of Long Bay Jail for old, sick prisoners. He has been in jail for 31 years and with all appeals now exhausted, that is where he will die.

Chapter Twenty

TEEN KILLERS: THE MURDER OF JANINE BALDING

On Friday, 9 September 1988, police were called to Cobham Youth Centre at St Mary's in Sydney's outer-western suburbs. A social worker at the drop-in centre had seen two unkempt boys hanging around. They had arrived in a car, but neither looked old enough to drive. The social worker had decided to call police, who arrived shortly afterwards and gave the two boys a once-over. A check of the car they were driving revealed that it had been stolen from Gosford on the New South Wales Central Coast earlier that day. They were taken into custody.

At St Mary's police station, the two youths were identified as Bronson Blessington and Matthew Elliott. Blessington was just 14 years of age and his mate was 16. A routine check told police that, despite their tender years, they had extensive criminal records. Blessington had several convictions for stealing. Elliott had convictions for arson, car theft, receiving stolen goods, false pretences, and breaking and entering and stealing. Both had been in and out of institutions and now lived on the streets. Police prepared to add a further charge of car theft to their burgeoning criminal inventories, but Elliott and Blessington had something more serious to tell them. The previous day, friends of theirs had killed a woman. They knew where the body was buried. They would take police there and show them.

Police drove Elliott and Blessington to the nearby suburb of Minchinbury. The youths directed them to a dam in a paddock sheltered from view by a series of tall gum trees. In the dead of night, police shone their torches around the dam, scouring the dam surface, before they located the body of a partially clothed young woman, lying face down in the shallows. There had been a crude attempt to conceal her body with foliage and tree branches. Immediately, it became clear to Detective Sergeant Sharp and his men that the woman had been murdered.

Elliott and Blessington had led police to the body of Janine Balding, a 20-year-old bank worker who had gone missing from Sutherland railway station on 8 September 1988. Police had been informed of her disappearance, and they had feared the worst from the outset. An autopsy revealed that Janine had died by drowning. Her lungs were filled with the muddy water from the edge of the dam. There was extensive bruising over her body. She had been beaten in the face and body with a blunt object or a fist. Further bruising around her face, neck, wrists and ankles indicated that she had been bound tightly and gagged. Bruising around her vagina and anus indicated that she had been sexually assaulted many times.

The police investigation proved that Elliott and Blessington's story was a concoction. Ultimately, Bronson Matthew Blessington, Matthew James Elliott and another man, Stephen Wayne Jamieson, 22, would be convicted of the abduction, rape and murder of Janine Balding. During sentencing in the New South Wales Supreme Court, Mr Justice Newman described the crime as 'one of the most barbaric killings in the sad criminal history of this state'. Amid calls for the reintroduction of the death penalty from the community, led by Beverley and Kerry Balding, Janine's grieving parents, Mr Justice Newman sentenced all three to life imprisonment, with the recommendation that they never be released.

⚰ ⚰ ⚰

On Thursday, 8 September 1988, the 4.22 pm train to Sutherland in Sydney's southern suburbs wound its way from the city, packed with commuters returning home after a day of work. Nineteen-year-old Kristine Mobberly was among them, and as she got off the train, she walked determinedly to her car in the railway station car park. Another day, another dollar, but now at least she could relax for the evening.

As she got to her a car, a bedraggled and unkempt youth approached her, asking for the time. Mobberly glanced at her watch. It was 20 minutes past five. She looked at the boy, who was wearing dirty clothes and looked like he hadn't had a wash in weeks, and told him what the time was. The youth continued to draw closer to her as she got into her car. 'Are you sure?' he asked. Mobberly looked at the clock in her car and confirmed the time. By now, she had a distinctly uneasy feeling, so she locked the car doors as the youth continued to walk towards the car. She rolled down the window. The grubby boy then asked her if she had any money. Mobberly looked again and saw that the young man had a yellow-handled knife concealed in his jacket sleeve. She did not wait around to engage in any more idle chat with the youth. She sped off, not waiting to see what the young man's real intentions were. Later, Mobberly would contemplate just how close she had come to meeting a violent death that day at Sutherland railway station.

⚰ ⚰ ⚰

Matthew Elliott and Bronson Blessington had met their accomplices earlier that day – 8 September – at The Station, a refuge for the homeless in Erskine Street, Sydney. The Station sits incongruously in the heart of Sydney's central business district. Surrounded by skyscrapers, the two-storey building with bars on the windows is dwarfed by the metal and steel giants. Workers at The Station, many of them volunteers, provide a hot meal or offer some comfort to the people that society has left behind. Many of those who visit The Station are down on their luck: jobless, homeless and without the basic necessities of life. On that day, five homeless youths met within The Station's bleak sandstone walls. They were street kids, living on their wits, and crime came easily to them. Elliott and Blessington met up with 15-year-old Wayne Wilmot; a girl he had known for only a few hours, 17-year-old Carol Arrow; and Stephen Jamieson, 22.

Wayne Wilmot was a ward of the state and had been in trouble with the police all of his young life. He had more than 12 convictions for sexual assault, indecent assault, stealing and robbery. Wilmot's family background was particularly troubled, and government social workers determined that he should be placed in a foster home. His behavioural problems meant that he would never find a caring family environment, so he turned to the streets to live.

Carol Ann Arrow had run away from her home in Leeton in the state's prosperous Riverina farming district. Turning to Sydney, she, too, made the streets her home, scrambling enough money to survive by prostitution and property crime. Desperate for attention and love, she had met Wayne Wilmot earlier that morning and had become deeply infatuated with him.

The eldest of the newly formed group was Stephen Jamieson, 22, an ill-fated individual. He, too, had a string of convictions for sexual assault, malicious wounding, robbery and theft. Jamieson was known as 'Shorty', but this only hinted at his appearance. For he had a simian countenance, a long face and down-turned mouth. While Jamieson was the eldest of the group, he was by no means the brightest. Later, psychiatric testing would determine that Jamieson possessed the intellectual and emotional capacity of a 10-year-old child.

At the trial, the prosecution claimed that all five had sat around The Station and plotted their heinous crime. Bronson Blessington was alleged to suggest, 'Why don't we get a sheila and rape her?' No-one disagreed. Not one was unsettled by the prospect. Indeed, the group eagerly made their plans. They decided to go to Sutherland railway station, 40 kilometres south of Sydney, as it provided a perfect location. There were parks nearby, and the group could abduct their victim there and rape and rob her in the parklands.

So four teenagers and one man with the intellectual age of a child set out on that fateful September day to abduct and rape a woman, on a whim. They had no idea, nor did they care, who their victim would be. She would be picked entirely at random: a woman who offered the slightest hint of vulnerability, someone they could snare in a moment and drag away to demean and brutalise. While other teenagers were planning their first awkward moments with the opposite sex or daydreaming about a conquest on the sporting fields around Sydney, Elliott and Blessington, with their new friends, colluded to commit a crime that would invariably lead to the vicious murder of Janine Balding.

Hopping onto the train in the mid-afternoon, the gang drew immediate attention to themselves. Their dirty clothes and untidy appearance stood out in the crowded train. Students returning home from school and workers who had finished their shifts early could not help but notice the gang. Elva Matyas was seated on the train after a shopping trip to the city. She recalled the gang being loud and vulgar. They menaced school students in their carriage. Matyas told police:

The gang told the students to give them their seats or they would bash their heads in. Jamieson seemed to be the centre of attention and he sat next to me. One of the others kept showing him a pornographic book and making filthy remarks about it. They were dressed in dirty clothes and it looked as though none of them had a bath in weeks. Jamieson talked about going on to Cronulla but they got off at Sutherland as planned.

Matyas would later identify the gang of five from photographs.

At Sutherland the gang loitered around the shops for a while before returning to the northern end of the railway station to stalk a victim. Just after 5.00 pm, a train pulled in to the station and people piled out of its carriages. One of them was Kristine Mobberly, and the gang followed her as she walked from the platform to the car park. But they had frightened Kristine away. She drove directly to her fiancé's home, a short distance away, and ran inside to tell him the story. Her fiancé, Barry Arkley, had a broken leg, but nevertheless got into the car with Kristine and went with her to Sutherland police station to report the incident. Kristine told police about the man who had approached her and the knife he was concealing under his jacket. Police took the report and said they would follow it up.

Shortly afterwards, they left the police station and drove back to Arkley's home. The drive took them past Sutherland railway station again, and Mobberly looked into the car park, hoping the nightmare had passed. But it hadn't. In fact, it was growing more terrifying by the moment. Mobberly was startled to see that two youths were accosting a young woman with blonde hair, near a blue Holden Gemini. The car's alarm system had been triggered, and the siren was blaring and the lights of the vehicle's headlights were flashing. One of the youths was getting into the car, while the other appeared to be wielding a knife. It was broad daylight. This couldn't be happening.

Kristine Mobberly and her fiancé knew the young woman was in trouble, but there was little they could do. Barry Arkley's leg was in a plaster cast and he was restricted to hobbling about on crutches. They turned their car around and raced back to the police station. Acting on the information, two squad cars rushed to Sutherland railway station, but by the time they arrived, the blonde woman and the youths had gone. The blue car was missing too. The image of the abduction would stay with Kristine Mobberly for life. She knew that it could just as easily have been her who was the victim that day.

⚰ ⚰ ⚰

Janine Balding had been working in the George Street branch of the New South Wales State Bank, a short distance from The Station, where the gang of five had set out earlier that day. She had been in this job for only a few weeks, but she had proven to be a popular and hard-working member of staff.

Janine had grown up with her sister, Carolyn, in Wagga Wagga. Their parents, Beverley and Kerry Balding, had provided both girls with a loving and stable family environment. Janine had decided to move to Sydney to further her career. Her parents bought an apartment in Cronulla, a short drive from Sutherland, and Janine and her sister lived there in the beachside suburb. Janine was engaged to be married to Steven Moran early the following year. They had purchased their own home in Wyong on the New South Wales Central Coast, in anticipation of spending many happy years there together. Steven lived nearby in Sutherland, and often Janine would spend the night there. When she planned to stay with Steven at his home, she would park her car at Sutherland railway station and catch a city-bound train from there.

On 7 September 1998, Janine had parked her car at Sutherland railway station and spent the night at her fiancé's home. Steven expected Janine to join him that night too. When she did not appear, he was not overly concerned. She might have gone out late-night shopping with her sister and decided to spend the night back at the apartment at Cronulla. He tried to call Janine the following day, but her sister, Carolyn, told him she had not spent the night there. Carolyn had, in turn, presumed that Janine had spent the night at Steven's place. Immediately, both were concerned. It was unlike Janine to stay out all night. Carolyn contacted her parents in Wagga Wagga and gave them the disturbing news. Janine had disappeared without a trace. Her loving family's worst fears would be realised after Blessington and Elliott took police to the murder scene at Minchinbury.

⚰ ⚰ ⚰

At St Mary's police station on Friday, 9 September, detectives began interrogating Elliott and Blessington at length. The pair stuck to their original story. They had only been along for the ride, they said. They claimed that a young street kid named Scott Agius and another man they knew only as 'Shorty' had been responsible for the abduction, rape and murder of Janine Balding. Two other street kids, Wayne Wilmot and his girlfriend, Carol Arrow, had been in the car too. Elliott and Blessington both said that Agius and the mysterious 'Shorty' had planned the murder. Blessington had produced a knife he said had been used to abduct Janine Balding. He told police that he had pinched the knife from Shorty's pocket afterwards, so that he could go to the police with proof that 'Shorty' and Agius had committed the murder.

The police scoured the streets looking for the other members of the gang. They soon had Wayne Wilmot and Carol Arrow in custody, picking them up from the streets of Kings Cross. Agius was known to frequent The Station, and police arrested him there shortly afterwards. Wilmot and Arrow both supported Blessington and Elliott: they also claimed that the man named 'Shorty' was responsible for the murder. But their stories were beginning to fall apart. Police did not believe for a moment that the four had no involvement in the murder, and all four were charged with the murder of Janine Balding.

Later, the police took Scott Agius into custody, but Agius claimed he had nothing to do with the murder. He had a watertight alibi and was released shortly afterwards. The hunt for 'Shorty' continued.

Through a series of lies and half-truths, Elliott, Blessington, Arrow and Wilmot kept the police guessing as to the real identity of the fifth member of the gang. Blessington told police that the 'Shorty' who had murdered Janine Balding was Mark Wells, a 28-year-old with schizophrenia who had a disposition towards violent crime. Wells lived in a world enveloped within his own delusions. He told anyone who would listen that he worshipped Satan and had killed a priest when he was just 15 years of age. He wore combat fatigues and a green beret, and was often seen muttering darkly to himself on the streets of Sydney. The police spotted him and took him into custody. Wells had no knowledge of the murder of Janine Balding. He, too, provided police with a perfect alibi and was released.

The police had photographs of 51 criminals who had the nickname 'Shorty'. Tirelessly, they showed these photographs to the four gang members, over and over again. All claimed that they were unable to identify the fifth gang member from any of the photographs they were shown. When the mug shot of Jamieson appeared, the four gang members did not bat an eyelid. No, he was not the one, they told police. They persisted in providing vague descriptions and false information in an effort to throw police off the trail. In the meantime, each persisted with the line that the fifth gang member, the 'Shorty' police were looking for, was singularly responsible for the murder of Janine Balding.

Ultimately, the lies of the four young people would be exposed. Within days of the arrest of Elliott and Blessington, Kristine Mobberly and Elva Matyas identified Steven Wayne Jamieson from the mug shots and police issued a warrant for his arrest. His alleged role in the despicable murder of Janine Balding shot Jamieson to number one on Australia's Most Wanted List.

⚱ ⚱ ⚱

On 22 September 1988, Steven Jamieson was spotted drinking with a group of transients in a park in Southport on the Queensland Gold Coast. Two Queensland police officers, Detective Sergeant Ray Wall and Detective Markey, went to the park. They pulled Jamieson aside and arrested him without any fuss. Within minutes, New South Wales Homicide Squad detectives were informed of the arrest. Detective sergeants Raue and Carroll flew to Queensland and shortly afterwards began questioning Jamieson.

Jamieson was asked questions in relation to the abduction, rape and murder of Janine Balding. 'I didn't kill anyone,' Jamieson told police. He said that he knew Wayne Wilmot and Carol Arrow. He knew a Bronson and a Matthew, but he didn't know their surnames. The police told him that these four youths had implicated him in the murder of Janine Balding. They said that he was the one who killed the young woman. In his record of interview, Jamieson allegedly confessed to raping Janine Balding.

'Did you rape her?' Detective Sergeant Raue asked.

'No, I didn't touch her. I was only with them,' Jamieson replied.

'Would you be prepared to undergo a blood test for comparison with samples taken from the dead girl?'

'I don't like needles,' Jamieson said. 'Do I have to? I did only root her once.'

Did this woman agree to have sex with you?' came the follow-up question.

'No,' Jamieson replied.

According to police, Jamieson then relented and gave a full confession. He told the two detectives that Janine Balding had been thrown into her Holden Gemini and that Arrow and Wilmot were in the front seat, with 15-year-old Wilmot at the wheel. Blessington held Janine at knifepoint while Elliott raped her. Jamieson said that he had held her legs while Elliott raped her. Later, Blessington took over, slashing at Janine's skirt with the knife and forcing her to perform oral sex on him. Arrow was sitting beside Wilmot as he drove, stroking his penis. As they headed out along the F4 Freeway towards Minchinbury, the violence continued. Janine Balding was raped repeatedly throughout the journey. As they drove down the freeway, one of the gang had remarked, 'It's a nice night for a murder.'

According to his statement, Jamieson directed Wilmot along the road towards a dam, near the Prospect Caravan Park. The dam was secluded and away from the prying eyes of others. They could do their worst here. When they arrived at the dam, Arrow and Wilmot remained in the car with Arrow fellating the 15-year-old on the front seat. In his confession, Jamieson told police:

> We all got out of the car. Then Matthew and Bronson had sex with her. The gag had come off. She was screaming. Then I had my turn. I had sex with her. She was pretty worn out by now and wasn't screaming as much. And then Bronson had sex with her again. He slapped her across the face because she wouldn't buck.
>
> Then after that Matthew and Bronson started talking about killing her. Then Matthew said: 'What the heck. If one's going to kill her, we're all going to go for a row.' Matthew asked me to see what was in the boot. I had a look and found some rope and gave it to Matthew and Bronson to tie her up.

Janine was raped again, and then tied in a crouched position, her knees drawn up around her chest and her arms behind her back. Her feet were bound and the rope wrapped tightly around her neck. If she had moved, she would have choked. Her face was covered, and a gag shoved into her mouth. She was then pulled and pushed through the paddock up to a barbed wire fence.

All the gang members provided conflicting statements. It was impossible to know which one of the gang members killed Janine. She was carried and dragged over the barbed wire fence, and then taken to the dam, where her head was forced into the shallows. She died with her face in the mud, clutching at the weeds that thrived in the dam, in a desperate attempt to hold on to her life.

After the murder, the gang took off in Janine's car. It broke down on the road to Mount Druitt, so the gang proceeded on foot. The gang members used Janine's ATM card to withdraw $300, and split the money among themselves before going their separate ways. Later, Elliott pawned Janine's engagement ring to a fence known as 'Goldfinger'. Arrow and Wilmot returned to The Station. Elliott and Blessington moved further away, stopping at Gosford where they stole a car, before returning to Sydney and the youth centre at St Mary's. They were placed under arrest the following night. Jamieson took flight to Queensland and spent the next fortnight there among the beaches and sunshine of one of Australia's most popular tourist resorts.

⚰ ⚰ ⚰

All five young people were charged with the abduction, rape and murder of Janine Balding. It was determined that Wilmot and Arrow had played no part in the murder, which forced the first trial to be aborted. Wilmot and Arrow were ultimately convicted of the abduction of Janine Balding. Wilmot was sentenced to ten years' imprisonment with hard labour, while Carol Arrow was put on a three-year good behaviour bond and allowed to walk free after having served 19 months on remand.

Blessington, Elliott and Jamieson were tried in the New South Wales Supreme Court. Their trial eventually commenced in June 1990. Although the three men faced the most serious charges possible and were all looking at long prison terms, they did not seem to be too bothered by it all. While they showed no remorse or regret for their awful crimes, Janine's parents and friends were spared the pain of a protracted trial when they pleaded guilty. All three stood in the dock, laughing and giggling throughout the sombre proceedings. Elliott amused himself by mouthing obscenities to the gallery and the press. Jamieson and Blessington made rude gestures. Their bizarre and callous behaviour served to strengthen the public mood to punish them severely.

The jury considered the verdict for two hours. When they returned to the courtroom and announced that they had found Elliott, Blessington and Jamieson guilty on all charges, the gallery cheered and applauded. Mr Justice Newman was forced to call the court to order. But the genuine outpouring of relief and emotion from Janine's family and friends was understandable.

Beverley and Kerry Balding lobbied the government to reintroduce the death penalty, but their pleas fell on deaf ears. Bev did not want retribution. She said:

> They should be put to death. I have no wish for revenge. People say that bringing back the death penalty is stooping to the level of the criminals. It's not. Stooping to their level would be to terrorise them as they did Janine. Often of a morning when the van was bringing them to court, I hoped it would run off the bridge or have an accident. They are just like wild animals.

Elliott, Blessington and Jamieson were sentenced on 19 September 1990. Mr Justice Newman offered the three young men no prospect of ever being released from jail. He stated:

> To sentence people so young to long terms of imprisonment is of course a heavy task. However, the facts surrounding the commission of this murder are so barbaric that I believe I have no alternative. So grave is the nature of this case that I recommend that none of these offenders should ever be released.

Stephen 'Shorty' Jamieson, the unfortunate-looking man with the mind of a child, and Matthew Elliott and Bronson Blessington, the youngest felons to be sent to prison without the possibility of parole in Australia's history, were led from the court. Elsewhere, teenagers pursued their ambitions. They studied at schools, colleges and universities. They sought romance. They chased their dreams, confronted the world and stumbled awkwardly through the rites of passage to adulthood. All the young murderers of Janine Balding could look forward to was four walls, a wash basin and a thin mattress with prison-issue blankets for the rest of their lives.

Over the years, various attempts have been made to have a release date set for Elliott and Blessington based on their young ages when they committed their crimes, but each time the prison doors have slammed shut. Now the appeals have run out and no matter what, they will die behind bars.

ABOUT THE AUTHOR

Paul B Kidd is a Sydney-based bestselling author, top-rating Radio 2GB talkback broadcaster, crime historian, ex-freelance *60 Minutes* researching producer and photojournalist who specialises in Australian true crime, big game fishing, adventure and humour.

Paul's stories, interviews and photographs have appeared in most Australian major outdoors and lifestyle publications, in numerous magazines and on *CrimeLibrary* websites worldwide.

The author of *Australia's Serial Killers; The Definitive History of Serial Multicide in Australia*, Paul is Australia's foremost authority on the history of Australian serial killers and criminals who have been sentenced to life imprisonment, with their papers marked never to be released.

Paul B Kidd is the past editor of *Fishing News Magazine*, *The Shimano Yearbook*, *The Tackle Trader* and *Rex Hunt's Fishing Australia Monthly* and is also a recognised authority on Australia's waterways and the creatures that inhabit them.

The author of 24 books on Australian true crime and fishing adventures, Paul lives in Sydney's eastern suburbs with his cat, Smiley.